How to Write a Statement of Work

Sixth Edition

How to Write a Statement of Work

Sixth Edition

Peter S. Cole, CPCM
Michael G. Martin, PMP

MANAGEMENTCONCEPTSPRESS

MANAGEMENTCONCEPTS PRESS
8230 Leesburg Pike, Suite 800
Tysons Corner, VA 22182
(703) 790-9595
Fax: (703) 790-1371
www.ManagementConceptsPress.com

Copyright © 2012 by Management Concepts, Inc.

All rights reserved. No part of this book may be reproduced or utilized in any form or by any means, electronic or mechanical, including photocopying, recording, or by an information storage and retrieval system, without permission in writing from the author and the publisher, except for brief quotations in review articles.

Library of Congress Control Number: 2012935936

ISBN 978-1-56726-364-0

Printed in the United States of America

10 9 8 7 6 5 4 3 2 1

About the Authors

Peter S. Cole, CPCM, had more than 37 years of experience in the field of acquisition and contracts management. During his military service he spent four years as a contracting officer in the Navy laboratory system; four years teaching basic and advanced procurement at the Army Logistics Management College (ALMC), Fort Lee; and four years at the headquarters staff level working on procurement policy matters.

Following his retirement from the Navy in 1979, Mr. Cole researched and developed textbooks and presented training programs in cost-plus-award fee contracting, competitive negotiation, implementation of OMB Circular A-76, FAR implementation, and contract management for technical personnel (COTR training). He provided consulting services to both government and commercial clients and wrote 20 manuals and handbooks for individual government agencies, including the Departments of Agriculture, Interior, Labor, and Treasury, the Central Intelligence Agency, and the National Institutes of Health. Mr. Cole also wrote 10 books on various aspects of government contracting.

Michael G. Martin, **PMP**, is an internationally recognized consultant, speaker, trainer, and author with extensive experience in portfolio, program, and project management as well as enterprise risk management. During his career Mr. Martin has been instrumental in helping organizations in both the public and private sectors worldwide achieve excellence in these disciplines.

A certified project management professional, Mr. Martin has authored several books, including *Federal Statements of Work: A*

Practical Guide and *Delivering Project Excellence with the Statement of Work, second edition.* He is also a contributing author of *The 77 Deadly Sins of Project Management* and the *Field Guide to Project Management, second edition.* He is the past President and Chair of the Atlanta PMI® Chapter, former member of the PMP® exam development committee, and Founding Chair of the PMI® Government Specific Interest Group.

Mr. Martin holds an MBA from the University of North Florida and a BS in Civil Engineering from West Virginia Tech. He is a frequent speaker at various companies, professional organizations, and universities.

In memory of Peter S. Cole

Table of Contents

Preface xv

CHAPTER 1. OVERVIEW 1
What Is a Statement of Work? 1
Importance of the SOW 4
Need for a Clear and Concise SOW 5
   Before Award 5
   After Award 6
   To Establish Performance Standards and a
      Contractual Baseline 7
   To Provide Prospective Contractors with a
      Basis of Estimate 7
   To Communicate Effectively 8
Relationship of the SOW to the Solicitation and Contract 9
   Format and Content of the Solicitation and Contract 10
   Relationship of the SOW to RFP Sections L and M 12
Use of the Proposal Preparation Instructions 13
   To Ensure Appropriate Coverage 14
   To Standardize Proposal Format 23
   To Require Specific Information 28
Formatting the Proposal Preparation Instructions 31
Need to Check Your Work Carefully 33

CHAPTER 2. PLANNING AND PREPARATION 35
Acquisition Planning 35
   What Is the Real Requirement, and
      When Is It Needed? 37
   How Will Success Be Measured or Determined? 38

What Is It Likely to Cost, and What Funds
  Are Available? 38
Market Research 39
Thinking the Project Through 45
Using a Work Breakdown Structure 46
Choosing the Contract Type 47
  Fixed-Price Contracts 47
  Cost-Reimbursement Contracts 49
  Time-and-Materials and Labor-Hour Contracts 50
  Indefinite-Delivery Contracts 51
Choosing the SOW Type 55
  Functional Descriptions 55
  Performance Descriptions 57
  Differences between Functional and Performance
    Descriptions 58
  Design Descriptions 60
Incorporating a Contractor's Proposal
  by Reference 61
Distinguishing Between Level-of-Effort (LOE)
  and Completion SOWs 63
  Level-of-Effort SOWs 63
  Completion SOWs 64
  Distinguishing between the LOE and Completion Forms . . 64
  Providing a Basis of Estimate for LOE and Completion
    Requirements 65
Personal Versus Nonpersonal Services 67
Sole-Source SOWs 69
Follow-on Efforts and Options 69

CHAPTER 3. WRITING A PERFORMANCE WORK STATEMENT FOR PERFORMANCE-BASED SERVICE CONTRACTING 73

What is Performance-Based Service Contracting? 73
  Performance Work Statement 74
  Quality Assurance Plan 75
  Incentive Plan 75

When Is It Appropriate to Use PBSC? 76
Developing a Job Analysis 77
    Organizational Analysis 78
    Data Gathering 79
    Directives Analysis 81
    Market Research 81
    Work Analysis 82
    Performance Analysis 82
    Cost Analysis 88
    For Defense Department (DoD) Readers 89
Developing a Quality Assurance Plan 90
    Types of Surveillance Methods 91
    Selecting Surveillance Methods 94
    QAP Example 95
Offering Incentives 99
    Formula Incentives 101
    Award Incentives 102
    Award Term Incentives 105
    Should Incentives Be Used in PBSC Contracts? ... 109
    Deductibles 112
Summary 115

CHAPTER 4. USING A STATEMENT OF OBJECTIVES (SOO) AND RELATED ISSUES 119
What Is an SOO? 119
SOO Format 121
    Section L 124
    Section M 124
Incorporation by Reference 125
Using an SOO 127
Competing the SOO 128
    Five-Step Approach 129
    Releasing Funding Information 140
Summary 141

CHAPTER 5. THE SOW FORMAT...................145
SOW Part I: General Information......................147
   Section A: Introduction.............................147
   Section B: Background.............................151
   Section C: Scope..................................153
   Section D: Applicable Documents....................154
SOW Part II: Work Requirements......................158
   Section A: Technical Requirements..................158
   Section B: Deliverables............................195
SOW Part III: Supporting Information.................198
   Section A: Security................................198
   Section B: Place of Performance....................199
   Section C: Period of Performance...................199
   Section D: Government-Furnished Property...........200
   Section E: Qualifications of Key Personnel............201
SOWs for Sealed Bidding............................203
   How the Differences between Sealed Bidding and
      Negotiation Affect the SOW.......................203
   Techniques to Support the SOW....................204
Summary..207

CHAPTER 6. COMMON PROBLEMS IN WRITING SOWS 209
General Writing Guidelines...........................209
Common Ambiguities in SOWS........................211
   Inconsistency of Requirements......................212
   Calling a Requirement by Different Names............213
   Conflicting or Unreasonable Schedules...............214
   Incomplete Description of Requirement..............216
   Vagueness and Generalized Language................217
   Use of Abstractions...............................220
   Unnecessary Comments...........................220
   Poor Sentence Construction........................220
   Typos or Missing Text.............................221
   Overly Complicated Vocabulary.....................222
   Excessively Long Sentences........................222

Conflicts Between the SOW and Contract Clauses 223
Obtaining Contractor Comments 228
    Draft Solicitations 228
    Preproposal Conference 229
    Proposal Preparation Instructions 230
Guidelines Related to the Use of Words 230
Guidelines Related to the Use of Phrases and Terms 232

CHAPTER 7. MANAGING CHANGES TO THE SOW 239
Legal Precedents Backing Change Management.......... 240
Identifying Changes................................... 242
Managing Project Changes 245
    Factors Affecting Change Mismanagement 245
Tools for Managing Changes.......................... 249
    Change Order Form 249
    SOW Change Order Tracker 252

APPENDIX A. SOW REVIEW 259

INDEX 317

Preface

This sixth edition of the classic *How to Write a Statement of Work* is dedicated to the late Peter Cole, a true thought leader who made a significant contribution to the literature on procurement management. I have a deep appreciation and respect for his work in this area and the value it has brought to both public and private sector organizations worldwide. Thus, it is my sincere pleasure to have the opportunity to update this book to reflect the current guidelines and references for government personnel to use when writing a statement of work (SOW), a performance work statement (PWS), or a statement of objectives (SOO) for use in a government contract.

This book is also useful for government personnel who must review or otherwise work with these documents. It is particularly useful for contractor personnel who must interpret and respond to government solicitations because it provides insights into government operations that are not generally available to contractors. It should be noted, however, that this book is generic in nature and must be used in conjunction with any specific agency instructions.

With the exception of Appendix A, which contains a detailed example of how to review and revise a functional SOW, this sixth edition of *How to Write a Statement of Work* has been updated to reflect new guidance and references, where applicable. This includes significant changes to Chapter 4, which addresses the SOO, as well as a new Chapter 7, which addresses the very important topic of managing changes to the SOW.

As in the earlier editions, the emphasis remains on providing practical, detailed guidance on writing and preparing a description of government requirements, whether the document used is an SOW, a PWS, or an SOO. The chapters included in this revised edition can be summarized as follows:

- *Chapter 1* provides an overview of SOWs, discussing the need for a clear and concise SOW and the relationship of the SOW to other parts of the solicitation and contract.

- *Chapter 2* addresses issues that must be considered when planning and preparing an SOW, discussing in detail topics such as choosing the SOW type (including functional and performance descriptions rather than design descriptions), distinguishing between level-of-effort and completion SOWs, and related considerations.

- *Chapter 3* discusses performance-based service contracting (PBSC), focusing on its use, how to develop the components of a PWS, how to conduct a job analysis, how to develop a quality assurance plan, and the use of incentives. It addresses how the PWS differs from the typical functional SOW and when the use of PBSC is appropriate.

- *Chapter 4* discusses the use of an SOO instead of a PWS in service contracting, and related issues. This contracting concept is not necessarily new; however, it is currently garnering a great deal of attention and is being applied frequently in the procurement of goods and services for public sector organizations. The use of the SOO requires a different approach to the presolicitation process.

Chapter 4 addresses the SOO concept, what the SOO is, and how to use it. The differences in acquisition planning, market research, and other presolicitation activities are discussed, as well as the evaluation, negotiation, and award of a solicitation based on an SOO. Potential problems and possible solutions are suggested. The chapter has been updated to reflect the current definition, references, and guidance regarding the development and application of the SOO.

- *Chapter 5* provides a sample SOW format to serve as the basis for discussion of which information is appropriate to include in an SOW, where the information goes in the SOW, and why. The information in this chapter applies equally to a functional SOW, a PWS, and, as appropriate, an SOO. This chapter also addresses the use of an SOW in sealed bidding.

- *Chapter 6* identifies common problem areas in writing SOWs and suggests how to deal with them. Writing guidelines, related primarily to the use of words, terms, and phrases in a contractual context, are also provided.

- *Chapter 7*, new to this edition, provides an overview of why change management is important on projects, legal precedents supporting change management, how to identify when a change occurs using the SOW, factors that could impede the acceptance and application of a change management process in an organization, and tools for documenting and managing project changes. The chapter also includes information on the federal government's Standard Form 30 (SF30) to provide perspective on how the change order is used and applied in the federal government.

- *Appendix A* contains a complete review and rewrite of an actual SOW. This appendix demonstrates how to analyze an SOW critically and how the SOW could be rewritten to describe the requirement more effectively.

The purpose of this book is to supplement existing government publications by providing greater depth and detail. Clearly, when developing a generic approach to such a multifaceted topic, some details will inevitably not be addressed, and suggestions may be made that are contrary to how you are accustomed to conducting a particular activity. Should you find that you do things differently, before you reject the ideas suggested in this book out of hand, please consider taking the following steps:

- Examine what you are doing and find out why.

- If your procedures are based on written agency or local directives, then follow the established procedures.

- If you cannot find a reason but are told, "This is the way we have always done it," there is a good chance that you should change, or at least carefully review, your current practices.

The point is that you should have a reason for what you do. This book provides suggestions about writing SOWs, PWSs, and SOOs and explains why, but it does not purport to be the final word on the subject. Use what applies now and keep the rest for reference in the event that the nature of your requirements changes.

Other sources of guidance for developing these documents are available. Agency sources include:

- Department of Defense, *Department of Defense Handbook for Preparation of Statement of Work (SOW)*, MIL-HDBK-245D, 3 April 1996. Online at *https://www.acquisition.gov. comp/seven_steps/library/DoDhandbook.pdf.*

- National Aeronautics and Space Administration, *NASA Guidance for Writing Statements of Work*, NPG 5600.2B, December 1997. Online at *http://www.hq.nasa.gov/office/ procurement/newreq1.htm.*

The following sources provide specific guidance for PBSC:

- Office of Federal Procurement Policy: *A Guide to Best Practices for Performance-Based Service Contracting,* Final Edition, October 1998. Online at *https://www.acquisition.gov/ bestpractices/bestppbsc.html.*

- Department of Defense: *Guidebook for Performance-Based Services Acquisition (PBSA) in the Department of Defense*, December 2000. Online at *https://www.acquisition.gov/comp/seven_steps/library/DODguidebook-pbsa.pdf.*

- *Seven Steps to Performance-Based Services Acquisition*, which can be accessed at: *https://www.acquisition.gov/comp/seven_steps/*. This website also provides links to numerous related publications.

I sincerely hope that each of you will garner some nugget of knowledge and value from the concepts and techniques described in this book. I hope that knowledge will make managing your contracts and projects more successful, and therefore make your professional life just a little bit easier.

Michael G. Martin
February 2012

1 Overview

A statement of work (SOW) is the written description of an agency requirement, used in the acquisition of supplies or services. The Federal Acquisition Regulation (FAR)[1] mandates that government requirements be described in a manner that promotes full and open competition to the maximum extent practicable and that restrictive provisions or conditions be used only to the extent necessary to satisfy the needs of the agency or as authorized by law. The FAR[2] goes on to say that requirements should be stated in terms of the functions to be performed, the performance required, or the essential physical characteristics of the requirements.

WHAT IS A STATEMENT OF WORK?

Although commonly used throughout the government, the term "statement of work" is not defined in the FAR. The FAR uses the term "work statement" when discussing research and development (R&D) contracting and uses the term "statements of work" in the coverage of performance-based contracting, but no specific definition is provided. For our purposes, the term "statement of work" is used in this book to refer to the document that completely describes the contractual work requirement. Unless otherwise noted, the term also encompasses the term "performance work statement" (PWS) used in performance-based service contracting (PBSC).

To put the term "statement of work" in the context of the FAR language, the following are some of the terms that the FAR uses when discussing the description of a work requirement:

- **Specification.** A specification is a description of the technical requirements for a material, product, or service that includes the criteria for determining whether these requirements are met. Specifications state the government's minimum needs and are designed to promote full and open competition, with due regard to the nature of the supplies or services to be acquired.

    The two sources of formal government-approved specifications are: (1) the *General Services Administration Index of Federal Specifications, Standards, and Commercial Item Descriptions*, which lists federal specifications and standards that have been implemented for use by all federal agencies, and (2) the *Department of Defense Index of Specifications and Standards (DODISS)*, which contains unclassified federal and military specifications and standards, related standardization documents, and voluntary standards approved for use by DoD.

- **Standards.** Standards are documents that establish engineering and technical limitations and applications of items, materials, processes, methods, designs, and engineering practices. Standards include any related criteria deemed essential to achieve the highest practical degree of uniformity in materials or products, or interchangeability of parts used in these products. Formal government-approved standards are found in the documents listed above.

    The FAR[3] states that agencies shall select existing requirements documents or develop new requirements documents that meet the needs of the agency in accordance with the guidance contained in the *Federal Standardization Manual*, FSPM-0001; for DoD components, *Defense Standardization Program Policies and Procedures*, DoD 4120.24-M; and for IT standards and guidance the *Federal Information Processing Standards Publications* (FIPS PUBS).

- **Voluntary Consensus Standards.** Voluntary consensus standards are standards established by a private sector body (other than a private standard of an individual firm) that are available for public use. The FAR[4] states that in accordance with OMB Circular A-119, *Federal Participation in the Development and Use of Voluntary Consensus Standards and in Conformity Assessment Activities, and* Section 12(d) of the National Technology Transfer and Advancement Act of 1995, Pub L. 104-113 (15 U.S.C 272 note), agencies must use voluntary consensus standards, when they exist, in lieu of government-unique standards, except where inconsistent with law or otherwise impractical.

- **Purchase Description.** A purchase description is a description of the essential physical characteristics and functions required to meet the government's minimum needs. A purchase description is used when there is no applicable specification that adequately describes the requirement. This term is usually associated with acquisitions using simplified acquisition procedures.

- **Product Description.** The term "product description" is a generic term for documents such as specifications, standards, and purchase descriptions.

Each of these terms addresses only part of a complete description of a contractual requirement, generally just the technical requirement. A complete description would include what you want to buy; why you want to buy it; where the work is to be performed; when the work is to be performed; what the work is to accomplish; what, how much, and when it is to be delivered; and how the government will determine that the work has been performed satisfactorily. The SOW encompasses all of these elements and may, as appropriate, include other documents such as specifications, standards, voluntary consensus standards, and purchase descriptions.

IMPORTANCE OF THE SOW

In the past, the government stressed the use of formal government-approved specifications and standards when describing requirements; however, that is no longer the case. Current policy encourages the acquisition of commercial items (i.e., any item, other than real property, that is of a type customarily used by the general public or by non-government entities for purposes other than governmental purposes) or non-development items (i.e., previously developed items or previously developed items that require only minor modifications of a type customarily available in the commercial marketplace). In other words, government agencies now must first consider acquiring supplies or services available in the commercial marketplace rather than using government specifications and standards.

Agencies are now permitted to choose whichever requirements documents they deem to be most suitable. They may use existing requirements documents (federal or DoD specifications and standards), modify or combine existing documents, or create new requirements documents. When creating new requirements documents, the FAR[5] cites the following order of precedence:

1. Documents mandated for use by law

2. Performance-oriented documents (e.g., PWS, SOO)

3. Detailed, design-oriented documents

4. Standards, specifications, and related publications issued by the government outside the Defense or federal series for non-repetitive acquisition of items.

This book is written primarily for those who develop SOWs for negotiated procurements. While the principles of developing an SOW are the same regardless of the method of procurement, certain caveats apply with respect to sealed bidding. These are addressed at the end of Chapter 5.

NEED FOR A CLEAR AND CONCISE SOW

An SOW is usually developed by the person responsible for ensuring that an activity's technical requirements are met (i.e., the requisitioner), with the support of contracting personnel. Because the SOW describes the contractual work requirements, it is the heart of the procurement action and must include a clear and concise description of the work requirement. Developing the SOW is, without a doubt, the most important step in the procurement process. A poor description of the work requirement is likely to be misunderstood, leading to—if not causing—problems throughout the procurement process and subsequent contract performance. Although a clear and concise description of the work does not guarantee the contract will be successful, it does significantly reduce the likelihood that problems will arise.

The author of the SOW is usually part of the organization for whom the work will be performed and therefore has a vested interest in the quality of the SOW. If the SOW does not work, the project may fail. Because it usually takes longer to solve a problem than it does to avoid one, it makes sense to take the time to do it right initially.

A clear and concise SOW is essential both before and after contract award and serves three main purposes:

- Establishing performance standards and a contractual baseline

- Providing the contractor with a basis of estimate

- Communicating effectively.

Before Award

Contractors must understand the SOW requirements to be able to develop their technical, management, and staffing plans and to price the proposal properly. The SOW in the request for proposals (RFP) is the only official description of the work requirement. Accordingly, it must provide prospective contractors enough information to develop and price the proposal—without the need for further explanation. A clear and concise SOW helps ensure the receipt of a well-written proposal. It also establishes a uniform basis for evaluating proposals (matching the proposed effort to the stated technical requirement) and for comparing prices.

If questions about the SOW arise during the solicitation process, you must answer them, but use care when providing explanations. Oral explanations, unless put into writing as an amendment to the SOW, are usually not binding. Refer the questions, along with the appropriate answers, to the contracting officer for an official response.

If deficiencies in the SOW are identified before award, the RFP must be amended to correct the deficiencies immediately and prospective contractors must be given additional time to consider the corrections and make appropriate revisions to their proposals. Do not wait and make the corrections after award. Keep the pricing of the corrections in the competitive pre-award environment; modifications after award are likely to cost more. Delaying changes until after award can also make your agency vulnerable to protests from unsuccessful offerors who perceive the delayed changes as favoritism to the successful offeror.

After Award

After award the contractor must understand the SOW requirements to be able to perform the work properly. The SOW in the contract is the only description of the requirement that the contractor is legally bound to follow. Accordingly, it must clearly and concisely describe what you want to buy and any special considerations or constraints that apply.

The SOW, as published in the contract, defines the contractual scope of work—the contractor is required to do *only* what is written into the contract. A poorly defined SOW therefore often results in a need for changes in the technical requirements, opening the contract to pricing and delivery changes. The number of changes and difficulties in negotiating their scope and price are usually directly related to the quality of the SOW. If the SOW is ambiguous or unclear and a dispute arises over contract interpretation, the courts will follow the contractor's interpretation, as long as it is reasonable. The courts generally hold the originator of the SOW responsible for its clarity.

To Establish Performance Standards and a Contractual Baseline

The SOW, through its description of the work requirements, establishes the standard for measuring performance effectiveness and achievement both during contract performance and upon contract completion. The work description establishes goals that become the standards against which contract performance is measured. The SOW is not complete unless it describes both the work requirements and the criteria for determining whether the work requirements are met.

The SOW also establishes the baseline from which the degree, extent, and ramifications of proposed contract changes are determined. Proposed changes are checked against the SOW to determine if they are within the scope of the contract. If the proposed change is within the scope of the contract, the change is handled by a contract modification. If it is not within the scope of the contract, a new contract is required. The clarity and conciseness of the SOW are, therefore, important throughout the life of the contract.

To Provide Prospective Contractors with a Basis of Estimate

Prospective contractors need sufficient information on which to base the estimated cost of contract performance. This information or "basis of estimate" is provided in the SOW through the description of the task requirements, a statement of the estimated level of effort required (when appropriate), or both.

Contractors develop cost estimates based on the work description in the SOW. First, they break the work description down into its smallest components, and then, starting from the bottom up, they develop estimates of the resources necessary to complete each component of each task. Cost figures are developed for the estimated resources required. Overhead and general and administrative (G&A) expenses are added to make up the total estimated cost. Profit or fee is then added to the total estimated cost to come up with the total estimated price.

Therefore, the work requirement must be described in a manner that will enable prospective contractors to develop an accurate cost estimate. This is important. If the successful offeror's estimate is too high, you will pay more than you should for the contract effort. If the estimate is too low, the contract requirement will be underfunded. If your contract is cost-reimbursement, underfunding usually results in a contract modification for additional funding or in contract termination. If your contract is fixed-price, underfunding puts the contractor in a loss position, because the contractor must complete the effort regardless of its own costs. Contractors in a loss position will try to minimize their losses by cutting corners or making contract changes, if they can. Cutting corners adversely affects the contract quality, and changes usually increase the contract cost. Neither of these actions is in your best interest.

A well-written SOW is no guarantee that the contractor will develop an accurate cost estimate. Many requirements (such as studies, analyses, R&D, and software development) are inherently difficult to estimate because of the nature of the work. Therefore, it is important to write the SOW as accurately as possible. A well-written SOW helps minimize the differences between estimated and actual costs by providing the offeror with the best possible basis for cost estimating.

To Communicate Effectively

The SOW is ultimately a vehicle for communication. It must communicate your requirement in a manner that can be understood by all personnel involved in the solicitation process as well as those involved in contract performance. This includes government as well as contractor personnel. Various people must read and understand the SOW during the course of the solicitation, award, and performance of the contract. These include the contractor's technical personnel, accountants, and cost estimators; government accounting and auditing personnel; government and contractor legal and contracting personnel; and subcontractors. Readers must be able to understand the requirements without having to interpret, extrapolate, or otherwise guess at the SOW's meaning.

It is a mistake to use the SOW language as a test of a contractor's ability to understand the requirements by writing a broad and generalized SOW just to see how contractors will respond. Misunderstandings may well be carried through into contract performance. The SOW must be written clearly and simply. The quality of the SOW directly affects the quality and pricing of the contractor's proposal and, eventually, the quality of the contractor's performance.

Before addressing how to write an SOW, however, it is necessary to discuss two other topics: the relationship of the SOW to the solicitation and contract, and the use of proposal preparation instructions with respect to the SOW. You need to understand how the SOW fits into the solicitation and contract and how it affects other parts of the solicitation. You also need to understand the relationship of the SOW to the proposal preparation instructions and how you can use them most effectively.

RELATIONSHIP OF THE SOW TO THE SOLICITATION AND CONTRACT

Two types of solicitations are used in government contracting (other than simplified acquisition procedures). If the procurement is negotiated, an RFP is used. If the procurement is by sealed bidding, an invitation for bids (IFB) is used. Both use the same format, but the contents—primarily the solicitation provisions and contract clauses—are different. This is true of both the solicitation and the resulting contract.

During the solicitation process, contractors use the SOW to develop and price their proposals; the government then uses the SOW in evaluating the proposals. The SOW also serves as the basis for information in other sections of the solicitation document. After award, the SOW becomes the only basis for contractual performance. Thus, the SOW is a key document from initiation of the procurement process through completion and final closeout of the contract. Understanding the format and content of the solicitation and contract is therefore crucial to developing an effective SOW.

Format and Content of the Solicitation and Contract

Solicitations and contracts are written using the uniform contract format established by the FAR.[6] This format organizes the solicitation and contract into four parts, as shown in Figure 1-1, and makes it possible to use the same document as both a solicitation and a contract.

Parts I–III of the RFP make up the contractual document. In Part I, Section A is a standard form; Section B itemizes the required supplies or services; Section C contains the SOW; and Sections D through H contain specific clauses related to the topic of each section. As part of the contractual document, the SOW describes only those actions that take place after contract award. Do not include any information related to the solicitation process in the SOW. Part II contains the standard contract clauses related to the type of contract and what is being procured. Part III contains a list of those documents or exhibits that are attached to the RFP. It is not unusual for a lengthy SOW to be referenced in Section C and included in Section J as an attachment.

Part IV of the RFP is the solicitation portion. It contains information related solely to the solicitation process. Section K describes the information that the contractor must provide to establish its eligibility for award of a government contract. Section L contains solicitation provisions related to the terms and conditions of the solicitation and the proposal preparation instructions

> **FIGURE 1-1**
> **Contents of the Request for Proposals/Contract**
>
> Part I—The Schedule
>
>   A. Solicitation/contract form
>   B. Supplies or services and prices/costs
> >>   **C. Description/specifications/statement of work**
>   D. Packaging and marking
>   E. Inspection and acceptance
>   F. Deliveries or performance
>   G. Contract administration data
>   H. Special contract requirements
>
> Part II—Contract Clauses
>
>   I. Contract clauses
>
> Part III—List of Documents, Exhibits, and Other Attachments
>
>   J. List of attachments
>
> Part IV—Representations and Instructions
>
>   K. Representations, certifications, and other statements of offerors or respondents
> >>   **L. Instructions, conditions, and notices to offerors or respondents**
> >>   **M. Evaluation factors for award**

(instructions related to the form and content of the contractor's proposal). Section M contains the evaluation factors and information about how the proposals will be evaluated.

The entire document (Parts I–IV) is used during the solicitation process by the prospective contractor to develop its proposal and pricing, and by the government to evaluate the contractor's proposal. When the contract is awarded, the solicitation portion (Part IV) is deleted. Section K is incorporated into the contract by reference and retained in the official contract file. Sections L and M can be discarded because they do not apply to contract performance. (In practice, however, a copy of Sections L and M is usually retained for reference purposes.)

As indicated by the arrows in Figure 1-1, the developer of the SOW is primarily interested in the development of Section C, the SOW, and Sections L (proposal preparation instructions) and M (evaluation factors). The contracting officer is responsible for developing the remaining coverage in the solicitation and contract; ultimately, the contracting officer becomes responsible for the entire solicitation and contract.

Relationship of the SOW to RFP Sections L and M

Responsibility for developing the SOW usually includes responsibility for developing the proposal preparation instructions in Section L and the evaluation factors in Section M. The SOW and RFP Sections L and M are directly related in several key ways, as illustrated in Figure 1-2. These relationships should be kept in mind when developing the SOW.

FIGURE 1-2
Relationship of the SOW and RFP Sections L and M

Section C	Section M	Section L
SOW	Evaluation Factors	Proposal Preparation Instructions
Describes the work to be performed by the contractor.	Based on the SOW, describes the evaluation factors, their relative importance, and how proposals will be evaluated.	Based on Section M and the SOW, describes the required proposal format and content.

Section M of the RFP contains information about how proposals will be evaluated, including the evaluation factors and their relative importance. The evaluation factors and their relative importance are developed by analyzing the SOW to identify those aspects of the requirement that are most important to the accomplishment of the work. These generally fall within the areas of technical, management, corporate experience, and cost, but the specific description and their relative importance depend on the contents of the SOW. The evaluation factors are set forth in Section M in descending order of importance, along with an indication of the relative importance of each factor. Publication of this information ensures that contractors understand how the proposals will be evaluated and that they will tailor their proposals to address those areas that you consider most important.

Section L contains the solicitation provisions appropriate to the requirement and the proposal preparation instructions. The proposal preparation instructions provide guidance on how you want contractors' proposals organized and how to identify information that you want the contractor to provide. The proposal preparation instructions are used to amplify the evaluation factors in Section M and the work requirements in the SOW. The proposal preparation instructions provide an outline for the proposal format based on the evaluation factors listed in Section M. They identify the specific information required in support of each evaluation factor and specify other constraints, such as page limitations.

USE OF THE PROPOSAL PREPARATION INSTRUCTIONS

The term "proposal preparation instructions" encompasses all information provided to a contractor regarding the format and contents of its proposal. Although this term is not in universal use in federal contracting, it is used here to describe the consolidation of all proposal preparation information in one clearly identifiable place in the RFP. If communication is to be effective, all information of a similar nature should be grouped and presented in the same place.

Proposal preparation instructions are used to ensure that prospective contractors submit proposals that facilitate full evaluation of each offeror's expertise and ability to perform the required work. Generally, these instructions are for guidance only, but you may want to make compliance mandatory for some instructions, such as paper size, type size, font style, and particularly page limitations. If you do, this must be spelled out in the proposal preparation instructions. While an offeror has the right to respond to a solicitation in any manner it sees fit, an offeror would be foolish to ignore the proposal preparation instructions; at the very least, doing so would reflect poorly on the offeror's ability to follow instructions.

Proposal preparation instructions are used to: (1) ensure appropriate coverage in the proposals, (2) standardize proposal format, and (3) require the submission of specific information.

To Ensure Appropriate Coverage

The primary purpose of proposal preparation instructions is to ensure that each proposal addresses your areas of interest as expressed by the evaluation factors in Section M. The contractor should be required to structure its proposal in the same order of importance as the evaluation factors listed in Section M. For example, if the following evaluation factors are listed in Section M in descending order of importance, require that the proposals address the same factors in the same order. This ensures that the proposals will discuss your areas of interest in the same order and with the same level of importance as you will use in evaluation. For example:

Technical Factors
    Technical Approach/Understanding the Requirement
    Technical Plan/Methodology
Management Factors
    Management Approach
    Staffing Plan
    Key Personnel

Corporate Experience
Past Performance
Cost

Presenting Primary Evaluation Factors

Section M presents each primary evaluation factor with a title and a short narrative illustrating the salient characteristics of the factor. Your proposal preparation instructions should present each *primary* evaluation factor in the same manner. This is redundant, but repeating the narrative description from Section M reinforces the connection between Section M and the proposal preparation instructions. You may choose simply to paraphrase the narrative description in Section M, but if you do this, exercise care in your wording. A paraphrased description can confuse the offeror, particularly if paraphrasing causes the requirement to appear different than in Section M.

Presenting Significant Sub-factors

Sub-factors are used to amplify the primary evaluation factors; therefore, the sub-factors should be presented somewhat differently. The subfactor narrative begins with a general statement (the same as used in Section M) followed by a statement of the specific information requirements that support the sub-factor. The specific information requirements will vary depending on the circumstances, but they should amplify the general statement, explaining what information you expect to see in the proposals.

Information requirements should specify both form and content. These requirements may address the submission of charts or graphs, a discussion of methods and methodology or specific technical considerations, technical or management plans and schedules, staffing levels and labor mix, and any other information you consider necessary to evaluate an offeror's response to a particular evaluation sub-factor. If certain tasks in the SOW require specific supporting information, you should reference those tasks to ensure that the connection is made.

For example, in a requirement for a study, the technical factors and significant subfactors could be presented as follows:

- **Technical** *[primary factor]*

    Proposals will be evaluated on the basis of the soundness and workability of the proposed technical approach, the demonstrated understanding of the requirement, and the validity of the technical plan and proposed methodology *[the same as set forth in Section M]*.

- **Technical Approach/Understanding the Requirement** *[significant subfactor]*

    The offeror shall demonstrate a sound and workable technical approach that ensures a high probability of successful performance. The offeror shall demonstrate its understanding of the requirement through the degree of thoroughness, soundness, and comprehension expressed by the proposed technical approach *[the same as set forth in Section M]*.

    The offeror shall describe its technical approach in sufficient detail to demonstrate its soundness and workability. Identify the scope of the study and how its purpose will be accomplished. Provide an analysis of the complexity of the requirement and indicate how any anticipated problems will be identified and resolved *[specific information requirement]*.

- **Technical Plan/Methodology** *[significant subfactor]*

    The offeror's technical plan, schedule, and the methodology to be employed to identify, obtain, research, and analyze articles, reports, and other information sources will be evaluated for its appropriateness for this study and the extent of effort proposed *[the same as set forth in Section M]*.

    The offeror shall fully describe its plan for its technical approach, demonstrating that it complies with the tasks set forth in the statement of work, including the phasing of tasks, scheduling of work effort, staffing, and the methodology to be employed. The discussion of methodology shall include the methodology to be used for data collection and that to be used to analyze the data and draw conclusions. Identify other methodologies that might have been applicable and indicate why they were not selected. Identify the proposed sources of information to be used and discuss the methods to be used to identify and obtain the information required. Indicate the volume of the anticipated research material and the research techniques to be used. Propose questions or areas of interest for the study when these are not provided in the SOW *[specific information requirement]*.

The specific information requirements for technical sub-factors vary considerably depending on what is being acquired. Information requirements that would facilitate the evaluation of the offeror's technical expertise and understanding of the requirement might include the following:

- Discuss specific work elements of particular interest (indicate if this information will be incorporated into the contract)

- Provide specific technical information such as graphs, drawings, charts, and other technical information needed for evaluation

- Discuss technical performance problems that the government has identified in the SOW or are otherwise known to the offeror and how they might be resolved

- Provide details of the proposed effort that demonstrate how the offeror will meet the requirement

- Discuss the proposed methodology or technical approach to be used, including an explanation of why the particular methodology or technical approach was selected, where more than one is available

- Provide a risk assessment that identifies risk areas and recommend approaches to minimize the impact of the risks on the overall success of the contract

- Provide a performance assessment, as appropriate, on past or current contracts that identifies contract performance problems and indicates how they were, or will be, corrected

- Define milestones or specific work schedules, including a work plan and performance schedule

- Propose details of scheduled technical meetings (e.g., purpose, when, where, who attends), when such meetings are dictated by the government in the SOW

- Discuss the technical data requirements and format

- Discuss the proposed quality assurance procedures

- Propose a test plan, including information on how the tests will be conducted and test results analyzed, if specific testing requirements are not dictated by the government in the SOW.

Providing a general statement followed by the specific information requirements ensures that the offeror understands how each sub-factor will be evaluated and that you get the information needed for evaluation. You must be as explicit as possible. Instructions that help offerors write their proposals are a plus, not a minus. You want offerors to write proposals that are responsive to your concerns. This makes the evaluation easier. At the same time, you should keep in mind that your job is to evaluate the offeror's technical expertise and ability to perform the contract, not its proposal-writing ability.

The following are examples of how other evaluation sub-factors could be presented and some of the types of information that might be needed for evaluation. Tailor the specific requirements to the procurement. Do not list something as a requirement unless you are sure that you know how you would evaluate the information submitted.

- **Management Approach**

    The general statement should require the offeror to provide a detailed discussion of its approach to overall management and integration of all activities required by the SOW. This discussion should also address the management objectives and techniques that demonstrate how the work requirements will be met.

    Specific information requirements might include the submission of organization charts, discussion of the lines of authority and responsibility, a demonstration of how the proposed organization will be prepared to respond promptly to problems or program changes, how the proposed project manager will obtain support from other corporate elements and subcontractors, and his or her ability to access higher levels of corporate management. Other useful information might be how the offeror prepares its internal management reports and how long after actual performance this information will be available (this helps in developing a meaningful schedule for submitting reports to the government).

- **Staffing Plan**

    The general statement should require the offeror to describe the proposed staffing plan, including how long it will take to staff the contract fully, and how peak workloads, overlapping or simultaneous task assignments, and sick and vacation leaves will be covered.

    The specific information requirements might include a discussion of how the offeror's resources are allocated, how the offeror plans to retain the proposed staffing levels, information on turnover rates and related recruiting efforts, and, when appropriate, how the offeror plans to maintain the required level of personnel with security clearances.

- **Key Personnel**

    The general statement should require the offeror to describe the educational background, directly related work experience, professional development, and demonstrated performance record of the proposed key personnel.

    Key personnel requirements and other resource requirements, such as minimum or maximum staffing levels, are not generally appropriate for performance work statements used in performance-based contracting (see Chapter 3). Such requirements tend to inhibit the contractor's ingenuity in developing its approach to meeting the contract requirements. (This does not, however, prevent the government from evaluating the key personnel or other resource requirements proposed by the offeror.)

    Specific information requirements usually include a description of what is required in the résumés of key personnel, such as information demonstrating that the individual meets the minimum qualification criteria described in the SOW. You should also obtain information on the current employment status of the proposed key personnel. If the individual is not currently employed full-time by the offeror, require a letter of intent or some other indication of the individual's commitment to work under the contract, as well as an authorization to use the individual's résumé in the proposal. You may also want the offeror to indicate the amount of time (usually as a percentage) that each key individual will devote exclusively to work under the contract. It is important to identify any other contracts to which the individual is committed, because you could have a problem if the individual is already fully or substantially committed to other work.

    If past performance is also an evaluation factor, require the offeror to indicate any involvement of proposed key personnel with any of the contracts referenced for past performance. You may want to question the offeror about the involvement of proposed key personnel in a contract that receives an adverse past performance report. Such questions, however, should be reserved for discussions (after establishment of the competitive range) because, while the offeror's response might require a proposal revision to name a different individual, it would not, in and of itself, require a proposal rejection.

- **Corporate Experience**

    The general statement should require the offeror to describe the corporate experience that demonstrates the contractor's ability to efficiently perform the tasks required under the contract.

    The specific information requirements usually include a requirement for the offeror to demonstrate previous experience similar to the current requirement. Require the offeror to identify the contract number, type of work done, contract type and dollar value, and name and telephone number of the contracting officer's technical representative (COTR) for each referenced contract. Require the offeror to demonstrate how each previous contract relates to the proposed effort. To ensure that the corporate experience is relevant, limit the time period for referenced contracts. The typical time periods used are three to five years, depending on how technological changes or other events may have affected the relevance of past contracts.

- **Past Performance**

    The general statement should require the offeror to identify current or past contracts that identify the offeror's ability to perform the required effort successfully.

    The specific information requirements usually include a requirement for the offeror to demonstrate previous experience similar to the current requirement. Require the offeror to identify current and past contracts for the same or similar work, including the contract number, dollar value, dates, name of the contracting agency, a contact telephone number, and a brief description of the work effort that demonstrates how the referenced contract relates to the proposed effort.

Require the offeror to identify any performance problems with the referenced contracts and the corrective action taken to resolve the problems. Inform the offeror that if past problems are not addressed fully, the government will assume that they still exist.

To ensure that the past performance information is relevant, limit the references to current contracts and contracts that have been completed within the past three to five years, depending on how technological changes or other events have affected the relevance of past contracts.

Although past performance information is similar to the information required for the corporate experience evaluation factor, it will be evaluated differently.

Corporate experience is used to assess a contractor's technical expertise and is typically evaluated on the basis of the contractor's experience with the same or similar work. It is related to whether the contractor has done such work in the past—not how well the contractor performed. Past performance is used to assess the quality of the contractor's performance and is typically evaluated on the basis of how well the contractor performed the same or similar work in the past and how that past performance is likely to affect the current effort.

- **Cost or Price**

    Under cost or price, you should describe how you want the contractor to present its cost or pricing proposal. These directions will vary depending on the contract type and the estimated dollar value. For example, if the requirement is expected to exceed $550,000 and a cost-reimbursement contract is contemplated, the following might be appropriate.

The general statement should indicate that cost data must be fully supported, documented, and traceable. The data must identify the basis of the estimate for each cost element, discuss how it was developed and calculated, and indicate which are based on actual and verifiable data and which are based on projections. For projected cost elements, the offeror must discuss the judgment factors used to project from the actual and verifiable data to the estimated value. Any contingencies or allowances used in developing the proposed costs and prices must be identified and discussed.

The specific information requirements vary. The FAR[7] states that if the submission of cost or pricing data is required, the contracting officer may require submission in the format indicated in Table 15-2 of 15.408, specify an alternative format, or permit submission in the contractor's format. If information other than cost or pricing data will be required, it may be submitted in the contractor's own format unless the contracting officer decides that use of a specific format is essential for evaluating and determining that the price is fair and reasonable, and the format has been described in the solicitation. If data supporting forward-pricing rate agreements are required, then the data supporting forward-pricing rate agreements or final indirect cost proposals should be submitted in a format acceptable to the contracting officer.

To Standardize Proposal Format

While the primary purpose of the proposal preparation instructions is to obtain information for evaluation, a secondary purpose is to make the evaluation process easier by standardizing the proposal format. Requiring adherence to the outline of the evaluation factors in Section M helps ensure that all proposals will present the information in the same format. Standardization makes the evaluation process easier because the evaluators will not need to search through differing proposal formats to find the necessary information. Standardization also assists offerors in their proposal preparation by eliminating the need for them to guess the proposal format that would be most acceptable to the government. This leads to better proposals.

Standardizing proposal format involves more than just providing an outline to follow. Standardization also includes establishing the number of proposal volumes, indicating the number of copies to be provided, setting page and type size preferences, and, when appropriate, limiting the number of proposal pages.

Proposal Volumes

Typically, the technical and management proposals are evaluated separately from the pricing proposals, by different evaluation teams. To permit both to be evaluated at the same time, offerors should be directed to divide their proposals into separate volumes. At a minimum, separate pricing and technical volumes should be provided.

Include a statement that pricing information is to be provided *only* in the pricing volume. This is necessary to protect the objectivity of the technical evaluation. Knowledge of the pricing can bias the results of the technical evaluation. In most instances, the technical evaluators know how much funding is available. It is difficult to evaluate a proposal objectively when you know that the proposal price is significantly higher or lower than the funds available.

As proposals become more complex, the need for additional proposal volumes increases. Often a management volume is required in addition to the technical and pricing volumes. Large, complex requirements may require additional volumes dealing with specific areas, such as specific tasks in a large, multi-tasked requirement. An examination of the evaluation plan can help determine how many volumes are required. If the plan indicates that a number of different evaluation teams will be evaluating different tasks, each team should have its own volume, if feasible.

In some instances you may want to include an executive summary as a separate volume. Be careful with executive summaries. They are not a substitute for close examination of the detailed proposal. Define this requirement carefully—make sure that offerors understand that the purpose of this document is simply to provide an overview of the proposal contents. Instruct offerors not to include pricing information in the executive summary. It is also a good idea to place a stringent page limit on this document.

Number of Copies

The number of copies to be provided is a function of the number of evaluation teams and how you will conduct the evaluation. Generally you should require enough copies so that each evaluator has a copy; however, if you do not plan to have each evaluator review each proposal, you will not need that many. Do not require more copies than will actually be used in evaluation. Proposals must be safeguarded in a manner similar to classified material—you do not want extra copies lying around.

Paper Size, Type Size, and Font Styles

Indicate the paper size, type size, and font style or styles to be used in the proposal. This helps avoid unnecessarily elaborate or hard-to-read proposals. Such standardization is also needed when page limits are used.

Paper size is usually established as the standard 8½ x 11 inches to discourage the use of legal-sized paper (which does not fit well into standard government files and provides an unfair advantage when page limits are dictated). You also may want to limit the size of fold-out pages. Fold-out pages are usually limited to non-text information, such as charts, tables, or diagrams, and the size is commonly 11 x 17 inches. Margins are often set at 1 inch. Some agencies require that proposal printing be double-spaced rather than single-spaced. Other agencies dictate the maximum number of lines that may be printed on a page.

Type size is usually set at no smaller than 10-point character height (vertical size) and no more than an average of 12 characters per inch to avoid the use of small print that is difficult to read.

Font styles are usually established only where provisions are made for proposals to be submitted in both hard copy and electronically or where page limits are set. If offerors will submit proposals electronically, the word processing program used must be compatible with your systems.

Page Limits

Page limits are used to preclude the submission of unnecessarily elaborate or lengthy proposals. A necessary prerequisite to the use of page limits is, of course, that you know how many pages constitute a reasonable proposal for your particular requirement. If you set the page limits too low, you may not get all the information you need. If you set the page limits too high, you are encouraging elaborate proposals. The best guideline to use is the complexity of your requirement. If you have a complex requirement (this will be reflected in the size of your SOW and the number of evaluation teams), you should probably establish a page limit. Examine previously submitted proposals for similar efforts to see if an average can be established, or simply use your best judgment. If the requirement is not complex, page limits are not necessary.

When using page limits, specify exactly what counts as a page. Generally, page limits are applied only against the basic text of the technical and management proposals. Attachments may or may not be included in the page limit. You may want to include page limits for attachments that amplify information in the technical and management proposals; otherwise, you may end up with slim proposals and fat attachments. You may also want to limit the types of information included in the attachments to technical supporting information that would not influence the evaluation of the technical and management proposals. *Pricing proposals are usually not included in page limits.*

In addition, you must state how you will determine which pages are excess and what will happen to excess pages. Typically, excess pages are determined by counting from the first page of the proposal. When the count reaches the page limit, the counting stops.

Pages in excess of the page limit are physically removed from the proposal (before the evaluation starts) and returned to the offeror. Offerors should be reminded that when excess pages are removed and not evaluated, this usually results in substantial proposal deficiencies, the correction of which is not permitted.

When you find formatting problems, such as the wrong type size, too many lines per page, and wrong page size, you should either recalculate the page count based on what it would be if done as directed, or simply remove the offending pages.

The use of page and format limitations depends on current circumstances. You should, however, have a valid reason for the limitations you do use. Keep in mind that when used, page limits *must* be followed in the evaluation and *cannot* be waived, unless the RFP is amended to revise the page limits for all offerors. If your limits are too restrictive or confusing, you may end up having to reject what might otherwise have been one of the most highly rated proposals.

You should note, however, that a proposal is not rejected simply because it exceeds page or format limitations. A proposal is rejected *only* when, after removing the excess pages, evaluation of the remaining proposal pages results in a determination that the proposal is technically unacceptable. *It is the deficiencies that result when only part of a proposal is evaluated that causes the rejection, not the failure to adhere to the page or format limitations.* Rejection is required because a technically unacceptable proposal is not subject to correction; to allow correction would give the offeror an unfair competitive advantage if it was permitted to have its noncompliant proposal evaluated as is, while other offerors adhered to the limitations in their proposals.

Figure 1-3 is an example of how a page limit could be established in the proposal preparation instructions.

To Require Specific Information

The proposal preparation instructions may also be used to elicit specific information that you need to amplify your initial SOW when you intend to incorporate all or part of the successful offeror's proposal into your final SOW. Incorporation by reference is accomplished by inserting a clause in the contract to the effect that all, or specified parts, of the contractor's proposal are incorporated into the contract by reference, and including the incorporated portions as an attachment to the contract. The incorporated portions become part of the contract, and the contractor is legally required to perform accordingly (contractors are required to do only what is written into the contract).

Generally, incorporation by reference is used in instances where the requirements are difficult to describe. You may not know how to go about meeting the requirement because of its technical complexity (as in software development). You may not be sure the requirement can be met, and part of the purpose of your requirement is to find out (as in R&D). There may be a number of ways to meet the requirement, and you do not want

FIGURE 1-3
Establishing a Page Limit

Offerors shall furnish proposals in two 3-ring binders in four sections, in the number of copies indicated, containing the following information:

SECTION	TITLE	NO. OF COPIES	PAGE LIMITS
Volume One		25	
I	Executive Summary		10
II	Management and Technical Proposal		80
III	Relevant Experience and Past Performance and Other Considerations		10
	Total Page Limit		100
Volume Two		25	
IV	Cost		None

RFP forms and Section K certifications required to be completed by the Offeror and Tables of Contents are excluded from the page limit. The proposal text shall be printed in not smaller than 12-pitch type (Elite) on standard 8 1/2 x 11-inch paper. Each volume of the proposal should be separate and complete within itself; however, discretionary references to another volume of the proposal may be appropriate to avoid duplication of the same material. Illustrations and forms shall be legible and no larger than 11 x 17-inch foldouts, as appropriate for the subject matter. Foldouts are considered two pages as part of the page limit. A sheet of paper printed on both sides is considered two pages.

The cost section, Volume Two, is not page-limited. However, the Cost Section is to be strictly limited to cost and price information. Information that can be construed as belonging in one of the other sections (in Volume One) will be so construed and counted against that section's page limit.

PAGES (ACTUAL OR CONSTRUCTIVE) SUBMITTED IN EXCESS OF THE PAGE LIMITS ENUMERATED ABOVE WILL NOT BE EVALUATED BUT WILL BE RETURNED TO THE OFFEROR.

to predetermine the way by specifying it in the SOW. You must, therefore, get the offerors to provide the necessary details in their technical proposals.

In such instances, you should provide a broad functional description of your requirement in the initial SOW and use the proposal preparation instructions to require offerors to explain the details of how the work will be done. The successful offeror's proposal would then be incorporated by reference (in whole or in part) into the final SOW.

To do this, you must tell the offerors the level of detail to be provided, such as the technical approach, work plans, methodology, analytic techniques, management reporting, and other details as to how the offeror proposes to meet the requirement. This is not dissimilar to what might be required in any event, but you must also indicate that the successful offeror's proposal will be incorporated by reference into the resulting contract and provide the offerors information about how to write a proposal to ensure that the wording used is contractually viable (see Chapters 4, 5, and 6).

It should be noted that you do not have to incorporate proposal detail by reference to include such information as a contractual requirement. You could amend the RFP to include the information in your SOW before award. To do this, the RFP must inform all offerors that you intend to revise the SOW to include certain information (specify the information) from the successful offeror's proposal. Or, you could simply revise the SOW in the award document for the successful offeror. You must be careful, however, to ensure that the revisions do not constitute a change to the nature of your requirement. Unsuccessful offerors can protest last-minute changes that could have affected the competitive standings.

A contractor's proposal is a promise to perform in a particular manner, but the contractor is not legally bound to perform in that manner as long as the contractor's performance meets the contractual requirements. If you want to hold the contractor to all or particular parts of its proposal, you must take action to include the pertinent parts of the contractor's proposal in the SOW. As noted, this can be done by incorporating by reference or by revising the SOW, but it must be done before contract award.

FORMATTING THE PROPOSAL PREPARATION INSTRUCTIONS

The purpose of proposal preparation instructions is to provide guidance on the format and content of proposals. How you provide this guidance is a matter of choice. The important thing to remember is that the instructions should be grouped together in a logical manner, clearly marked as proposal preparation instructions, and contain only information related to the development of the offeror's proposal. Do not include any information that applies to activities taking place after contract award. Information of this nature belongs in either the SOW or a contract clause, as appropriate.

There are a number of ways to present the proposal preparation instructions. Figure 1-4 provides one example of how it could be done.

FIGURE 1-4
Sample Format for Proposal Preparation Instructions

Introduction
- Make a statement to the effect that unnecessarily elaborate or lengthy proposals are not desired and will reflect adversely on the evaluation of the contractor's understanding of the requirement.
- Require the contractor to provide the technical and management information in a separate volume from the pricing information. Additional volumes may be required as necessary.
- Indicate the number of proposal copies required.
- If you intend to limit the number of proposal pages, indicate the page limit, how it will be applied, and how you will handle excess pages.

continues

continued

FIGURE 1-4
Sample Format for Proposal Preparation Instructions

Note: The information is often presented in a table, such as:

Volume	Title	No. Copies	Page Limit
I	Technical Proposal	10	100
II	Management Proposal	10	15
III	Corporate Experience	10	2
IV	Past Performance	10	2
V	Cost Proposal	4	None

Instructions
- Require the contractor to present the proposal in the same format as the evaluation factors listed in Section M. For example, if the following evaluation factors were listed in Section M, the instructions should require that the proposal format follow the same order and address the same factors:

Technical Factors
  - Technical Approach
  - Understanding the Requirement

Management Factors
  - Management Approach
  - Staffing Plan

Corporate Experience

Past Performance

Cost

- For each evaluation factor and sub-factor, identify the data or other information required. This includes such information as staffing plans, organization plans, graphs, charts, and other technical information that you need for evaluation purposes. It also includes information needed to complete the description of your requirement, such as work plans and schedules, proposed methodologies, proposed test plans, and other necessary information.

NEED TO CHECK YOUR WORK CAREFULLY

The proposal preparation instructions are an important part of the solicitation process. The contractor relies on this information in preparing its proposal. The efficiency of the evaluation process depends on how well the proposal preparation instructions direct the contractor to provide relevant information and a proposal format that facilitates the evaluation.

Check your proposal preparation instructions carefully before the RFP is issued to ensure that they are properly presented. Ambiguities, inconsistencies, or outright errors in the proposal preparation instructions can cause considerable confusion among the competing offerors and can result in the disqualification of an otherwise qualified offeror.

Check the proposal preparation instructions against the RFP as a whole, but pay particular attention to ensuring that the SOW requirements and the evaluation criteria and procedures listed in Section M are compatible.

Most offerors follow the proposal preparation instructions because they realize that proposals tend be scored lower if the evaluators have difficulty locating pertinent information due to a differing format or if required information is not provided.

An offeror appreciates and benefits from clear and thorough proposal preparation instructions because the more an offeror knows what the government wants to see in the proposal, the better it can respond to the government's concerns. Both the government and the contractor benefit from a responsive proposal.

The proposal preparation instructions are the final part of the evaluation plan. Keep in mind that the evaluation factors, their relative importance, and the proposal preparation instructions are published in the RFP. This enables you to influence the structure and content of the proposals and to expedite the evaluation process by reducing the possibility of confusing and conflicting proposal structures.

This concludes the introduction to the SOW and how it interacts with the other parts of the RFP. Chapter 2 addresses the planning and preparation necessary before you begin writing the SOW.

NOTES

[1] General Services Administration, Department of Defense, and National Aeronautics and Space Administration, *Federal Acquisition Regulation,* vol. 1–51, March 2005. 11.002(a)(1). Page 11.1-1. Online at *https://www.acquisition.gov/far/current/pdf/FAR.pdf* (accessed February 2011).

[2] FAR 11.002(a)(2).

[3] FAR 11.102.

[4] FAR 11.101(b).

[5] FAR 11.101(a).

[6] FAR 15.204-1.

[7] FAR 15.403.5(b)(1)(2)(3).

2 Planning and Preparation

It is essential to plan and prepare the description of the requirements carefully if they are to be translated successfully into an effective statement of work (SOW). Writing an SOW is not simply a matter of drafting a memo saying "I want what I want when I want it." The government's needs must be analyzed, the work requirements identified, the marketplace researched, and the requirements described in contractual language.

Today's marketplace is dominated by technological advances and innovations that make planning and preparation more important than ever to ensure that government acquisitions take full advantage of what the marketplace has to offer. Two key elements of planning and preparation are acquisition planning and market research. Acquisition planning identifies the agency requirement and its initial description and is accomplished before the statement of work or performance work statement is developed. Market research develops information about marketplace capabilities and processes and refines the description of the requirement by correlating the government need with what industry can provide. Market research takes place both before and during the preparation of the statement of work or performance work statement.

ACQUISITION PLANNING

"Acquisition planning should begin as soon as the agency need is identified, preferably well in advance of the fiscal year in which contract award or order placement is necessary."[1] To accomplish this goal, a planner is needed. The FAR defines a planner as "the designated person or office responsible for developing and maintaining a written plan, or for the planning function in those acquisitions not requiring a written plan."[2] Depending on the size or importance of a pending acquisition, an individual may be specifically appointed as the planner, or the function may be assumed to be part of a person's job description.

Generally, the planner is a technical person in the office or program generating the requirement. There are, however, a number of other persons whose expertise will be required during the course of the acquisition, such as contracting, fiscal, and legal personnel. Consideration should also be given to consulting users (personnel who will be using the product or receiving the services resulting from the acquisition) as well as other technical personnel, from within the agency or from other agencies with similar requirements, who can provide necessary expertise.

Acquisition planning is best accomplished using a team approach, either formally or informally. Major acquisitions are planned using a formal approach with appointed members and a structured approach. Less-than-major acquisitions are generally planned informally using an ad hoc approach. While the term "team approach" brings to mind an image of endless meetings, this need not be the case. The planner should be the coordinator and information gatherer, interfacing with the other personnel as needed to gather the information necessary to put together an initial picture of the pending acquisition. Generally meetings are needed only when decisions must be made.

To plan an acquisition, certain questions must be addressed initially:

- What is the real requirement, and when is it needed?

- What results are required, and how will success be measured or determined?

- What is it likely to cost, and what funds are available?

What Is the Real Requirement, and When Is It Needed?

Generally, when acquiring equipment, supplies, or other hardware items, the requirement is readily apparent, but this is not always the case. When what you want is what you bought before, the requirement is easily defined, but consideration should always be given to whether you really need something better, different, or more refined. Consider the effect of technology changes since the previous procurement as well as the possibility that the utilization of the product has changed. User input can be important to the determination of the real requirement.

When acquiring services, the need to carefully consider the real requirement is even greater, because how the requirement is stated can affect how offerors respond. For example, stating a services requirement as a requirement for information technology (IT) resources instead of describing the requirement in terms of what those resources are expected to do can limit offerors to responding in terms of bodies rather than technology.

Do not automatically use the same description of the requirement that was used on a previous acquisition. Even if it appears that the agency's requirement has not changed, technological advances or innovations may have changed how that requirement can be met. Using the previous description of the requirement may inhibit offerors from proposing the latest advances. Proper planning and preparation will ensure that the description of the requirement is flexible enough to take advantage of what the marketplace has to offer.

To obtain the best results from a "team" approach, the planner should query those who would be involved in both the procurement and the resulting contract to get their concept of what the requirement is and the results intended. These varying concepts can then be brought to the table for a common resolution.

Initially, acquisition planners must ensure that they have accurately identified both the need to be satisfied by the acquisition and what must be acquired to meet that need. Except when necessary for program purposes, planners should identify the requirement in terms of the required results rather than how the work is to be accomplished.

The planners must also determine when the users need the requirement and the projected term of the contract. This is necessary for developing a timeline for accomplishing the various tasks necessary to complete the acquisition, such as conducting market research, developing a description of the requirement (e.g., a statement of work, performance work statement), conducting the competition, source selection, and contract award.

How Will Success Be Measured or Determined?

Acquisition planning must include a determination of how contract success will be measured. Specifics are not necessary in the initial acquisition planning, but the required capabilities or performance characteristics of equipment or supplies should be determined. When acquiring services, advance planning should identify the broad performance standards of the services being acquired and whether or not performance-based contracting methods will be used. The initial determinations will be enhanced by the results of market research before development of the SOW or performance work statement (PWS).

What Is It Likely to Cost, and What Funds Are Available?

Once the requirement is identified, the planners must develop an estimate of what it might cost. This cost estimate must then be reconciled with the agency's projected budget to determine what funds are likely to be available when the requirement enters the procurement process. During the planning process, cost estimates are adjusted frequently to reflect budget fluctuations and refined as the requirement itself is more clearly defined. The availability of funds may require an adjustment to the requirement, but it is better to make such adjustments after the requirement is fully defined rather than try to build a requirement to a projected budget figure.

The answers to these questions will form a basis for the acquisition planning. Acquisition planning is not done overnight. It is a step-by-step process that takes time to accomplish. FAR Part 7 provides guidance on what areas should be considered and what should be in a written acquisition plan. Most agencies have adopted local procedures to implement FAR Part 7; however, FAR Part 7 is only part of the picture. FAR 7.102 states that agencies shall perform acquisition planning *and conduct market research* for all acquisitions. Market research is addressed in FAR Part 10, but it is an integral part of the acquisition planning process.

MARKET RESEARCH

Market research is the process of collecting and analyzing information about commercial capabilities and practices to determine the capability of the marketplace to satisfy agency needs. Generally, market research is conducted before developing new requirements documents and soliciting offers for acquisitions in excess of the simplified acquisition threshold of $150,000, and for acquisitions of less than $150,000 when adequate information is not available and the circumstances justify the cost.[3] Market research may also be conducted on an ongoing basis within a segment of industry. This is done to keep up with changes in the marketplace that might affect future agency requirements and not as part of a specific acquisition plan.

It is important that *all* market research activity be documented and maintained in the acquisition file. Agencies should document the results of market research in a manner that is appropriate to the size and complexity of the acquisition being performed.[4] This will permit easy access when planning future acquisitions and by other agency personnel with similar acquisition requirements.

Market research is most effective when conducted after the agency has made an initial determination of what it needs, when it needs it, how the agency will define contract success, and roughly how much it might cost. This information provides direction to the researchers regarding what to look for in the marketplace. Generally, market research is done during the initial stages of acquisition planning or, if this is not possible, at least before a final statement of work or performance work statement is developed.

Market research is conducted to obtain information about what the marketplace has to offer—its capabilities, practices, and pricing policies. The results of market research are used to enhance the final description of the agency requirement.

When acquiring equipment or supplies, market research information includes who manufactures or can otherwise provide the required items, if there have been technological or other changes in how the items are manufactured or utilized, and if such changes would affect how the current requirements are described. It may also indicate that the current items are obsolete and that something new or different would better serve to meet current requirements.

When acquiring services, the key concerns are how the same or similar commercial services are organized and staffed, the work outputs or products, performance indicators, performance standards, acceptable quality levels, and if technological advances and other innovations have changed how the services are performed.

The first step, however, is to conduct a desk audit, which is essentially a review of the information available in-house, and a literature search of appropriate trade publications and contractor marketing literature. A request for information (RFI) or a sources-sought synopsis may also be used in conjunction with the initial market research.

It is not unusual for an agency to revise its initial description of the requirement as a result of market research. Effective use of market research will allow the planners to meld agency requirements with industry capabilities and practices to produce a statement of work or performance work statement that permits industry the greatest flexibility to provide innovative solutions to meet the agency's requirements.

The FAR does not address who should conduct market research. While technical and program personnel continually do informal market research through their professional reading and contacts with their industry counterparts, this information is rarely recorded and much of its value as market research is typically lost. Successful market research requires that the information be recorded and made available to others. This is why market research should be conducted as part of acquisition planning and based on the contributions and participation of the pertinent planning team members.

For example, the technical or program personnel need to know about the technical aspects of how industry goes about providing the goods or services in question, such as technological advances, innovative processes or practices, and performance metrics and measurements. Contracting personnel need to know about pricing, warranties, and other commercial terms and conditions that might affect how the goods or services are to be procured. Users will have their own set of concerns related to the practical use of the goods or services. These varying concerns must be coordinated as part of the planning process before actually conducting the market research so that all members of the acquisition planning team understand what the market research is to accomplish.

FAR 10.002(b)(2) suggests how market research might be conducted, identifying the following techniques:

- Contacting knowledgeable individuals in government and industry regarding market capabilities to meet requirements

- Reviewing the results of recent market research undertaken to meet similar or identical requirements

- Publishing formal requests for information in appropriate technical or scientific journals or business publications

- Querying government databases that provide information relevant to agency acquisition

- Participating in interactive, online communications among industry, acquisition personnel, and customers

- Obtaining source lists of similar items from other contracting activities or agencies, trade associations, or other sources

- Reviewing catalogs and other generally available product literature published by manufacturers, distributors, and dealers or available online

- Conducting interchange meetings or holding presolicitation conferences to involve potential offerors early in the acquisition process.

FAR Part 10 is not the only reference to market research techniques. FAR 5.205(a) addresses the use of R&D advance notices ("Research and Development Sources Sought") to obtain information about the capabilities of R&D firms, and FAR 5.205(c) states that contracting officers may transmit to the government-wide point of entry (GPE) special notices of procurement matters such as business fairs, long-range procurement estimates, pre-bid or pre-proposal conferences, meetings, and the availability of draft solicitations or draft specifications for review.

In addition, FAR 15.201(c) identifies the following techniques to promote early exchange of information:

- Industry or small business conferences

- Public hearings

- Market research, as described in Part 10
- One-on-one meetings with potential offerors
- Presolicitation notices
- Draft RFPs
- RFIs
- Presolicitation or preproposal conferences
- Site visits.

These techniques should all be considered, used as appropriate, and documented as market research. There is no single way to conduct market research. It is a continuing process, starting during acquisition planning and continuing until the solicitation is released.

After conducting a desk audit and literature search, the next step is to do basic research about the marketplace related to your requirement (e.g., who are the likely sources and what is known about their capabilities) using a combination of the techniques listed in FAR 10.002(b)(2). Then contact the likely sources to request information about their capabilities to meet your requirements.

Keep in mind that market research is a presolicitation activity. Your requirement is not yet defined sufficiently to begin the solicitation process. Market research can be conducted through telephone calls, letters, questionnaires, and personal contacts, as appropriate. Develop a list of questions to be asked before making any contacts and document the answers received.

When your likely sources are contacted, the requirement should be described in general terms, such as a need to improve the capabilities of a particular piece of equipment or services to accomplish certain types of tasks. The description should provide enough information for the sources to decide if they are interested in pursuing the matter. Your initial query (generally by letter) should ask for an expression of interest and identification of the respondent's capabilities to meet the requirements. Depending on the responses, you may want to pursue more information using some of the techniques identified in FAR 15.201(c).

The most effective method to elicit information about a firm's capabilities is through one-on-one meetings between the agency's technical or program personnel and their counterparts in the firm (marketing or sales personnel not included). This can be done after an initial contact has established that the firm is interested and has the capabilities to meet the requirement. The primary purpose of these meetings is to discuss the firm's capabilities to meet the requirements as outlined in the initial contact letter and to learn more about the firm's procedures, processes, and policies.

Later, more definitive information can be obtained by using a draft SOW or RFP where the firm is asked to comment on the draft with the assurance that its comments will not be made available to other firms. These methods are effective because they ensure confidentiality; thus, the firm is free to talk about its technical and business practices without fear of compromising its market position. When using a draft SOW or RFP, ensure that respondents are told that the draft is subject to change and that comments on different or innovative approaches are encouraged.

Techniques such as presolicitation or preproposal conferences, or any other meeting where a number of firms will be attending, are less effective because participants will be reluctant to talk about their firm's innovations or unique capabilities due to the presence of their competitors. Such meetings do, however, tend to reveal weaknesses in the agency's description of its requirements because the participants are not reluctant to point out such problems (unless they plan to take advantage of the weaknesses if they receive the contract award).

Chapter 4 addresses market research as it relates to the use of a statement of objectives (SOO). That discussion also applies to all market research, particularly with respect to information exchanges with industry before the receipt of proposals.

THINKING THE PROJECT THROUGH

Before starting to write the SOW (or PWS), it is important to think through the entire project, from solicitation and contract award through contract performance, delivery, acceptance, and use. What is required to initiate and sustain the contract effort? What is going to happen once the contract product is delivered and accepted? What is the intended end use of your product? What should be put in the SOW to ensure that the product is usable? When acquiring IT systems or software, for example, consider system or software maintenance for at least the first year of operation.

Planning and preparation are possibly the most important steps in the SOW process. It is essential not to be rushed and to get experienced help when necessary.

One approach to this planning process is to review the requirement as though you were going to do the work in-house and had all the necessary resources. Identify the key activities or tasks, and any related subtasks, on the basis of how you would organize the effort. Then determine the essential requirements, such as quantity, quality, capability, and any other salient characteristics that must be in the finished product or completed service. You also need to determine what must be accomplished during contract performance to produce the required end product and identify problems that are likely to be encountered.

Consider what information you have and what you will need from the contractor to describe your requirement. Some of the needed information can be obtained from market research, RFIs, draft RFPs, or direct contact with potential contractors. In some instances, you may want to request specific information in the proposal preparation instructions. Finally, you should develop an outline of the technical requirements by task. This is the foundation for your SOW.

Scope the requirement to your actual needs, not to your anticipated budget. The scope should allow for sufficient effort to address all project issues. If it turns out that the requirement exceeds the budget, you have a sound basis for requesting additional funds or for revising your requirement to bring it in line with the budget. If you initially scope the project to the anticipated budget, budget shortfalls may preclude accomplishing all of your project goals.

It is essential to ensure that the effort can be performed as described. Do not ask a contractor to take on a requirement that will exceed its capabilities or capacity. Consider breaking large or complex requirements into smaller packages that can be performed in phases or awarded to multiple contractors. If it appears that significant subcontracting will be required, consider indicating which efforts must be performed by the contractor and which may be subcontracted.

USING A WORK BREAKDOWN STRUCTURE

If the work requirements are complex, you can use a work breakdown structure (WBS) to model the requirement. The WBS can be developed manually or by using commercially available planning software.

To develop a WBS, each of the key activities or tasks to be performed must first be identified. Next, the related subactivities or subtasks within each key activity that are necessary for successful completion should be identified. This breakdown helps ensure that all activities within the technical requirement have been identified and described in the SOW. In most cases, you will not need to structure your WBS beyond the third level to describe your requirement adequately. The WBS also serves as the basis for developing the independent government cost estimate.

Generally, the WBS serves only as an internal planning document. Do not use the WBS in your SOW or anywhere else in the solicitation. Dictating a WBS in the SOW inhibits a contractor's flexibility in developing its proposal because the contractor will assume that its proposal must conform to your WBS. This may preclude a proposal that sets forth a better way to do the job.

CHOOSING THE CONTRACT TYPE

Before deciding on the type of SOW you will write (functional, performance, or design), you need to consider the type of contractual pricing arrangement to be used. You must have a general idea of the contract type before beginning to write your SOW so that its contents will support your preference. The contracting officer will make the final decision regarding contract type but will usually follow your preference, as long as it makes sense.

Choosing the most effective contract type involves considering how the contract type will affect the description of your requirement. For each contract type, your SOW must be definitive enough to achieve the intended result.

Fixed-Price Contracts

In a fixed-price contract, the contract price is fixed at the time of contract award. This price cannot be changed unless the scope of work is changed, and the contractor is entitled to payment only if the contract is completed successfully. The contractor makes its profit by completing the work at a cost less than the fixed price.

Fixed-price contracts are used only when the SOW is definitive enough for the contractor to price the cost of contract performance accurately and have a high degree of confidence that the work can be completed within that price. Fixed-price contracts are generally used for commercial or commercial-like equipment or services available in the open market.

In a fixed-price contract the contractor guarantees performance at the fixed or ceiling price. If the contractor cannot complete performance at this price, the contractor must complete the work at its own expense. This puts a significant burden on the author of the SOW to ensure that a fixed-price SOW is definitive enough for the contractor to estimate accurately the costs of performance. For example, the following was taken from a fixed-price solicitation for training services:

> 0001AN   New course development as specified in 3.6 of the statement of work   1 Lot
>
> 3.6   The contractor agrees to undertake new course development as required by the Government pursuant to the terms of this contract. When the Contracting officer determines that such services are required, he will issue an order for such work.

The SOW did not provide any further discussion of new course development. The RFP required a fixed price for each line item. How can a contractor put a fixed-price on such an ill-defined requirement? This is not the way to describe a requirement for a fixed-price contract. Needless to say, this solicitation and the resulting contract had a lot of problems.

When you have a requirement that involves performance uncertainties or risks, a fixed-price contract is usually inappropriate. Performance uncertainties are present when you are uncertain about the final outcome or your requirement cannot be defined except through contract performance, as in a research and development effort. Performance uncertainties are also found in requirements for studies and analytic effort when you are uncertain as to the extent of effort required. Requirements for creative effort, such as the development of computer software, training courses, manuals, or handbooks, also involve performance uncertainties because creative efforts often require flexibility in the extent of effort required.

Fixed-priced contracts are inappropriate for efforts of this nature because the fixed price limits the extent of the contractor's efforts. If performance proves to be more difficult or extensive than anticipated, and the contractor's costs are approaching the fixed price, the contractor's options are limited. The contractor can continue to strive for a quality product, at its own expense, or the contractor can cut corners and do whatever is necessary to finish the contract within the fixed price.

The first option is not popular with contractors—a contractor cannot stay in business for long unless it makes a profit. The second option is not popular with the government—cutting corners and taking other actions designed to "finish the contract" usually have an adverse effect on the quality of the final product. Problems such as these can be avoided by carefully assessing the performance uncertainties of your project and using a fixed-price contract only when performance uncertainties are minimal.

Cost-Reimbursement Contracts

In a cost-reimbursement contract, the contractor is reimbursed for the costs it actually incurs. In addition, the contractor is usually paid a fee for contract performance. This fee may be fixed or variable. The maximum fee amount is fixed at the time of contract award and cannot be changed unless the scope of work is changed.

The contractor is required to expend its *best efforts* to complete the contract within the funds initially obligated. The contractor is not required—or expected—to complete the work at its own expense as in a fixed-price type contract. The contractor recovers its actual costs incurred regardless of contract performance. When it appears that the obligated funds are not sufficient to complete the contract effort, the contractor should notify the contracting officer and provide an estimate to complete the effort, indicating if, and how much, additional funding will be required. The contracting officer may or may not add the required funds, as appropriate. When the funds are fully expended, the contractor should stop work. Any continued work is at the contractor's own expense, unless the contracting officer adds funds before all the originally allotted funds are expended.

Cost-reimbursement contracts are designed for efforts that contain performance uncertainties. This type of contract accommodates those uncertainties by basing the price on estimated costs (plus the fixed or variable fee) and permitting additional costs (but not fee) to be funded without the need for a corresponding change in the scope of work. Cost-reimbursement contracts are used when the work cannot be fully defined, the nature of the work is uncertain, or creative effort is required. Cost-reimbursement contracts are typically used in R&D, studies, analytic effort, and software development.

The funding flexibility in cost-reimbursement contracts, however, does not lessen the SOW requirements. An SOW for cost-reimbursement work must be as definitive as possible so that the contractor's cost estimate is as accurate as possible. Otherwise, you will be creating a cost-overrun situation in your initial SOW. The SOW must be written to minimize overruns, not create them.

Time-and-Materials and Labor-Hour Contracts

In a time-and-materials (T&M) contract, the contractor is paid a fixed hourly rate for each labor category set forth in the contract. The fixed rate includes direct labor, overhead, general and administrative expenses, and profit. Materials used in contract performance are reimbursed at cost. The T&M contract has some characteristics similar to both cost-reimbursement and fixed-price contracts.

The T&M contract is worked on a best-efforts basis like the cost-reimbursement contract, but this is its *only* resemblance to a cost-reimbursement contract. The T&M contract has a price ceiling, but this is its *only* resemblance to a fixed-price contract. Payment is for the hours worked, not for the delivery of a specific product. The T&M contract is a *fixed-rate* contract, and the total amount paid depends on the number of hours worked plus material at cost. The labor-hour contract is exactly the same as a T&M contract, except that no materials are involved.

T&M contracts are used when it is not possible to estimate the extent or duration of the work or to anticipate the total costs, and the use of a cost-reimbursement contract is not feasible. T&M contracts are used for repair, maintenance, or emergency services requirements, or for service contracts with small businesses or individuals who lack an accounting systems sophisticated enough to use a cost-reimbursement contract.

The SOW for a T&M contract must be as definitive as possible. The overall effort is restricted by the ceiling price, which is usually the sum of the total estimated hours at the fixed rates plus materials at cost. The work requirements must be described in sufficient detail for the contractor to estimate accurately the extent of effort and the amount of materials required.

Indefinite-Delivery Contracts

Indefinite-delivery contracts are used when the exact time of delivery or the quantities of supplies or services to be delivered are not known at the time of award. In effect, the government uses the contractor as a warehouse, drawing the necessary supplies or services as the specific requirements develop. There are three types of indefinite-delivery contracts: definite-quantity, requirements, and indefinite-quantity contracts. Requirements contracts and indefinite-quantity contracts are also known as delivery-order contracts (for supplies) and task-order contracts (for services).

- **Definite-quantity contracts.** This arrangement provides for the delivery of a definite quantity of specific supplies or services for a fixed period, with deliveries or performance to be scheduled at designated locations upon order. Definite-quantity contracts are used when a definitive quantity of the supplies or services will be required during the contract period and are regularly available or will be available after a short lead time. Orders are placed for delivery or performance at the designated locations as the requirements develop during the contract term.

- **Requirements contracts.** This arrangement provides for the delivery of all actual requirements of specific supplies or services by designated government activities during a fixed period. Generally, the contract will state the maximum amount the contractor is required to deliver and, within that amount, that the government is required to purchase *all* of its actual requirements for the specified supplies or services from the contractor. Deliveries are ordered by issuing delivery or task orders when the supplies or services are needed. Under a requirements contract, the contractor is the sole source of supply during the term of the contract.

- **Indefinite-quantity contracts.** This arrangement provides for the delivery of an indefinite quantity, within stated limits, of supplies or services during a fixed period. Deliveries are ordered by issuing a delivery or task order when the supplies or services are needed. Under this arrangement, the government is required to order the minimum quantity stated in the contract, and the contractor is required to provide the maximum quantity stated in the contract, if ordered, at the stated price.

The basic difference between a requirements contract and an indefinite-quantity contract is that while the government *must* order all of its actual requirements from the contractor under a requirements contract, once the minimum quantity has been ordered under an indefinite-quantity contract, the government is not obligated to place further orders with the contractor and could, for example, place any further orders with another contractor offering lower prices. Once the maximum quantity has been ordered, the contractor may renegotiate the prices for any further orders.

The FAR[5] states a preference for making multiple awards of indefinite-quantity contracts under a single solicitation for the same or similar supplies or services to two or more sources, but does permit single awards under certain circumstances. The decision whether or not to use multiple awards must be documented in the contract file. Generally, when multiple awards are made, the individual delivery or task orders must be competed among the awardees, but the FAR does allow orders to be placed on a sole-source basis under certain circumstances.

The FAR[6] also states that performance-based work statements must be used to the maximum extent practicable when procuring services (see Chapter 3).

The primary characteristics of indefinite-delivery contracts are that government funds are obligated upon issuance of each delivery or task order rather than at contract award, and the government does not have to order the supplies or services until the actual requirement materializes.

While any appropriate cost or pricing arrangement under FAR Part 16 may be used for indefinite-delivery contracts,[7] delivery-order contracts (for supplies) are usually priced on the basis of a fixed price per line item, and task-order contracts (for services) are usually priced on a cost-reimbursement or time-and-materials basis. However, commercially available services with established pricing may be priced on a fixed-price basis.

When using a delivery-order contract, the SOW for the basic contract describes the specific supplies required. The delivery orders simply cite the contract line item numbers and the nomenclature of the supply item. Another complete SOW is not required.

Under a task-order contract, multiple SOWs are usually required. An SOW is required for the basic contract, and another SOW is required for each task order issued. The contract SOW describes the general nature of each task but not the specific work requirements (which are not usually known at the time of contracting). The contract SOW describes the general nature of the tasks required, describes the required resources and facilities, and provides an estimate of the required level-of-effort for each general task. The contract SOW must describe the tasks sufficiently for the contractor to estimate the extent of effort required and provide an overall price estimate. The basic contract is negotiated and priced based on the contractor's response to the contract SOW.

As each specific work requirement is known, a task-order SOW is required. Each task-order SOW must describe the specific work requirement in sufficient detail for the contractor to submit a priced proposal. This must be a complete SOW, as though it were the SOW for a contract. Keep in mind that the contract SOW is very general in nature. If you want to hold the contractor to your work requirements, the task-order SOW must adequately express these requirements.

Inadequate task-order SOWs are a common problem. Task-order SOWs are often written with the assumption that the basic contract SOW adequately covers the work. This is not the case. The basic contract SOW provides only a general description; it is the task-order SOW that provides the details. If the task-order SOW is not complete, it is likely that the work will also be incomplete or otherwise unsatisfactory. The contractor is required to submit a priced proposal in response to the task-order SOW. Once the price and technical details are negotiated, the task order is issued.

When writing an indefinite-quantity contract, you must explain how the delivery or task orders will be handled. The FAR clauses that are used are general in nature and must be supported by either language in the SOW or a locally developed clause that provides the specific details. Addressing these details in the SOW permits you to tailor the ordering procedures to your specific needs. Locally developed clauses tend to get out of date and are often too generalized for specific needs, so they must be examined in each instance and tailored as required.

CHOOSING THE SOW TYPE

There are a number of ways to write an SOW. You can write an SOW in terms of a functional description, a performance description, or a design description. You can write a stand-alone SOW or one that contemplates the incorporation of all or part of the contractor's proposal into the final SOW. If you are using a cost-reimbursement contract, you can describe your requirement as a level-of-effort (LOE) or a completion effort. Regardless of the approach you choose, to ensure consistency in your writing techniques, you should make your choice before you start writing the SOW.

Functional Descriptions

The FAR[8] states that requirements are to be expressed in terms of the functions to be performed, performance required, or essential physical characteristics. A functional description addresses what is to be done rather than how it is to be done. It specifies what the contractor is to accomplish, such as collecting data and performing an analysis, but does not get into the precise details of how to collect the data and perform the analysis.

Generally, a functional SOW describes the required effort in terms of what, when, where, how many, and how well the work must be performed, without describing exactly how to perform the work. A functional description can best be developed as an extension of the WBS. The WBS graphically displays the activities to be performed (the what), but to ensure an accurate work description, the functional description must describe each task and subtask in terms of the following:

- **Work Input**—Determine what activity triggers initiation of the work effort. This could be the submission of a request, the issuance of a task order, the occurrence of a particular event, or any other activity that authorizes the contractor to begin work. Also identify any physical items (government forms, documents, reports, etc.) used to signal the contractor's authority to begin. These may be items provided by the government or a third party, or work products previously produced by the contractor.

- **Work Effort**—Determine the steps required to perform the work, such as what has to be done to process particular documents, analyze specific input, or otherwise perform each task. Keep in mind, however, that these steps are described in terms of what must be done rather than how the work is to be accomplished. The description of the work effort would include, as applicable, where and when the work is to be performed.

- **Work Output**—Determine what is to be produced or provided by each task or subtask. The description of the work output should also address "how much" or "how many" are required as well as the criteria for determining whether the requirements are met.

Each task and subtask description should indicate what initiates the work effort, what effort must be undertaken, and what must be produced or provided by the work effort. The development of this information is similar to the job analysis performed when developing a performance work statement (PWS) for a service contract under the performance-based service contracting (PBSC) concept (see Chapter 3).

A purely functional description is rarely appropriate; usually, certain constraints must be described to ensure that the contractor produces a useful end product. These constraints can be physical characteristics, such as size or weight, or can relate to how the contractor performs, such as restrictions on the use of specific techniques. Only those constraints necessary to ensure contractor understanding of the complete requirement should be described. The use of a functional description permits the contractor to use its own approach as long as it is within the constraints you have established.

A functional description encourages contractor creativity and the use of innovative techniques or methodologies, allowing your project to benefit from the latest developments in the state-of-the-art. A functional description is also appropriate when several ways are available to perform the requirement and you do not want to dictate the approach used.

When a functional SOW is used, the contractor must respond with a technical proposal that shows how the work will be performed. This enhances your ability to evaluate the contractors' expertise and understanding of the requirement and to make an award based on the best technical and price combination. By proposing how the work will be done, the contractor assumes responsibility that the proposed effort will produce an acceptable result.

Performance Descriptions

The SOW for a performance description is referred to as a performance work statement (PWS) and is used in conjunction with performance-based service contracting (PBSC) because performance descriptions are usually more appropriate for service contracts than supply contracts.

A performance description is similar to a functional description in that it describes the requirements in terms of "what" is to be required rather than "how" the work is to be accomplished, the number of personnel to be assigned, or the number of hours to be provided. As with the functional description, the performance description also contains the necessary design constraints to ensure an acceptable end product. The performance description, however, provides much greater detail as to the expected performance outcomes and how they are measured. The differences between the functional and performance descriptions are summarized in the following paragraphs and addressed in greater detail in Chapter 3. Despite the differences, the general concepts regarding the format and contents of the PWS and the functional SOW are the same (see Chapter 5).

Differences between Functional and Performance Descriptions

The basic differences between functional and performance descriptions are in the level of specific detail provided. Functional descriptions are more generalized, and conformance to the requirements is usually measured by a subjective assessment of the contract monitors. Performance descriptions are more detailed and provide an objective means of measuring contract compliance. The specific differences are as follows:

- **Statement of the required services in terms of output.** Both the performance and the functional descriptions describe the requirements in terms of "what, when, where, how many, and how well" the work is to be performed rather than "how" the work is to be performed.

    The performance description, however, goes further and describes the work requirements, or outputs, in terms of specific performance indicators. The term "output" means an expression of the work requirements in terms of the results of the work (i.e., what the services are to produce or provide). Output is described in terms of objective, measurable performance indicators, such as rooms cleaned, equipment repaired, or requests processed.

The functional description is less specific, usually describing the work in terms of what is to be accomplished or the functions or tasks to be performed, but not to the detail of specific, measurable performance indicators.

- **Use of measurable performance standards for the required outputs.** Both the performance descriptions and the functional descriptions must describe the criteria for determining whether the requirements are met. The performance description lays out such criteria in terms of performance standards. Performance standards are linked to the performance indicators and expressed in quantifiable terms, such as a rate of performance (e.g., x number per hour, x minutes per job), quantities, time, events, or any other terms that can be measured objectively.

  The functional description spells out the criteria for determining successful performance in terms of the characteristics or features of successful contract performance and indicates how they will be measured. While similar to the standards in the performance descriptions, these criteria are less specific, particularly in terms of how they will be measured.

- **Use of acceptable quality levels (AQL) or allowable error rates.** In addition to establishing measurable performance standards, a performance description must also establish an acceptable deviation from the standard (an AQL or allowable error rate) that will still result in an acceptable level of quality. It is not realistic to expect 100 percent compliance in all cases.

  A functional description rarely establishes an acceptable quality level except where it is necessary to set performance standards for certain tasks.

- **Use of a quality assurance plan (QAP) and surveillance.** In addition to the PWS, a performance description contains a QAP, which defines what the government will do to ensure that the contractor's performance is in conformance with the established PWS standards. The QAP includes a surveillance schedule and must clearly state the methods of surveillance to be used. The QAP will be discussed in greater detail in Chapter 3.

A functional description might address contract surveillance in the SOW, but not in the detail set forth in a QAP.

- **Use of incentives.** The PBSC concept encourages the use of incentives for all PBSC contracts (discussed in Chapter 3). Contracts using a functional SOW may, when appropriate, use incentives, such as cost-plus-award fee (CPAF) incentives in acquisitions of significant dollar value, but the use of incentives is not mandated.

Design Descriptions

A design description details exactly how the contractor must perform the work by providing precise details on materials, methods, processes, and procedures. In essence, all competing contractors are required to perform exactly the same effort. Deviations from the requirements of the design description are not normally permitted. Each contractor must provide a proposal demonstrating that it can do the work, with price being the primary consideration for award. Generally, a design description is appropriate only when the work must be performed in a particular manner.

When a design description is used, the government assumes responsibility that the work can be successfully performed as described. This is one of the primary differences between design descriptions and functional or performance descriptions. When functional or performance descriptions are used, the contractor assumes the responsibility that the work can be successfully performed as proposed. This is the reason that the use of design descriptions is not encouraged.

INCORPORATING A CONTRACTOR'S PROPOSAL BY REFERENCE

Some requirements are difficult to describe, for a variety of reasons. You may not know how to go about meeting the requirement because of its technical complexity (as in software development). You may not be sure that the requirement can be met (as in R&D) and part of the purpose of your requirement is to find out. A number of different ways to meet the requirement may be possible, and you are reluctant to predetermine the approach by writing the SOW around a particular method.

In such instances, the SOW should be treated as a two-part document. Use performance-based or functional terms to describe what the contract effort is to produce or accomplish in the initial SOW (in the RFP). At the same time, use the proposal preparation instructions to require offerors to explain how the work will be performed. The successful offeror's proposal is then incorporated (in whole or in part) in the contract by reference and becomes part of the final, or contractual, SOW. This is done just prior to award by inserting a clause into the contract that identifies the successful offeror's proposal and makes it a part of the contract.

You cannot, however, incorporate or otherwise use any portion of a proposal *other than that of the successful offeror.* You cannot use the "good" portions of an unsuccessful proposal to improve your SOW. To do so would invite protests from the unsuccessful offerors, and such protests are usually sustained.

Moreover, you cannot use this process to *change* your requirement. This process may be used only to incorporate those parts of a successful offeror's proposal that amplify or provide greater detail on how your requirement will be met. A change in your requirement requires an amendment to your solicitation that is provided to all offerors in the competitive range.

Do not automatically incorporate the entire proposal by reference. Use only those parts pertinent to the performance of the work requirement as described in the SOW. The successful offeror's proposal should be reviewed carefully and the offeror required to revise the wording as necessary to make it contractually acceptable. Agreement should be reached on the specific wording of those parts that are to be incorporated in your SOW before contract award. You do not want to incorporate loopholes or ambiguities into your SOW through the wording of the successful offeror's proposal.

After contract award, those parts of the contractor's proposal incorporated in the SOW become part of the government's requirement. If a dispute arises over interpretation of the SOW, the government is responsible for any ambiguities or other problems. This responsibility cannot be avoided by using an "order of precedence" clause to resolve conflicts between the initial SOW and those parts incorporated by reference. The final SOW is totally the government's responsibility.

You are not required to incorporate all or part of the successful offeror's proposal in your SOW. This is a matter of choice. You should, however, make at least a tentative decision before writing your SOW. Your decision does not affect how the initial SOW is written, but it will affect how the proposal preparation instructions are written. If you are considering incorporating all or part of the successful offeror's proposal in the SOW, ensure that the proposal preparation instructions require offerors to provide the necessary details.

The concept of incorporating all or part of a contractor's proposal by reference is commonly used in sole-source procurements when you want the contractor to discuss certain aspects of the requirement to fill out the details of your SOW. It is also used in competitive procurement, but not as often, because of the danger of inadvertently incorporating something that changes a key aspect of your requirement. There is a performance-based concept, however, in which a statement of objectives (SOO) is used in the solicitation instead of an SOW. Each offeror, in effect, writes the contractual SOW in its proposal and the successful offeror's proposal is then incorporated by reference into the contract (see Chapter 4).

DISTINGUISHING BETWEEN LEVEL-OF-EFFORT (LOE) AND COMPLETION SOWS

Cost-reimbursement contracts are appropriate when it is not possible for the contractor to estimate accurately the costs of contract performance. This can occur, for example, when the contract product is uncertain (R&D), the amount of effort required is uncertain (technical support services), or creative effort is required (software development, studies, analytic effort). The cost-plus-fixed-fee (CPFF) contract is the most commonly used cost-reimbursement type contract. CPFF contracts have two forms, LOE and completion.

When writing an SOW for a CPFF contract, you must ensure that the requirement is precisely defined as either an LOE or a completion effort. LOE and completion efforts have different funding requirements and use different clauses; moreover, LOE efforts involve personal versus nonpersonal services considerations. The contracting officer must be able to distinguish between the two forms to construct the contract properly.

Level-of-Effort SOWs

The LOE form calls for the contractor's services (time and effort) to perform a task. The purpose of the contract is to obtain the contractor's time and effort rather than a concrete end product. The SOW describes the requirement and obligates the contractor to devote a specific level-of-effort for a stated time period.

It describes the categories of personnel required, their expertise, and the specific tasks to be accomplished. When the level-of-effort form is used, the contractor is reimbursed its incurred costs and paid a fixed fee if the performance is deemed satisfactory. The level-of-effort form is appropriate, for example, for maintenance of IT software and equipment and ongoing technical support that cannot be specifically defined at the time of contracting.

If the specific tasks to be performed cannot be adequately described initially, which is often the case when procuring technical support services, a task order contract may be used.

Completion SOWs

The completion form calls for the contractor to provide a concrete end product rather than a level-of-effort. The SOW describes the work by stating a definite goal or target and specifying a product that demonstrates successful performance. The SOW describes the requirement in terms of the production or development of a deliverable product—something that will be used, as delivered, to meet the requirement. The contractor is reimbursed its incurred costs and paid a fixed fee if it delivers an acceptable end product (e.g., a final report). Use of the completion form is preferred because it gives the government greater control over the contractor's efforts than an LOE form does.

The completion form is appropriate for studies, analytic efforts, IT equipment, and the development of software in which a concrete end product can be defined.

Distinguishing between the LOE and Completion Forms

Unless the SOW is written carefully, it is often difficult to distinguish between an LOE and a completion effort. In both cases, there is work to be completed and often a reported result. The basic difference between these forms lies in the purpose of the contract. If the contract is to buy a contractor's time and effort to perform a single or multiple tasks and the government's need will be met by the performance of that work, the level-of-effort form should be used. If the purpose of the contract is to buy a specific end product and the government's need will not be satisfied until that product is delivered, the completion form should be used.

The SOW must clearly identify the purpose of the contract by the way in which the work is defined. A completion SOW must describe the requirement in terms of the completed end product, and a level-of-effort SOW must describe the requirement in terms of the services to be performed. The SOW should not be labeled as one form or the other and then the requirement described in a manner inconsistent with that label. The contracting officer must be able to identify the form readily to ensure that the appropriate contract clauses and funding provisions are used.

Providing a Basis of Estimate for LOE and Completion Requirements

The SOW must provide the contractor sufficient information on which to base the estimated cost of contract performance. A properly described completion requirement usually provides a sound basis for the contractor's cost estimate because it describes the work in a manner that facilitates the contractor's development of its WBS, around which the cost estimate can be built. However, some efforts (such as studies or analytic effort) are completion efforts only because the resulting report is the concrete end product. The description of such requirements often resembles a level-of-effort rather than a completion description. In such instances, a scope statement (see Chapter 5) should be used to provide the basis for an estimate.

A level-of-effort requirement, even when fully described, does not provide as sound a basis for an estimate as a completion description. For example, assume that the first contractor task is to gather data to serve as a database for the analytic effort to follow. This task is usually described by identifying the kind of data to be collected and, when appropriate, the sources to be used. The description of the data to be collected, no matter how detailed, does not provide much of a basis for the contractor to develop a cost estimate.

To estimate this effort the contractor must first develop its data collection methodology and sources, and then estimate the resources and materials required. This procedure can produce wide variances in cost estimates, depending on the data collection methodology and the sources selected by each contractor. When the work requirement can be described but the description cannot define the amount of effort required to accomplish the work, you must provide a scope statement that contains your estimate of the level of effort required to accomplish the work. This is normally described in terms of work days or work months, either for the total effort or for each task, whichever you deem appropriate.

The use of a scope statement provides the contractor with a basis for estimating, but also serves to define the extent or scope of the anticipated contractor effort. This information helps define the total effort and enhances the contractor's understanding of the requirement. When it is applied to each individual task, it serves also to indicate the relative importance of each task with respect to the total effort. This indication of relative importance can be a significant benefit to both the contractor and the government when the work requirement contains tasks, such as data collection or database management, that could go on indefinitely if not limited.

To develop a scope statement, however, you need your own basis for estimating the amount of effort. Your best basis of estimate is what would be required to do the work in-house. Assume that the requisite expertise is available, determine how each task would be organized and staffed, and estimate how much effort is required to accomplish the task. Use the resulting figures in the scope statement.

Another method of estimating the scope is to examine similar efforts accomplished under previous contracts and use the level of effort actually experienced in the scope statement. A problem with this method is that contractors tend to work to the level permitted by the contract. If a contract permits the use of four people for five months, generally that is what the contractor provides. There is no direct relationship between the optimum level of effort necessary to accomplish the work and the level of effort actually expended.

An examination of past contract files will show what was done, but not necessarily how well it was done. In addition, other unstated factors or requirements that are not evident in the written record may have affected the level of effort provided. Examination of previously accomplished effort is a valuable tool in the development of a scope statement, but it should not be relied on as the sole criterion.

PERSONAL VERSUS NONPERSONAL SERVICES

When acquiring services, you must consider the issue of personal versus nonpersonal services. The typical service contract is for nonpersonal services. The contractor is awarded the contract and provides the services. The SOW defines what services the contractor must perform, but the contractor is responsible for determining how to perform the services. Under a nonpersonal services contract, the contractor performs the work free of daily government supervision over its personnel.

Personal services contracts are different—they permit direct government supervision of the contractor's employees. In fact, being able to supervise contractor employees is one of the primary reasons the government uses a personal services contract. Personal services contracts are characterized by the development of an employer-employee relationship between the government and the contractor's personnel.[9] The government treats contractor personnel as though they were federal employees, usually through the manner in which those personnel are supervised. Agencies must have specific statutory authority to use personal services contracts,[10] and these contracts include special terms and conditions not found in nonpersonal services contracts.

If a nonpersonal services contract is found to be for personal services, the contract can be deemed illegal and can be voided. To avoid this problem, some federal agencies require that their personnel office write all personal services contracts and that their procurement office write all nonpersonal services contracts. Nevertheless, the problem persists: A nonpersonal services contract can inadvertently be turned into an improper personal services contract by the way the contract is written or managed. It is therefore essential to use care when writing an SOW for nonpersonal services to ensure that it is written properly.

It is often difficult to distinguish between personal and nonpersonal services contracts, particularly when contractor employees must work at a government facility. Mixing government and contractor employees makes it difficult to maintain the proper relationships. The main issue is government supervision of contractor employees. If a nonpersonal services SOW calls for contractor employees to work at a government facility—with their daily work assignments and supervision provided by government employees—the contract may be deemed an improper personal services contract. If the contract is silent on these matters, but during contract performance it is found that the government is providing daily supervision, the contract may be deemed an improper personal services contract.

The best way to avoid inadvertently creating an improper personal services requirement is to ensure that the SOW clearly indicates that the contractor must supervise its own employees. The SOW should be written so that it requires the contractor to: (1) provide an on-site supervisor and (2) ensure that, during contract performance, all government direction is provided through the on-site supervisor. The on-site supervisor is intended to inhibit the development of an employer-employee relationship between the government and the contractor's personnel. It is necessary, however, to be vigilant in contract management to ensure that the SOW requirements are followed.

SOLE-SOURCE SOWS

Many government contracts are awarded on a sole-source basis, usually because of the contractor's unique capabilities. Often, a sole-source RFP is not issued until after you and the contractor have discussed and mutually understood the requirement. In such instances, however, there is a tendency to write the SOW based on your mutual understanding rather than to write a complete description of the requirement. This often results in an inadequate SOW because details that have been discussed get left out of the SOW on the assumption that they are not needed.

There should be no difference between an SOW written for a competitive procurement and one written for a sole-source procurement. All SOWs must fully describe the work requirement, even if the procurement is sole-source. A complete description of the work requirement is necessary to protect the government's legal right to enforce contract performance. When government or contractor personnel changes occur, previous "understandings" are not necessarily passed along to successor personnel. This leaves gaps in the SOW coverage that may lead to misunderstandings and disputes. The SOW, which describes the contract work requirements, must survive the personnel changes that may occur during the solicitation process or during contract performance. The contractor is required to do only what is written in the contractual SOW. Understandings not expressed in the SOW lack legal standing and are therefore usually unenforceable.

FOLLOW-ON EFFORTS AND OPTIONS

As part of thinking your way through the project, you should determine the likelihood of a follow-on effort resulting from the work performed under the proposed contract. A follow-on requirement can be either a continuation of the effort or an advancement to another stage of the project; it may be competitive or sole-source. If the follow-on effort will be competitive, planning should begin as soon as you can identify the requirement. A competitive follow-on requires a new solicitation and a new contract. Creating the necessary documentation and obtaining approvals takes time, so effective planning is necessary to avoid project delay at the end of the current contract.

If the follow-on effort is anticipated and is clearly sole-source, an *option* can be used to cover this effort. An option is a clause that obligates the contractor to provide the specified supplies or services if the contracting officer exercises the option within a stated time frame. Options provide an expeditious means to move on to additional or extended efforts.

Options are exercised by a unilateral modification of the current contract and are usually priced at the time the current contract is awarded. An *unpriced option* may be used if the option cannot be sufficiently described for pricing purposes at the time of original award. If the option is unpriced, the contractor is still obligated to perform, but only if a reasonable price can be negotiated. An unpriced option must establish how the option effort will be priced. For example, the option could require the contractor to submit a price proposal by a certain time; exercise of the option would be dependent on successful price negotiations. Do not use an option, however, unless there is a reasonable expectation that the option will be exercised.

If you fail to consider a follow-on option, you risk delaying the project at contract completion while a modification or new contract is processed. During this processing period the contractor may not be able to hold its project team together, and key personnel may be lost. When you know a follow-on effort is required and can describe it, you may create a follow-on option task to be exercised at some point before the end of the contract.

If you know a follow-on effort is required but cannot describe it, consider using an option to bridge the period between the end of the current contract and the beginning of the follow-on effort. It could, for example, require several months' effort to develop an SOW or project plan for the follow-on effort. However, this is a valid procedure only if the follow-on effort is clearly sole-source. If the nature of the work permits, you may include an option that simply calls for a continuation of the effort. Be careful with options, however; it is not proper to create an imaginary or "make-work" option just to keep the contractor under contract. There must be a valid effort for the contractor to perform.

Once you have concluded your planning and preparation effort, you are ready to begin writing your SOW. Chapter 5 will provide a model SOW format and discuss what kind of information belongs in an SOW, where it goes, and why. But first, Chapter 3 discusses performance work statements used in performance-based service contracting, and Chapter 4 addresses an emerging concept: the use of a statement of objectives in lieu of a performance work statement.

NOTES

[1] FAR 7.104(a).
[2] FAR 7.101.
[3] FAR 10.001(A)(2).
[4] FAR 10.002(e).
[5] FAR 16.504(c).
[6] FAR 16.505(a)(3).
[7] FAR 16.501-2(c).
[8] FAR 11.002(a) (2)(i).
[9] FAR 37.104(a).
[10] FAR 37.104(b).

3 Writing a Performance Work Statement for Performance-Based Service Contracting

Performance-based service contracting (PBSC) is a new term for a contracting technique that has been in use for years. Recently, however, PBSC has become a preferred technique for service contracting, and detailed guidance on its use has been published. The new emphasis may make it seem that the performance work statement (PWS)—which is essentially the SOW for PBSC—is something totally different from a typical SOW. This is not the case, however. While there are some differences, they are found primarily in documents attached to the PWS, rather than in how the PWS is written. This chapter discusses the PBSC concept, and Chapter 5 will cover the format and contents of any SOW, including the PWS.

WHAT IS PERFORMANCE-BASED SERVICE CONTRACTING?

Performance-based contracting can be defined as the structuring of all aspects of an acquisition around the purpose of the work to be performed, with the contract requirements set forth in clear, specific, and objective terms with measurable outcomes as opposed to either the manner by which the work is to be performed or broad and imprecise statements of work. The FAR states that:[1]

Performance-based contracts for services shall include —

(1) A performance work statement (PWS);

(2) Measurable performance standards (i.e., in terms of quality, timeliness, quantity, etc.) and the method of assessing contractor performance against performance standards; and

(3) Performance incentives where appropriate. When used, the performance incentives shall correspond to the performance standards set forth in the contract.

PBSC is a contracting concept in which the contractor is paid based upon its attainment of predetermined contractual goals. The PBSC work requirement is described in terms of what is to be accomplished, the performance standards the contractor is to meet, how these performance standards will be measured, and how the contractor's performance will be monitored with respect to the performance standards. This concept is designed to ensure that:

(1) Contractors are free to determine how to meet the performance objectives

(2) Appropriate performance quality levels are achieved

(3) Payment is made only for services that meet the performance quality levels.

PBSC involves significantly more planning and development effort than that required for a typical service requirement using a functional SOW, and sufficient time must be allowed for this activity. If the initial planning effort is not done well, the resulting contract will pose continuing problems and probably result in a much lower quality of services than anticipated.

The success of PBSC depends primarily on careful development of three specific components: a PWS, a quality assurance plan (QAP), and, when appropriate, an incentive plan.

Performance Work Statement

The PWS is a document that describes the required services in terms of the expected results or work outputs. The PWS is similar to the functional SOW in that it includes such elements as "what, when, where, how many, and how well" the work is to be performed. However, it goes into greater detail than the functional SOW by expressing the work outputs as performance indicators with objective, measurable performance standards and associated acceptable quality levels (AQL) that express the allowable variance from the performance standards. This approach facilitates assessment of the quality of work performance. Other than how the work outputs are described, the contents of a PWS are the same as those found in a functional SOW.

Most government service requirements are similar to those provided in the commercial marketplace. The PWS should reflect the terms and conditions and the performance standards of the commercial marketplace to the maximum extent practicable rather than establishing unique government requirements and performance standards. Reserve unique requirements or standards for those instances where they are critical for successful contract performance.

Quality Assurance Plan

The QAP addresses what the government must do to ensure that the contractor has performed in accordance with the performance standards. It reflects the established performance indicators and related performance standards and states how contractor performance will be monitored and measured (i.e., surveillance methods) to determine the extent to which the contractor is in compliance with the performance standards. The QAP may be incorporated into the PWS but is usually described in a separate document as an attachment to the PWS. It is not unusual to have multiple QAPs, each reflecting different surveillance methods for different tasks.

Incentive Plan

When PBSC is used, the FAR[2] encourages the use of financial incentives in a competitive environment to encourage contractors to develop innovative and cost-effective methods of performing the work. The incentive structure should relate the contractor's performance to the PWS and QAP to reward contractors who perform well and penalize those who do not perform to the required standards. It should be noted, however, that incentives should be used only when appropriate.[3]

The incentive plan may be included as part of the QAP or set forth in a separate document as an attachment to the QAP. Generally, if deductibles are used, they are addressed as part of the QAP; if award, formula, or term incentives are used, they are addressed in a separate document attached to the QAP. The use of incentives is addressed in greater detail at the end of this chapter.

WHEN IS IT APPROPRIATE TO USE PBSC?

Service contracts usually involve the contracting out of a function previously performed by government personnel or one that supports a government function. The use of PBSC is most appropriate for services that can be defined in terms of objective and measurable performance outcomes, such as guard services, transportation services, maintenance and repair services, administrative services, and some technical services. Services that are repetitive in nature and represent a continuing requirement are particularly appropriate for PBSC because the time and effort to establish the initial contract can be amortized over time. Moreover, the PWS for successor contracts will need updating only to the extent that actual experience or changed requirements dictate.

Do not, however, simply copy the RFP/PWS from a previous contract. At a minimum, market research and analysis, as well as a review of how the work is actually being accomplished, are required to ensure that there have not been changes since the last contract was awarded.

Services that require creative thinking (such as R&D) or a highly skilled technical effort often do not have definable outcomes in terms of measurable performance outcomes. If the end product of the work effort cannot be specifically defined at the onset of the procurement (i.e., in the RFP), it does not lend itself to the detailed definition required for the successful use of PBSC (but see Chapter 4 on the SOO concept). Do not try to force-fit an inappropriate effort into a PBSC mode. This will only cause problems.

DEVELOPING A JOB ANALYSIS

The PWS describes the required services in terms of the expected work outputs (performance indicators) of each task, the performance standards (required quality level) for each output, and any permissible deviations (acceptable quality level) from the established performance standard. These are determined through job analysis (DoD uses the term "performance requirement analysis"). Job analysis involves examining the requirement and the kinds of services and outputs needed and provides the basis for establishing performance indicators and related performance standards.

Job analysis examines how a service requirement is currently performed (plus any known changes to be implemented during contract performance), either by in-house staff or the incumbent contractor, to determine the actual work results or products. When conducting job analysis, it is essential to distinguish between what is actually being done and your perceptions of what is being done. Organizations, missions, and how work is performed can change over time, both formally and informally. Job analysis should be performed on the basis of an onsite audit of what is actually being done.

Some sort of job analysis is required for the development of any SOW. The job analysis required for a PWS is more detailed than that required for a functional SOW because of the need to develop performance indicators, standards, and acceptable quality levels; a QAP; and, when using incentives or deductibles, performance values to tie into the incentive structure.

Job analysis involves:

- Organizational analysis

- Data gathering (workload, facility, and resource)

- Directives analysis

- Market research

- Work analysis

- Performance analysis

- Cost analysis.

Organizational Analysis

Organizational analysis is an internal activity (as opposed to external activities, which examine the commercial marketplace) that involves an examination of the organizational unit supported by the required services to see how it is organized (i.e., its place in the agency's organizational structure and its relationship to other organizational units), its mission (i.e., what services the organizational unit provides as its work product), and what services it currently provides and how it provides them (i.e., by in-house or contractor personnel).

Organizational analysis involves the following steps:

1. Examine the organizational unit to be supported by the required services.

2. Examine the service function as it is currently performed to see how it is organized and what kind of services it provides.

3. Identify the organizational unit's mission, the other organizational elements supported, and the services currently performed by each element of the organizational unit.

4. Identify the services performed in terms of routine services and contingent or emergency services, as appropriate.

5. Distinguish between what is currently being done and any changes in the workload or work processes that will be required during the period of contract performance.

Organizational analysis focuses on the activity to be contracted out. The analysis of other organizational functions should be limited to a general description sufficient to identify any interfaces of the unit in question with other organizational units.

Data Gathering

Data gathering is also an internal activity. It is the process of obtaining as much information as possible on anticipated workloads and facilities or resources required. The following types of data are usually collected:

- **Workload Data.** The contractor must be provided an estimate of the anticipated workload for use in preparing and costing its proposal. The government also uses this information to develop the government cost estimate and to analyze the facilities and resources necessary to perform the work. Workload estimates must be as accurate as possible. Examine available historical information on the workload of the organizational unit involved as well as how this workload was measured (this may affect how the job analysis is conducted). Then determine if there are any changes anticipated in the workload during the period of the contract. Changes in organization, mission, laws or regulations, processes or procedures, and technology are just some of the changes that can affect the workload during future contract performance. These changes should be identified, and how and when they might affect contract performance should be determined.

- **Facility Data.** The contractor must also be informed of any government-furnished facilities, equipment, data, or services that will be provided during contract performance. The contractor needs this information for proposal preparation, and the government needs it to make arrangements for delivery of the government-furnished items. Examine the facilities, equipment, data, and services currently used in performing the effort to be contracted out, and determine the benefit to the government of providing all or some of these items. If anticipated changes will affect the facility data, this should be reflected in the data collected.

- **Resource Data.** Determine the number and types of in-house personnel (or incumbent contractor personnel) currently used. This information is needed to prepare the government cost estimate and to provide a basis for evaluating proposals. The government must have its own idea of the resources necessary to do the work in order to evaluate what the contractors propose.

This resource information should not be provided in the PWS. Identifying the number and types of personnel required (using job titles or other qualifiers such as college degrees or years of experience) is not appropriate for performance-based contracting because it may inhibit the contractor's ability to propose its own methodology and resources for meeting the requirement. Contractors often believe that they cannot deviate from the requirements set forth in the RFP and therefore may not propose innovative methodology using different resources.

The PWS should describe the requirement in a manner that permits the contractor to propose whatever number and types of personnel it believes will best meet the requirement.

Once the proposal is submitted, the evaluators will assess the proposal, including the proposed resources, to determine the feasibility of what is proposed and eventually which proposal offers the best value.

Resource requirements should be examined to determine if there are any constraints, such as the need for security clearances, that might affect the resources the contractor proposes to provide. Such constraints must be set forth in the PWS.

Directives Analysis

A directives analysis involves examining all currently applicable directives relevant to the operation of the services to be contracted out to determine which must be identified in the PWS. Directives that govern how the contractor must perform and would therefore affect how the contractor prepares its proposal must be identified. (See Chapter 5, Applicable Documents, for how this information should be presented).

Market Research

Market research is critical for the development of a PWS. The key concerns are how commercial services are organized and staffed, the work outputs or products, performance indicators, performance standards, and acceptable quality levels (performance metrics and measurements), particularly if the services have not been previously procured on a performance-based basis. Even if the services have been previously procured using a PWS, market research will reveal if there have been changes in techniques or methodology that will benefit the current acquisition.

Basic market research was discussed in Chapter 2, and certain other market research aspects are addressed in Chapter 4. All of this information applies to the development of both a PWS and a standard SOW.

Work Analysis

The organizational analysis, data gathering, directives analysis, and market research provide the basis for the work analysis. Work analysis is the process of identifying the required work products (or outputs), breaking them down to their lowest task level, and linking them in a logical flow of activities. In essence, this is a work breakdown structure expressed in terms of the work product or output required. The result is the identification of those work products expected of the contractor.

Work analysis identifies the three components of a work requirement (by task, and subtask if appropriate):

- **Work Inputs.** Work inputs are those actions or documents needed to initiate the work activity.

- **Work Steps.** Work steps are those actions that must taken to actually accomplish the work.

- **Work Outputs.** Work outputs are those items produced by the work steps. They provide the means to quantify and measure the contractor's performance.

This information is needed to develop an overall picture of the requirement, what needs to be accomplished, and any constraints that might apply. Work outputs are the primary product of work analysis. The work outputs provide the basis for performance analysis.

Performance Analysis

Performance analysis is the process of examining the results of the work analysis and determining how the key work outputs of each task or subtask can be measured (developing a performance indicator), developing the acceptable performance level (the performance standard), and determining the permissible deviations (the acceptable quality level, or AQL). Work analysis has identified the tasks/subtasks that must be accomplished to meet the government's requirements. Performance analysis provides the means to determine if the contractor has satisfactorily met those requirements.

Performance Indicators

Generally, performance indicators are the work output for each task, expressed in terms of something that can be measured, such as quantities or quality. Performance indicators must not only be realistic and meaningful in terms of the effort being performed, but must also indicate accomplishment of a significant event in terms of the task or subtask involved.

Performance indicators are developed by dividing the overall work requirement into tasks (and subtasks, as necessary) and analyzing each task or subtask to determine its required outputs or results. Some outputs are difficult to express in measurable terms, and others do not represent critical factors in successful performance. Work outputs that are not significant or that are difficult to express in measurable terms should, if possible, be included as part of another output that can be quantified. Performance indicators should be developed only for those outputs that demonstrate accomplishment of a significant task or subtask. Keep the number of performance indicators to a minimum, because too many will unnecessarily complicate contract administration.

The PWS must fully describe each task and subtask (see Chapter 5) in terms of what is to be accomplished. The performance indicators, performance standards, and AQL should be expressed at the end of the task or subtask description as the criteria for determining whether the requirements are met.

One of the dangers in PBSC is the development of a complicated contract that contains so many different elements to monitor that the agency resources to administer the contract are overwhelmed and cannot adequately perform the task. For example, imagine a requirement to provide on-base personnel transportation at a large military installation. The requirement has two tasks: (1) Operate Vehicles and (2) Maintain Vehicles. The Operate Vehicles Task has three subtasks: (1) On-Call Taxi Service, (1) Scheduled Bus Service, and (3) Unscheduled Bus Service (for special occasions, i.e., conferences, tours). Figure 3-1 shows the subtask On-Call Taxi Service, broken down into four performance indicators: response time, accidents per mile, operational cost per mile, and taxi in-commission rate. All of these are indicative of how well a taxi operation is performed.

Subtask 1 contains four performance indicators, each of which could also apply to subtasks 2 and 3. Thus the overall requirement for personnel transportation could contain 12 performance indicators, each of which must be monitored during contract performance. What if Task 2: Maintain Vehicles also had three subtasks, each of which had four performance indicators? This would total 24 performance indicators, each of which must be individually monitored throughout contract performance. The point at which the requirements become too much to handle will vary, but most agencies would be reluctant to dedicate more than one or two people to monitoring a contract.

This problem can be avoided by exercising discipline when conducting a performance analysis and identifying only those

FIGURE 3-1
Subtask 1: On-Call Taxi Service

Performance Indicator	Standard	Acceptable Quality Level
Response Time	4 minutes	5%
Accidents Per Mile	0	0%
Operational Cost Per Mile	$0.14	20%
Taxi In-Commission Rate	80%	10%

activities that are critical to the work at hand. In the Figure 3-1 example, which of the four performance indicators is most important to assessing the success of the taxi service? If a team was used to identify the performance indicators, the customer representative might choose response time, the safety representative might choose accidents per mile, the comptroller representative might choose cost per mile, and the maintenance representative might choose the in-commission rate. Each group has its own perceptions of a successful operation, but it is not practical to try to satisfy everyone.

Once all the possible performance indicators have been identified, the next step is to analyze objectively what is really important, considering the other tasks and associated performance indicators that must be covered in the contract. The answer is easy in this instance. The primary success indicator for a taxi service is response time. The accidents per mile and in-commission rate are subsets of the response time in that problems in these areas will adversely affect the response time. The cost per mile depends on who is footing the bill; if the contract is cost-reimbursement, this could be an important factor and might be included as a second performance indicator. Otherwise, response time is the only performance indicator needed.

The same thought process applies to the bus subtasks. The only critical performance indicator is response time. Thus, instead of 12 performance indicators for vehicle operations, only three need to be monitored. This eases the monitoring resource requirements significantly.

Performance Standards

Performance standards express the level of performance required by the government. They are the yardsticks used to measure performance indicators and determine the extent to which the contractor is producing a quality output. Performance standards must be realistic (i.e., attainable) and generally should not exceed the level of performance considered acceptable when the work is performed by government personnel or by the incumbent contractors. Performance standards are expressed in quantifiable terms, such as a rate of performance (x number per hour, x minutes per job), quantities, time, events, or any other term that can be measured objectively.

Generalized standards, such as cleanliness or workmanship, can be used, but they require subjective evaluation on the part of the government. If they are used, the PWS should define the terms used and explain how the standard will be measured. This may prove difficult to do because generalized terms are most often used when a definitive standard cannot be developed. Generalized standards should be avoided in PBSC (but see Chapter 4 on SOOs).

Performance standards can be designed specifically for the work at hand or can come from published sources, such as government standards, industry-wide standards (e.g., ISO 9000, 9001, and 9002), standards established by industry associations, government regulations or directives, or locally developed standards. Generally, industry-established standards should be used, if available, because contractors understand and accept these standards and their use will enhance the competition.

Setting reasonable performance standards is very important in PBSC. If the standards are complicated and difficult to measure (e.g., require a lot of ongoing contract surveillance, time-consuming testing), contract administration will be burdensome for both the contractor and the government. If the standards are too high, their attainment will be more costly than necessary. If the standards are too low, the government may not receive the benefits it should from contract performance.

In the taxi example, the performance standard is expressed in terms of how quickly the taxi responds (i.e., four minutes). This number, however, must be reasonable and must have a rational basis. Some of the factors to be considered, for example, should be the distance to be traveled, speed limits, traffic congestion, road conditions, and any other local factors that might affect the response time.

The performance standard should be based on an achievable average time under any conditions. Do not establish a time frame that might require the taxi driver to speed or otherwise drive in an unsafe manner. While it is possible to develop multiple response times (for example, to take into account rush hour or adverse weather conditions), this is usually not a good idea because it overcomplicates the standards. Keep in mind that government personnel must be assigned to monitor the contractor's performance and to measure its compliance with each of the standards. Multiple standards unnecessarily complicate contract administration.

Acceptable Quality Level

The AQL expresses the allowable variation from standard that will still result in an acceptable level of quality—that is, the maximum allowable error rate or variation from the standard. The AQL is usually expressed as a percentage variance from the standard; for example, an AQL of 5 percent means that the work must be performed to the standard 95 percent of the time. The AQL recognizes that despite a contractor's best efforts, things do go wrong, and 100 percent compliance with the performance standard (an AQL of 0 percent) is often an unrealistic and expensive goal. There are, however, instances where an AQL of 0 percent would be appropriate; for example, for health and safety tasks or other tasks that, for project purposes, must be performed to standard. Each performance standard must be assessed and an AQL assigned that recognizes the realities of contract performance.

A published standard will usually indicate the AQL. If a published standard is not available, historical workload data should be examined to determine what variance has been acceptable in the past. Generally, the AQL should reflect the same variance from the standard that was applied when the government (or incumbent contractor) performed the work. It would be a good idea to document (for the file) how the AQL was established, particularly if the AQL has been changed from that previously used.

Performance Requirements Summary

The results of the organizational analysis, data gathering, directives analysis, market research, and work analysis represent the end products of job analysis and provide the information needed to accomplish the performance analysis. This information is usually presented in a performance requirements summary.

The performance requirements summary presents the performance indicators (work requirements expressed in terms of the work output), the performance standards (how the performance indicators will be measured to determine successful performance), and the AQL (allowable variance from the performance standards) in a table format, usually as an attachment to the PWS. A performance requirements summary table would be required for each contract task. When a deductible is used, a percentage is used to note the value of the performance indicator and the amount to be deducted for services not provided or not meeting acceptable quality standards.

Figure 3-2 is an example of a performance requirements summary table taken from one of the model PWSs that can be obtained from the Office of Federal Procurement Policy (OFPP). This example shows only one of the seven tasks under the contract.

Cost Analysis

Cost estimates, based on available data, should be prepared for each service or output on a continuing basis as the requirement is refined. The cost estimates are used in preparing the government estimate, determining incentive structures when the use of incentives is appropriate, and evaluating proposals.

FIGURE 3-2
Performance Requirements Summary Table

1. Contract Requirement: Entry/Exit Control Services

Work Requirement	Standard	AQL
Entry/Exit Control Services	Post manned, proper procedures (C.15a & b)	1%
Communications	Able to establish within standards (C.10)	1%
Conduct	Meets required standards (C.8)	1%
Uniform	Complete and neat (C.9)	1%
SOP	Current copy available, guard knowledgeable of and understands procedures (C.2b)	1%

For Defense Department (DoD) Readers

It should be noted that the foregoing information is presented somewhat differently by DoD.[4] DoD refers to the analytical process as performance requirement analysis and describes it in three steps:

1. **Define the desired objectives.** *What must be accomplished to satisfy the requirement?* List what needs to be accomplished to satisfy the overall requirement. Techniques: (1) Use an interview or brainstorming approach with the customer (user) to determine all dependent variables (what, when, where, who, quantity, quality levels, etc.) or (2) review previous requirements for validity and accuracy.

2. **Conduct an outcome analysis.** *What tasks must be accomplished to arrive at the desired outcomes?* Identify specific performance objectives for those outcomes defined in the previous step. Techniques: (1) Segregate desired outcomes into lower task levels and link those tasks together

into a logical flow of activities or (2) use a tree diagram to outline each of the basic outcomes.

3. **Conduct a performance analysis.** *When or how will I know that the outcome has been satisfactorily achieved, and how much deviation from the performance standard will I allow the contractor, if any?* Identify how a performance objective should be measured and what performance standards are appropriate (including acceptable quality levels).

The DoD guidebook also suggests a more extensive performance requirements summary (PRS), saying that the PRS is the baseline for the PWS and that the PRS should be brief and should capture the salient elements of the requirement. In the actual PWS, the acquisition team will elaborate on and describe the requirement in greater detail. The ultimate goal is to describe the requirement in a way that allows an offeror to understand fully what will be necessary to accomplish the requirement. The guidebook suggests using a PRS matrix with the following headings: performance objective, performance standard, acceptable quality level (AQL), monitoring method, and incentives.

While the DoD language is somewhat different from that in this chapter, the intent and the results are the same.

DEVELOPING A QUALITY ASSURANCE PLAN

In PBSC, the government must ensure that it receives the quality of services called for under the contract and pays only for the acceptable level of services received. The QAP is used to inform both contractor and government personnel how the government will monitor the contractor's performance to determine the extent of the contractor's compliance with the established performance standards. The QAP summarizes the quality requirements (i.e., performance indicators, performance standards, and AQL) for each task, indicates the type and level of surveillance (including the sampling procedures, as appropriate), states how the surveillance results will be evaluated and analyzed, explains how these results will affect contract payments, and includes samples of the forms to be used. The government also uses the QAP to determine the resources and procedures needed for contract administration.

Because the QAP is based on the performance indicators and standards established in the PWS and because the methods of surveillance for each task may differ, there may be a need to develop a QAP for each task. The QAP commits the government to a particular course of action during contract administration, and the government must monitor the contractor's performance in accordance with each published QAP. Keeping the number of performance indicators to a minimum will simplify contract administration.

Because of the close relationship of the PWS and the QAPs, both should be developed within the same time frame. Generally, the QAPs should be included as an attachment to the PWS to ensure their visibility.

Do not confuse the QAP with a contractor's internal quality control or quality assurance plan, which is a contractor's internal plan for how it will ensure that a quality product is delivered—it is entirely separate from the government-developed QAP.[5] DoD uses the term "performance assessment plan" instead of "quality assurance plan" and the term "assessment" instead of "surveillance" to avoid confusion between the terms.

Types of Surveillance Methods

Surveillance methods are a key part of the QAP. They describe how and when the government will monitor contractor performance. Surveillance methods must be tailored for the specific requirements, using the method or methods most appropriate for the specific activity to be monitored. A number of different surveillance methods are available. The following are the more commonly used methods:

- **100-percent inspection.** This method is appropriate for infrequent tasks or tasks with stringent performance requirements where complete compliance is critical to success, such as tasks involving health and safety issues. With this method, performance is monitored at each occurrence. Because 100-percent inspection is administratively expensive in terms of time and manpower during contract administration, this method should be used only when absolutely necessary.

- **Random sampling.** This is the most commonly used method for recurring tasks, probably because the use of tables and mathematical formulas gives an impression of accuracy not found in the other methods. With this method, services are sampled to determine if the level of performance is acceptable. Random sampling works best when the number of instances of the services being performed is very large and a statistically valid sample can be obtained.

    The problem with this method is that it can lead to a complicated surveillance process. Moreover, if the number of samples to be observed exceeds the manpower available to make the observations, contract administration can be difficult.

- **Periodic inspection.** This method calls for the surveillance of tasks on other than a 100-percent or random basis. It is appropriate for tasks that occur infrequently and do not require 100-percent inspection. Periodic inspection, or planned sampling, involves the development of a surveillance plan based on subjective judgment and an analysis of available agency resources to determine which tasks to inspect and how frequently to inspect them.

This method requires careful assessment of the various tasks and informed judgment regarding what to inspect, how to inspect it, and the frequency of inspection. While this method permits the tailoring of the surveillance to the available resources, it often appears more difficult to develop than the use of random sampling and related mathematical formulas. Periodic inspection is often overlooked for this reason, even though it can simplify contract administration.

- **Customer input.** This method can be used as a supplement to the other methods, but it is rarely appropriate as the primary surveillance method. Basically, it is a customer complaint system. Contractor performance is measured by the number and types of customer complaints about contractor performance. This is done through customer surveys and the use of customer complaint forms. It can be a valuable support method for services that are rendered to third parties, such as repair or janitorial services.

  However, this method requires extra administrative effort. Procedures must be developed and personnel assigned to manage the complaint system. Customer complaints must be documented, preferably through the use of standardized forms either provided to the customers or used to record verbal complaints and, as appropriate, validated. When a customer complaint system is used, it must be managed in a manner that clearly demonstrates that the complaints are being acted upon. If the customers perceive that their complaints are not being remedied, they will cease making formal complaints regardless of the quality of the services.

- **Unscheduled inspections.** Unscheduled (surprise) inspections are observations made at the times and places deemed appropriate by the contract monitors. In theory, such inspections provide an unbiased picture of contractor performance because the contractor has no way of anticipating when they will occur.

Unscheduled inspections should be relied on only to provide a snapshot of an instance of contractor performance and not to provide a continuing performance picture. PBSC contracts should be monitored on the basis of the contractor's overall performance, not isolated instances of performance. For this reason, unscheduled inspections should not be used as a primary surveillance method. They are effective, however, as a support method used when the primary surveillance method indicates problems.

Selecting Surveillance Methods

Surveillance methods and schedules are influenced by a number of factors, including the number (population) of different service activities (performance indicators) to be inspected; the importance, characteristics, and locations of the activities to be inspected; and the criticality and cost of the activity. In a contract with multiple tasks and subtasks, each task/subtask should be examined and an appropriate surveillance method selected. This will probably result in a number of different methods being employed under the same contract.

When selecting the surveillance methods, available resources should be kept in mind. The surveillance process includes scheduling, observing, documenting, accepting service, and determining payment due. If available resources are not sufficient to monitor the contract properly, a functional SOW should be used instead of PBSC. The benefits of PBSC are realized only when the contract is structured properly and monitored effectively.

Surveillance should be comprehensive, systematic, and well documented. This does not mean, however, that the process must be complicated. Cumbersome and intrusive process-oriented surveillance methods that are difficult to administer and interfere unduly with contractor operations should be avoided. It is important to keep the contract monitoring process and its documentation as simple and cost-effective as possible.

If development of the surveillance process starts to get complicated, the PWS should be reviewed and the performance indicators (what is being measured) simplified. The key to simplification is to keep the number of performance indicators—not the different surveillance methods—to a minimum.

QAP Example

Figure 3-3 is an example of a QAP. It is based on one of OFPP's model PWSs. The model PWS is for a guard services requirement consisting of seven work requirements:

1. Entry/exit control services

2. Roving patrol services

3. Courier services

4. Scheduled escort services

5. Miscellaneous services

6. Administrative requirements

7. Indefinite quantity work.

The PWS contains a QAP for each of these requirements, reflecting the differing surveillance plans for each requirement. The following example QAP is based on the first work requirement. Certain changes have been made for readability, but these changes do not affect the substance of the QAP.

This is just one example of how a QAP might be structured; the actual structure and content of a QAP should be tailored to the specific services required. There is no official format, but a typical QAP should:

FIGURE 3-3
Quality Assurance Plan #1
Entry/Exit Control Services

1. *Contract Requirement.* Entry/Exit Control Services

Work Requirements — **Standards of Performance**

- a. Entry/Exit Control — Post manned, proper procedures (PWS C. 15 a & b)
- b. Communications — Able to establish within standards (PWS C.10)
- c. Conduct — Meets required standards (PWS C.8)
- d. Uniform — Complete and neat (PWS C.9)
- e. SOP — Current copy available, guard knowledgeable of and understands procedures (PWS C.2b)

2. *Primary Method of Surveillance.* Random sampling supported by unscheduled inspections and validated customer complaints.

3. *Acceptable Quality Level (AQL).* The AQL for all work requirements is 1%.

4. *Quantity of Work.* The quantity of work is based on the number of 30-minute periods in which entry/exit control services are provided during the month. The quantity will vary from month to month based on the actual number of calendar and working days. The following example is based on providing services at four posts during a month in which there are 30 calendar and 19 working days.

Post	Location	Hours/Day	Days/Month	Units/Month
1	Main Gate	24	30	1,440
2*	South Gate	12 (0600–1800)	19	456
3	East Gate	18 (0600–2400)	30	1,080
4*	West Gate	4 (0600–0800) (1600–1800)	19	152
		Total quantity of work		3,128

*Gates are not opened weekends or holidays.

continues

continued

FIGURE 3-3
Quality Assurance Plan #1
Entry/Exit Control Services

5. *Sample Size.* Based on an average of 3,128 services per month for a 12-month contract term, the sample size is:

   For the normal level of surveillance   203

   For the minimum level of surveillance   65

6. *Level of Surveillance.* The normal surveillance (sampling) level will be used initially. If the observed defect rate (ODR) is less than one-half of the AQL for the entry/exit control work requirement during any given evaluation period, the minimum surveillance level will be used during the following evaluation period. If, at the minimum surveillance level, the ODR exceeds the AQL for entry/exit control, the normal surveillance level will be resumed.

7. *Sampling Procedures.* Prior to the beginning of the evaluation period, the Quality Assurance Evaluator (QAE) will generate the appropriate number of samples, based on the level of surveillance to be used, through the use of a table of random numbers or a calculator or computer that has the capacity to generate random numbers. A number matrix (which assigns a specific number to each 30-minute unit of work) will be used to determine the specific units of work to be evaluated. The time, date, and location of each unit of work will be recorded on the QAE's inspection schedule for the evaluation period.

8. *Evaluation Procedures.* During the evaluation period, the QAE will visit and observe entry/exit control services at each of the times/locations selected and evaluate each of the work requirements listed in paragraph 1 as either satisfactory (S) or Unsatisfactory (U) on the Evaluation Worksheet. A brief description of any observed defects and action taken will also be noted. Copies of the Evaluation Worksheets will be provided to the contractor at the end of each working day.

Initially the post will be monitored at a distance, if possible, before the QAE's presence is known by the guard. After the initial observation, the post will be inspected for its general appear-

continues

continued

**FIGURE 3-3
Quality Assurance Plan #1
Entry/Exit Control Services**

ance, whether the guard is properly equipped with a weapon and communications equipment, whether the guard's uniform and personal appearance are neat and complete, whether a current copy of the SOP is available and the guard is aware of its requirements, and whether or not communications have been established with base station or supervisor, as appropriate.

    a. *Customer Complaints.* The QAE will record and attempt to validate each customer complaint received on the standard customer complaint form. All complaints, even if not validated, will be recorded and reviewed to determine if there is a trend or pattern of complaints concerning specific posts or individual guards. Only those complaints validated by the QAE will be used when determining contract payments.

    b. *Unscheduled Inspections.* Unscheduled inspections may be conducted at any time, but will be limited to posts of particular importance, posts where problems have been noted in the past, and posts for which complaints have been received. Unscheduled inspections will be documented on a separate evaluation worksheet from those used for random sampling.

    c. *Rework.* Rework will not normally be allowed because it is not practical for most entry/exit control services.

9. *Analysis of Results.* At the end of each evaluation period, the QAE will summarize the results of the inspections, calculate ODRs, and recommend payment amounts.

    a. If the ODR for a work requirement is equal to or less than the AQL, performance of that requirement (Contractor's Rating) is satisfactory. If the ODR is less than one half of the AQL, the minimum surveillance will be used for the following evaluation period (see paragraphs 5 and 6).

    b. If the ODR for a work requirement is greater than the AQL, the performance of that requirement is unsatisfactory. The QAE will recommend that a Contract Discrepancy Report (CDR) be issued or stronger action taken, and surveillance will be returned to the normal level for the next evaluation period.

- Describe the work requirements in terms of performance indicators, performance standards, and acceptable quality levels (or maximum error rates)

- Identify the surveillance methods to be used

- Describe how performance will be measured (e.g., evaluation periods, sample size, sampling procedures, level of surveillance)

- Describe how the performance measurements will be evaluated

- Describe how the evaluation results will be analyzed

- Describe how the evaluation results will affect contract payments

- Provide samples of the forms to be used, such as evaluation worksheets, customer complaint forms, and the forms used to calculate contract payments (these forms will differ depending on the contract type and incentive used).

OFFERING INCENTIVES

The use of incentives in performance-based service contracting is encouraged but not required by the FAR. Generally, contractors are self-incentivized to provide something more than just satisfactory services to improve their competitive position. Contractual incentives seek to enhance this self-motivation and encourage contractors to increase efficiency and maximize performance to an extent that might not otherwise be emphasized. To be effective, contractual incentives must meet *all* of the following criteria. They must:

- Motivate the contractor to the desired level of performance

- Clearly communicate what is desired

- Be measurable in a quantitative sense

- Be realistic and achievable—the contractor must be able to attain the highest level of performance

- Be controllable—the contractor must be able to control or influence the incentivized elements.

The application of an incentive arrangement will not automatically bring about improved performance. For example, if the services are already being performed at a high level of quality, it is unlikely that the use of an incentive will result in a yet higher level of quality. If, given the nature of the work, it is unlikely that performance can be improved by innovative concepts, incentives will not be effective. If the contract funds are not sufficient to generate an incentive amount large enough to encourage the contractor to change its procedures and develop more efficient and effective performance methods, the incentives will not bring about improvements. If the contract represents a small percentage of the contractor's total sales, the contract may not receive the management attention necessary to bring about improvements in the incentivized areas.

The use of incentives is based on the assumption that a contractor is motivated primarily by profit. While this is true with regard to a contractor's overall business, a contractor is not necessarily motivated by the profit possibilities of an individual contract. Non–profit-oriented reasons that might motivate a contractor to compete for a contract include:

- The business prestige and reputation related to holding the contract

- As an aid in the recruitment and retention of key personnel

- The attraction of new business

- An interest in entering or becoming stronger in a particular field

- The need for a broader business base to control overhead costs.

If a contractor wants a contract for non–profit-oriented reasons, it may be willing to take the contract for little or no profit just to get the business. While the contractor will naturally seek to perform well (to be in a position to attract future business), specific incentives may not be effective.

Before constructing an incentive arrangement, you must consider how contractors' business strategies might be motivated by the incentives. Effective incentives are difficult to construct; if not done properly, they can bring more trouble than they are worth. A PBSC incentive should be used only when it is determined that the incentive arrangement will motivate contractor performance that might otherwise not be achieved.

Formula Incentives

The fixed-price incentive (FPI) contract and the cost-plus-incentive fee (CPIF) contract are formula-type incentives. These are arrangements in which positive and negative incentives are based on target numbers and applied by a mathematical formula, depending on the extent to which the contractor exceeds or fails to meet the target numbers.

All formula incentives must contain an incentive on cost. If incentives are desired on other areas, such as performance quality and timely delivery, these must be in addition to the cost incentive. This is necessary to prevent a contractor from concentrating its efforts on the other incentive areas at the expense of cost. Multiple incentive contracts are very difficult to develop because the relative value of the various incentives must be continuously balanced, one to the other, to ensure a proper incentive application. For example, if quality and cost were incentivized, you would have to strike a balance between the increments of quality improvement and the increased cost of such quality improvements.

Add a delivery incentive, and you would have to strike a balance among the increments of quality improvement, the increments of delivery improvement, and the associated cost increases.

A major problem with formula incentives is that they are applied mechanically and do not necessarily reflect the realities of contract performance, especially when there have been a number of contract changes during the course of contract performance. This is particularly true of multiple-incentive contracts because contract changes will affect the balance among the various incentives, jeopardizing the effectiveness of the entire incentive arrangement.

FPI contracts can become disastrous to a contractor if performance costs reach the price ceiling and further modifications to bail out the contractor are not possible. Without a contract modification that increases the price ceiling, the contractor must complete the contract at its own expense. This has happened on a number of major systems acquisitions in the past. This is not a problem with CPIF contracts because there is no price ceiling, but cost overruns, particularly when there are numerous contract changes, can be anticipated.

Over the years, numerous studies have been conducted to quantify the effectiveness of formula incentives. These studies have either been inconclusive (because contract changes during performance made such quantification impossible) or have found that incentives had little or no direct effect on a contractor's performance.[6] Despite the fact that the FAR and policy makers tout the use of FPI and CPIF contracts, these incentives offer little definitive payback, particularly in service contracts.

Award Incentives

The cost-plus-award fee (CPAF) contract is the most commonly used award incentive, but an award package may also be used with a fixed-price contract. Award incentives are arrangements in which the incentive is expressed as a total dollar amount to be divided up and paid out periodically during contract performance. The amount of the available award fee to be paid after each award fee period is based on the government's subjective assessment of the quality of the contractor's ongoing performance in relation to stated evaluation factors. These factors can include cost control, performance quality compared to stated performance factors, and delivery performance. If structured and administered properly, an award incentive can bring about improved quality in contractor performance, particularly with respect to services.

Award incentives work because they are flexible (incentive goals and criteria can be changed during contract performance to reflect the realities of contract performance), the award amount is determinable (the contractor can calculate the portion of the award amount available for each portion of contract performance), and the increased management attention required by this arrangement—on the part of both the contractor and the government—can create a team approach that in itself increases the likelihood of improved efficiency and effectiveness.

High-level management attention is critical to the success of an award fee arrangement. The award fee determination (payment) is made by an agency official at a level higher than both the contracting officer and the project manager, and this determination, which is in essence a report card on the contractor's performance, is provided to a similarly placed contractor official at a level higher than the contractor's program manager. Reporting contract performance at a level higher than the project manager is likely to get everybody's attention, particularly if there are problems (the boss wants to know why), and this increases the potential for an effective dialogue between the government and the contractor personnel that will enhance contractor performance.

While award fee arrangements are effective incentives, their use is not without problems. A problem common to all award fee arrangements is the high cost of administration. Award fee administration requires the appointment of award fee evaluation boards and performance monitors who must stay familiar with the contractor's ongoing performance. If an agency is not willing and able to devote the appropriate assets to the administration of the award fee throughout contract performance, the use of an award fee arrangement would be a mistake.

While award fee incentives are effective when administered properly, this does not always happen. A common problem is late payment of the award fee. Care must be taken to ensure that the incentivized areas are evaluated and the award fee amount is determined promptly, coupled with a procedure that ensures prompt payment to the contractor. Incentives do not work well with contractors who are paid late.

Another potential problem is the inflation of award fee payments. These payments are based on subjective evaluations; in long-term contracts when the contractor performs well and pleases the government evaluators, there may be a tendency to upgrade the contractor's performance to a higher level or to fail to downgrade the contractor if the quality of the contractor's performance deteriorates in a given performance period. This tends to negate the effect of the incentive because the contractor will get used to being paid more for less effort.

Given the minimal value of the formula-type incentives, award incentives, despite the potential problems, are still the most effective incentive for PBSC contracts. This is because the administrative effort necessary to monitor a PBSC contract mirrors that needed to administer an award incentive. Thus there would be little, if any, added administrative cost. The other potential problems can be handled through effective high-level contract management.

The only drawback to using award incentives for PBSC is that they are generally not viable for contracts of low dollar value because they do not generate sufficient award funds to motivate the contractor to improve performance. However, even in the lower-value service contracts, there is enough value in the feedback inherent in award arrangements to at least warrant consideration of using of this type of incentive.

The advantages of award fee contracting accrue primarily to the government and are applicable only if the government manages the contract properly, that is, uses appropriate award fee evaluation criteria, uses conversion techniques (from evaluation points to award fee dollars) that appropriately reward contractor performance, monitors the contract properly, and ensures that award fee amounts are paid promptly.

Award Term Incentives

Award term incentives "reward" a contractor for excellent performance with an extension of the contract term instead of an additional fee. Satisfactory performance results in no change in the contract term, and unsatisfactory performance results in a reduction of the current contract term.[7]

Award term incentives are not contract options; the exercise of an option is a unilateral government right to be exercised solely at the government's discretion. Contractors do not have a "right" to an option. An award term incentive provides the contractor with a legal entitlement to a contract extension when all conditions are met (i.e., the contractor has provided excellent performance, the government has a continuing need for the services and has sufficient funds available, and the contractor has met any other specific conditions set forth in the contract). When these conditions are met, the government must either extend the contract term or terminate the contract.

Generally, award term contract arrangements work like award fee contract arrangements. The process is established in an award term plan that is implemented by a contract clause. The clause and plan should establish:

- The organization and responsibilities of the personnel who will conduct the award term evaluation.

- When and how the evaluations will be conducted.

- The evaluation criteria to be used.

- The basis for either a contract term extension or reduction, depending on the quality of the contractor's performance.

- How the evaluation criteria or other parts of the plan can be changed.

- How disputes over the process will be handled. It should be noted that the DoD *Guidebook for Performance-Based Services Acquisition* indicates that the government's decisions on award term are not subject to dispute. This might not be valid, however, because there are court rulings[8] to the effect that similar statements (that the contractor cannot dispute award fee determinations) are not valid. Therefore, award term clauses should provide for a disputes process.

There are no published policies or procedures on the use of award term incentives and there have not been any significant rulings by GAO or the federal courts on this concept. Several problems immediately come to mind:

1. FAR Part 6 requires full and open competition when acquiring goods or services. Would award term contract extensions, which could extend the contract term for five to ten years, violate the requirement for full and open competition?

2. While award term incentives are technically not options, to what extent will the concepts set forth in FAR subpart 17.2—Options be applied to award term? For example, solicitations including options must indicate the entire possible contract term, and options must be priced and the option prices evaluated prior to contract award. How the options concepts will apply to award

term has yet to be decided. Pricing will certainly be a problem with award term, particularly with respect to the out years when they could extend well beyond five years. Generally, with the exception of economic price adjustment clauses, contract prices cannot be renegotiated during the term of the contract unless the contract has been modified, and then only with respect to the modification itself.

3. While award term will provide for long-term relationships with contractors who continue to perform in an excellent manner, are such relationships necessarily a good thing? In theory, long-term contractual relationships can result in increased efficiency and effectiveness as the contractor gains familiarity with the government project and the government processes and becomes more of a partner in the project. Government project managers would prefer to have a continuing relationship because changing contractors is disruptive and could have an adverse effect on the program.

Such long-term relationships, however, can become incestuous. Service contracts require close cooperation between the government and contractor personnel. Over time these relationships can become personal, and the objectivity of government evaluators can become questionable. If the contractor is not performing poorly, there may be a tendency to rate the contractor's performance higher than really warranted. This has been a problem with award fee contracts (consistently high award fee payments that do not necessarily reflect actual performance) and could become a problem with award term contracts.

4. Another problem would be how to evaluate excellent performance over a long term. How often can a contractor perform in an excellent manner before such performance becomes standard? How long can a contractor improve upon its performance before it becomes impossible to make any further improvement? If satisfactory performance brings no further contract term extensions, award term could self-destruct over a period of time.

5. What if the government or the contractor wants to get out of the contract? Long-term contractual relationships can become a problem for both the government and the contractor. The government always has the option to unilaterally terminate for convenience, but contractors generally do not have the right to quit a contract when it is no longer to their advantage to continue performance. Business situations can change over time, and what was a reasonable arrangement could become less advantageous over a long term. It would probably be necessary to provide the contractor a contractual way out of the contract. Otherwise contractors who want out of an award term contract would have to reduce their performance to satisfactory, which does not extend the term of the contract, or to unsatisfactory, which acts to reduce the term of the contract. In such instances, the award term would turn out to be a disincentive to excellent performance.

Before attempting to make an award term contract, you should consult with agencies that have awarded such contracts, such as the Air Force, NASA, and GSA. There are also a number of publications that address award term contracting. Some of these are:

- "Award Term: The Newest Incentive," by Vernon J. Edwards, October 30, 2000, published in the February 2001 issue of *Contract Management* magazine, page 44. This article can also be accessed at *http://www.wifcon.com/anal/analaterm.htm* (accessed February 2012).

- "The Award Term Incentive: A Status Report," by Vernon J. Edwards, February 2000, published in the February 2002 issue of *Contract Management* magazine, page 22. This article can also be accessed at *http://www.wifcon.com/anal/analaterm2.htm* (accessed February 2012).

- *Guidebook for Performance-Based Services Acquisition (PBSA) in the Department of Defense,* December 2000, page 13 and Appendix I. This publication can be accessed at *http://www.acq.osd.mil/dpap/Docs/pbsaguide010201.pdf* (accessed February 2012).

- *AFMC Award-Fee and Award Term Guide,* Department of the Air Force, November 2000. This publication can be accessed at *https://www.acquisition.gov/comp/seven_steps/library/AFMCaward-fee-guide.doc* (accessed February 2012).

Should Incentives Be Used in PBSC Contracts?

If the coverage in this section on incentives appears to be negative, that is because since the 1960s studies on cost incentives (FPI and CPIF contracts) have shown that they have little or no effect on a contractor's performance. If cost incentives do not work, it is not likely that performance incentives will have a material effect on contract performance. There does not appear to be much research on the effect of performance incentives, probably because of the complexity of multiple incentive contracts (the FAR requires a cost incentive in multiple incentive contracts) and the fact that contract changes generally erode the relationships between the various incentive elements, making it difficult to determine the effect of the incentive on contractor performance under FPI and CPIF contracts.

There are, however, published accounts[9] of the successful use of multiple incentives in service contracts. In most cases such contracts are large dollar value, multi-tasked efforts, and the contracts used a combination of contract types to achieve their goals. The key to success was careful preparation and effective contract management.

As noted earlier, award fee incentives are probably the most effective incentive for PBSC contracts. Effective management of award fee incentives requires continuing communication between the government and the contractor, as does the management of a PBSC contract. Because the resources necessary to manage an award fee contract mirror those required for the management of a PBSC contract, the administration costs are not increased. However, award fee incentives will work *only* if structured and administered properly.

Contracting officers are not limited to those incentive arrangements set forth in the FAR. Other incentive arrangements, if they make sense and do not violate any prohibitions set forth in law or regulation, may be used. A word of caution, however: FAR 16.402-4 states that "all multiple-incentive contracts must include a cost incentive (or constraint) that operates to preclude rewarding a contractor for superior technical performance or delivery results when the cost of those results outweigh their value to the Government."

Award term is an example of an innovative incentive concept that is not covered by the FAR, and since it is not a multiple-incentive arrangement, a specific cost incentive is not required. It should be noted, however, that cost control should be a primary evaluation criteria in the performance evaluation of an award term contract.

Service contracts tend to be long term, and this could be a problem with respect to the use of incentives. One of the primary purposes of an incentive is to motivate the contractor to a desired level of performance (i.e., encourage contractors to improve their performance). But at what point does this end? How should incentives be applied in the long term? If the basis for the incentive is satisfactory performance and the contractor is paid a bonus for performance above satisfactory, does a contractor who routinely performs at a level above satisfactory continue to receive the bonus over the term of the contract? If the incentive is supposed to be used to encourage improved performance, shouldn't the bar be raised for the continuing performance (i.e., at some point the contractor's routinely excellent performance would be considered to be satisfactory in order to encourage incrementally better performance)?

On the other hand, if the bar is raised and the contractor is not paid the continuing bonus, this would, in effect, be penalizing the contractor for its excellent work. There is a limit to how much performance can be improved. There is also a cost to the contractor for improved performance, such as training of its personnel in new methodology and research to find ways to improve performance. Generally, these are acceptable costs if they serve to improve the contractor's competitive position and bring in new business. But on the individual contract level, how long will the incentive be effective if each year the contractor is expected to incrementally improve its performance to earn the incentive?

The practical solution would be to keep the definition of satisfactory performance stable and to, in effect, pay the contractor extra for its continuing excellent performance. This tacitly recognizes that the contractor is performing at a level higher than anticipated and therefore is earning the incentive amount, even if there are no longer any incremental improvements in contract performance. The incentive is now operating to encourage the contractor to continue its excellent performance rather than improve its performance. Whether the contract is still an "incentive" contract is debatable, but it does get the job done.

Long-term incentive contracts, if not managed well by the government, can become problem contracts. The following is a possible scenario: After several years the contractor's project manager realizes that further performance improvements are not practicable and continues performance at the same (albeit high) level. Over the next several years, the contractor continues to receive the incentive amounts because the government program personnel are pleased with its performance and routinely give the contractor high grades. Over time, however, the contractor's performance deteriorates because either: (1) the contractor's more experienced personnel are transferred to newer projects that need their experience, or (2) the contractor personnel grow complacent because the contract is "safe" and they are not being challenged. It will take some time for the government personnel to react to the deteriorating performance. When they do begin complaining, the contractor changes program personnel and performance begins to improve. Improvements are possible because the bar (for satisfactory performance) has been lowered due to the deteriorated performance, and there is room for improvement—back to the level where further improvements are no longer practicable. And the cycle repeats itself.

This is a possible, but not necessarily probable, scenario for a long-term incentivized service contract. Incentives could be described as follows: *Donkeys are not dumb. If you dangle a carrot in front of a donkey's face, it will not be long until: (1) the donkey grabs the carrot and eats it, or (2) the donkey realizes that it cannot get the carrot and stops trying.* Incentives have a shelf life, the duration of which is dependent on the type of services being acquired and any practical limitations on performance improvements. When deciding whether to incentivize a PBSC contract, consideration must be given not only to the type of incentive to use but also to how the term of the contract might affect the effectiveness of the incentive arrangement. This is particularly true of the award term incentive because the contractor must provide "excellent" performance to earn an extended term—how "satisfactory" and "excellent" will be defined in the out years should be a matter of concern.

Deductibles

The term "deductibles" refers to a procedure, used primarily in service contracts, to ensure that the government does not pay for something it does not receive. While technically not an incentive, this process does act as a negative incentive. Deductibles are used to reduce the contract price (or fee) when the required level of services is not provided or does not meet the required quality levels.

In Part 46, Quality Assurance,[10] the FAR addresses nonconforming supplies or services, stating: "For services, the contracting officer can consider identifying the value of the individual work requirements or tasks (subdivisions) that may be subject to price or fee reduction. This value may be used to determine an equitable adjustment for nonconforming services."

Deductibles are developed by determining values for the services to be rendered, usually on a line-item (per performance indicator) basis. This process was discussed in detail in OFPP's Pamphlet No. 4, *A Guide For Writing and Administering Performance Statements of Work for Service Contracts*. Figures 3-4 and 3-5 are examples from this pamphlet that illustrate generally how this is done. [NOTE: This pamphlet and OFPP Policy Letter 91-2, *Service Contracting*, have been rescinded (but still may be available on bookshelves or libraries) because the subject matter has been covered in the FAR and OFPP's *A Guide to Best Practices for Performance-Based Service Contracting*. The examples in Figures 3-4 and 3-5 were not included in the newer coverage but are still valid examples of how to develop deductibles.]

The deductible value is often based on payroll costs to reflect the value of each performance indicator. The number of personnel and the associated payroll costs can be determined using government staffing and payroll costs or those of an incumbent contractor. The value of each performance indicator is shown as a percentage reflecting the relationship of the payroll costs of that activity to the total payroll costs. If the services are not rendered,

FIGURE 3-4
Deduct Analysis

[Shows how the value of a service can be calculated]

Job: Vehicle Operations	Personnel	Payroll	% of Total
Operate Vehicles	xxxxxxx	xxxxxx	xxxxxxxx
Operate Taxi	5	$5,000	19.2%
Operate Scheduled Bus	4	$4,000	15.4%
Operate Unscheduled Bus	1	$1,000	3.8%
(etc.)	(etc.)	(etc.)	(etc.)
(etc.)	(etc.)	(etc.)	(etc.)
Total	28	$26,000	100%

FIGURE 3-5
Deducting for Non-Performance

[Shows how an actual deduction might be calculated when, based on sampling, the services were determined to be unsatisfactory]

If: Quality of completed work is unsatisfactory (AQL of 6.5% exceeded)
and: Contract price is $100,000 per month
and: Quality of completed work deduct percentage is 10%
and: Sample size is 50
and: Number of defects in the sample is 10 (reject number is 8)
Then: Deduction from the current month's invoice is:

```
    Contract price                    = $ 100,000
    x Deduct percentage               =       .10
                                      $    10,000
    x Percent of sample defective            .20
    Deduction                         = $    2,000
```

---

or performance is unsatisfactory, the percentage figure represents the percentage to be applied when calculating how much is to be deducted from the monthly invoice.

To summarize (since the two examples are not related), the value of each performance indicator is determined based on the relation of the payroll cost of that activity to the total payroll cost. For taxi operations, the value is 19.2%; in the deduct formula, this would be the quality of completed work deduct percentage. The payroll costs are used only to determine a value for the performance indicator. In the deduct formula application, the dollar figure used is the total monthly contract price.

It is not a good idea to use both a deduction schedule and an incentive in the same contract because the application of both can be complicated and lead to problems. The primary problem with combining deductions and incentives is that it would not be proper to reduce the contract price for services not received, or received but not with an acceptable quality, and then make a further reduction for the same reason under the incentive arrangement. If both are used, the deductible should be applied first and then the incentive applied to whatever is left. It would be better to decide early to use either a deductible or an incentive arrangement, but not both.

Another problem with deductibles lies in their application. A common mistake when dealing with a task comprising multiple subtasks is to indicate that a failure to complete one subtask satisfactorily will cause the entire task to be rated as unsatisfactory. For example, in a contract for hospital janitorial services, where a number of different areas were to be cleaned, a failure to clean one area satisfactorily would have resulted in an unsatisfactory rating (and a contract deduction) for all room-cleaning services. The problem was that there were different cleaning standards: sterile for operating rooms, while administrative areas were judged on such factors as ashtrays and waste receptacles emptied. GAO[11] ruled that an overall deduction could not be applied in light of the different standards. The application of deductibles must be reasonable and must have a sound and documented basis.

SUMMARY

Developing the PWS, QAP, and incentive structure can get complicated. When examining each task to develop performance indicators, there is a tendency to use every possible factor involved in task performance. It is important to keep the process simple. Only those factors most significant with respect to successful completion of the task should be included. In developing performance standards and AQLs, the standards and deviations should be realistic and should reflect a satisfactory operation rather than a perfect operation.

Every factor used to measure contractor performance must be monitored in accordance with the published surveillance plan.

This will significantly affect the number and quality of personnel assigned to contract administration. Once the surveillance plan is published in the QAP, it becomes a contractual requirement on the part of the government. If the government fails to adhere to the plan, the government's ability to enforce the contract terms will be adversely affected.

A PBSC contract requires a more extensive planning and development effort than that required for a typical service contract using a functional SOW, and sufficient time must be allowed for this effort. A PBSC contract also requires significantly more contract administration effort because the contract must be monitored in accordance with the QAP.

These problems notwithstanding, PBSC offers an opportunity to develop a service contract that explicitly requires the delivery of services of a predetermined quality. PBSC works best when used for services of a continuing nature, where the services can be defined in terms of objective and measurable performance standards and the cost of developing the initial contract can be amortized over a number of contracts.

The difference between PBSC and a service contract using a functional SOW lies primarily in the PWS requirement for specific, measurable performance standards and acceptable quality levels; the use of a QAP to summarize the performance standards and establish the surveillance methods and schedule; and the preference for the use of incentives.

While agency-developed procedures may differ somewhat from this book, the details of how to structure a PWS are not significantly different from those of a functional SOW.

The information set forth in Chapter 5, The SOW Format, and Chapter 6, Common Problems in Writing SOWs, is applicable to both the PWS and the functional SOW. Chapter 4, Using a Statement of Objectives (SOO) and Related Issues, addresses a new concept as a substitute for the use of a PWS.

NOTES

[1] FAR 37.601.

[2] FAR 37.602(b)(3).

[3] FAR 37.601(b)(3).

[4] *Guidebook for Performance-Based Services Acquisition (PBSA) in the Department of Defense*, December 2000. Online at *http://www.acq.osd.mil/dpap/Docs/pbsaguide010201.pdf* (accessed February 2012).

[5] Ibid.

[6] For some examples of these studies, see the article "Award Term: The Newest Incentive," by Vernon J. Edwards, pages 2–4, which can be accessed at *http://www.wifcon.com/anal/analaterm.htm* (accessed February 2012).

[7] For a good discussion of award term contracts, see *https://www.acquisition.gov/comp/seven_steps/step5_consider.html* (accessed February 2012).

[8] See *Burnside-Ott Aviation Training Center v. John H. Dalton, Secretary of the Navy*, U.S. Court of Appeals for the Federal Circuit No. 96-1227, 2/25/97. Online at *http://www.ll.georgetown.edu/federal/judicial/fed/opinions/96opinions/96-1227.html* (accessed February 2012).

[9] See "Performance-Based Contracting Incentives: Myths, Best Practices, and Innovations," by Gregory A. Garret, *Contract Management*, April 2002, and "Strategy-Driven Service Contracting," by Lyle Eesley, *Contract Management*, March 2002. See also "A Case for Multiple Incentives," by Tom Dickinson, *Contract Management*, February 2001.

[10] FAR 46.407(f).

[11] *Environmental Aseptic Services Administration and Larson Building Care Inc.*, B-207771, 2/28/83, 83-1 CPD ¶194.

4 Using a Statement of Objectives (SOO) and Related Issues

This chapter addresses the statement of objectives (SOO) concept and other issues related to competing an acquisition using an SOO. Because this is an emerging concept, this chapter will go beyond "how to write" an SOO and discuss the process itself and some of the ramifications related to the SOO concept.

WHAT IS AN SOO?

Section 5 of the 1996 Department of Defense handbook for preparing SOWs defines the SOO as follows:

> The SOO is a Government prepared document incorporated into the RFP that states the overall solicitation objectives. It can be used in those solicitations where the intent is to provide the maximum flexibility to each offeror to propose an innovative development approach. Offerors use the RFP, product performance requirements, and SOO as a basis for preparing their proposals including a SOW and CDRL. Note: The SOO is not retained as a contract compliance item.
>
> The program SOO should provide the basic, top-level objectives of the acquisition and is provided in the RFP in lieu of a Government-written SOW. This approach provides potential offerors the flexibility to develop cost effective solutions and the opportunity to propose innovative alternatives meeting the stated objectives. It also presents the Government with an opportunity to assess

the offeror's understanding of all aspects of the effort to be performed, by eliminating the "how-to" instructions to accomplish the required effort normally contained in the SOW the Government provides to prospective offerors.[1]

In 2001, a group of volunteers from across the federal government joined together to participate in a project known as the *Seven Steps to Performance-Based Acquisition*.[2] This project also addressed the SOO concept and defined it as follows:

> The alternative process—use of a SOO—is a more recent methodology that turns the acquisition process around and requires competing contractors to develop the performance work statement, performance metrics and measurement plan, and quality assurance plan...all of which should be evaluated before contract award. If the SOO approach is used, FAR 37.602(c) directs us to remove the SOO when the contract or task order is awarded, and replace it with the awardees' winning PWS.
>
> The SOO is a very short document (e.g., under ten pages) that provides the basic, high-level objectives of the acquisition. It is provided in the solicitation in lieu of a government-written statement of work or performance work statement.
>
> In this approach, the contractors' proposals contain statements of work and performance metrics and measures (which are based on their proposed solutions and existing commercial practices). Clearly, use of a SOO opens the acquisition up to a wider range of potential solutions.[3]

The SOO does not replace the SOW. MIL-HDBK-245D also states:

The SOO should not address each WBS element, but each WBS element should be traceable to something in the SOO. For example, a SOO may instruct the bidder to address his engineering approach. That is not a particular WBS element, but several WBS elements might be created to breakout the engineering tasks. Generally, a broad and sweeping objective statement will trace to more WBS elements than would be the case for a very narrowly focused objective statement.[4]

Potential offerors use the SOO, along with other information and guidance provided in the RFP, to develop the contract work breakdown structure, SOW, and other documentation supporting their proposals. The SOO should be clear and concise in defining the objectives of the work effort, and it should provide potential offerors with sufficient information to structure a sound response and satisfy the government's objectives. Once the contract is awarded, the SOO is replaced with the offeror's proposed SOW.

SOO FORMAT

There is no set format for an SOO, but the SOO should, at a minimum address the following:

Purpose—The purpose should be a short statement that describes why you need to acquire the services, usually in terms of what you want accomplished. In the *Seven Steps* example from a VA SOO[5], the purpose was succinctly stated:

> The purpose of this task order is to obtain loan servicing in support of VA's portfolio that will significantly improve loan guaranty operations and service to its customers.

Background—Provide the background to the requirement and the current environment and its relationship to the project it supports. In the VA SOO example, the background statement included sections on:[6]

- VA loan servicing history

- Current VA portfolio origination/acquisition process

- Overview of the current servicing process.

The background should specifically include reference to any problems the government or previous contractors have encountered in the past that might affect how the services are provided. Of particular interest would be problems with methodology that did not work or otherwise created performance difficulties. You want to put offerors on notice of past problems so the problems will not be repeated.

Scope or mission—A scope statement is necessary to help offerors to get an overview of the size and range of the services needed. The *Seven Steps* VA SOO example contained the following scope statement:

> The purpose of this [task order] is to provide the full range of loan servicing support. This includes such activities as customer management, paying taxes and insurance, default management, accounting, foreclosure, bankruptcy, etc., as well as future actions associated with loan servicing. This Statement of Objectives reflects current VA policies and practices, allowing offerors to propose and price a solution to known requirements. It is anticipated that specific loan servicing requirements and resulting objectives will change over the life of this order. This will result in VA modifying this order to incorporate in-scope changes.[7]

The scope statement may also include information on the amount of funding available (see Releasing Funding Information at the end of this chapter).

Performance Objectives—Describe project objectives and performance requirement plans, including how project quality, cost, and adherence to the schedule will be measured. Success criteria may also be defined to ensure that potential offerors clearly understand the objectives that must be met for the work to be considered successful. The *Seven Steps* VA SOO example set forth the following performance objectives:

> The VA expects to improve its current loan servicing operations through this task order in several ways. Primary among these is to increase the number and value of salable loans. In addition, VA wants to be assured that all payments for such items as taxes and insurance are always paid on time. As part of these activities, the VA also has an objective to improve Information Technology information exchange and VA's access to automated information on an as required basis to have the information to meet customer needs and creditors' requirements.[8]

Period and Place of Performance—Indicate the period of performance, including any options. As appropriate, indicate the place of performance if it could affect how an offeror might propose to do the work.

Constraints—Identify any constraints that could affect the offeror's proposed performance work statement and how the performance might be measured. For example, acquisitions related to information technology will need to conform to the agency's information technology architecture and accessibility standards. There may be other constraints, such as security, privacy, safety, and accessibility to government facilities. Identify any government policies, directives, standards, or regulations that an offeror must comply with. If appropriate, identify any government property to be provided. Potential constraints should be a matter of interest for the program and contracting personnel, and particularly the users of the services, when initially developing the SOO. Contractor input with respect to potential constraints should be obtained during market research.

Section L

The government-prepared SOO is published in Section L of the RFP. When using an SOO, Section L of the RFP must inform offerors that if they receive the award, their proposal will be incorporated into the contract by reference. Section L must also provide offerors with a common outline or format to follow—otherwise the structure of offerors' proposed PWSs will vary considerably, making a comparative assessment difficult. Require offerors to provide a performance work statement complete with the performance metrics and measurement plan, and a quality assurance plan that addresses how performance assessment (surveillance) will be conducted.

Section L must also provide directions on how to write the PWS, including direction on the common *do*s and *don't*s of SOW/PWS writing (see Chapter 6). It is in the government's best interests to ensure that potential offerors are provided sufficient information to write their proposals in a manner that will be contractually acceptable.

Section M

Special care must also be taken when writing the evaluation criteria in Section M of the RFP. The technical evaluation criteria and their respective weights should center on those things that demonstrate how well the offeror understands the requirement, how well the contractor's proposal will meet the requirement, the validity of the proposed performance metrics and measurement, the viability of its quality assurance and performance assessment plan, and whether the government has sufficient resources to monitor and assess the offeror's performance in accordance with the offeror's proposal.

The technical evaluation plan (and to the extent possible, the description and weighting of the evaluation criteria) must recognize that the content of offerors' proposals may vary widely as they propose their own way of meeting the government's requirements. The plan must establish the value of the services and provide a tradeoff method for determining the respective values of the differing performance levels. The technical evaluation plan itself is not provided in the RFP, but, if appropriate, Section M could provide offerors with a target performance level along with a minimum acceptable performance level. This would help avoid having to evaluate clearly unacceptable offers.

Past performance is an important evaluation factor when using an SOO. How well an offeror has performed similar government or commercial work provides a good indicator of how well it might perform to its current proposal.

Evaluation criteria should not be structured in a manner that inhibits offerors' creativity. Take particular care with the wording of evaluation criteria related to staffing plans, labor mixes, the experience of key personnel, and other resource-related evaluation criteria to ensure that such criteria do not directly or indirectly restrict how an offeror might propose to do the work.

In standard services acquisitions, manpower requirements are commonly prescribed in terms of "required number of bodies" or by other qualifiers such as college degrees or specific years of experience. In an SOO, prescribing manpower requirements in this manner limits the ability of offerors to propose their best solutions and could preclude the use of qualified contractor personnel who may be well suited for performing the requirement but may be lacking, for example, a complete college degree or the exact years of specified experience. Offerors should be free to propose whatever resources they deem appropriate. However, if a resource must have a specific skill set or certification, then it should be duly identified.

INCORPORATION BY REFERENCE

A contract will be awarded to the offeror whose proposal is determined to offer the best value. Award is made in the usual fashion after including a clause in the contract identifying the contractor's proposal and incorporating it into the contract by reference.

The concept of incorporating an offeror's proposal into the contract by reference (in whole or in part) is not new. It has been used in the R&D community for years in situations where the government knew what it wanted as an end product but either didn't know how to get there or knew that there were a number of solutions and didn't want to fix on one solution without seeing what else industry could come up with. The RFP outlined what was wanted as a result of the contract and set forth any constraints that might apply (much like an SOO). The RFP invited offerors to provide complete proposals to accomplish the purpose of the contract and informed them that their proposals would be incorporated by reference into the resulting contract. Award would be made to the offeror proposing the best combination of technical value and price. It was not unusual during negotiations to direct an offeror to make specific wording changes to ensure that what was incorporated by reference was contractually viable.

Even though the contractor's proposal is incorporated into the contract by reference, it should *also* be included as an attachment to the contract. This document will become the only contractual requirement (the government's SOO is deleted along with the rest of Section L) and should be made available to those government and contractor personnel who will be involved in contract performance and administration.

Because the proposals will become the contractual requirement, they must be examined closely during the evaluation process to ensure that they do not contain loopholes, inconsistencies, vagueness, or other problems that will adversely affect contract compliance. Problems with the wording of an offeror' s proposal should be considered deficiencies, and offerors who are included in the competitive range must be informed of such deficiencies during negotiations and given an opportunity to correct them.

Correction of the wording of an offeror's proposal may generate new protest grounds. Under the current rules, offerors must be informed of the deficiencies and significant weaknesses in their proposals, but agencies *cannot* tell offerors how to correct them. When using an SOO, however, the wording of an offeror's proposal may have inadvertently created loopholes, inconsistencies, or vagueness that is contractually unacceptable but does not go to the essence of the proposal (i.e., would not affect the offeror's competitive position if corrected). In such instances, agencies should not only identify the deficiencies but should also tell the offeror the corrections that must be made if the offeror is to remain in the competition. This is likely to draw protests, but it is the only way to ensure that the government does not incorporate a proposal by reference that contains contractually unacceptable wording.

USING AN SOO

Two questions must be addressed when deciding on the acquisition approach during acquisition planning: "What is the contract supposed to achieve?" and "Does market research indicate that innovative or different approaches might be available?" The first question is addressed during the budget process but should be reexamined at the initiation of acquisition planning. The second question should be critically examined during market research. The market research should focus on what is available in the commercial marketplace that might satisfy the government requirement.

The results of the market research will bring about a third question, "Do we want to consider innovative or different approaches?" The fact that there are "other" ways to get the job done does not necessarily mean that such approaches must be considered. There may be reasons to continue doing the work as it has been done before. Market research may reveal that the "other" approaches are too expensive; risk analysis may indicate that the "other" approaches are too risky—innovations are not risk-free. Then there is the old adage, "If it ain't broke, don't fix it." In other words, do not change something unless there is a clear benefit to making the change.

The SOO approach is viable when there are clear benefits to be achieved. For example, market research reveals that "other" approaches may result in cost savings or will bring about greater efficiency, even if at acceptably greater cost or that it is not possible for the government to develop performance standards and assessment methods without inhibiting competition because of the variety of "other" approaches available in the marketplace. The SOO approach permits the offeror to develop the performance metrics and measurements in accordance with how the offeror proposes to accomplish the work.

COMPETING THE SOO

In a typical services acquisition, the government issues an RFP containing a statement of work or performance work statement that describes the work requirement, identifying the kinds of services required and what they are to accomplish. The RFP contains all the information an offeror needs to know to develop a competitive proposal.

The SOO, however, provides only the basic, high-level objectives of the acquisition. Will this be enough information to serve as the basis for a competitive proposal? In many cases it will be enough information. When dealing with commercial or commercial-like services, offerors already know how to perform the work and only need to know what it is that you want. This may not be the case, however, for complex or multi-task services or for service contracts where the performance requirements are continually evolving.

Five-Step Approach

In "An Innovative Approach to Performance-Based Acquisition Using a SOO," Chip Mather and Ann Costello suggest a five-step approach to conducting a services acquisition using an SOO:[9]

1. Conduct market research

2. Develop a statement of objectives and identify constraints

3. Conduct initial "competition"

4. Support contractors during the "due diligence" phase

5. Conduct best value evaluation and make award.

Step 1: Conduct Market Research

While market research is part of the normal process for conducting acquisition planning, it is critical to the success of an acquisition using an SOO. The authors recommend a particular process:

> The right kind of market research, in our view, is one-on-one market research sessions with industry leaders (practitioners, not "marketers") to learn about the state of the marketplace, commercial practices, and commercial performance metrics. Especially with regard to the latter, asking contractors to provide performance measures and collection methods they are using on their existing contracts (both commercial and government) reveals what the contractors consider important in service delivery.

As noted in Chapter 2, market research is conducted in a variety of ways. Generally, one-on-one market research should be the last step in the market research process, after the research has examined the marketplace, looked at the various commercial practices, and identified the industry leaders. The industry leaders should then be approached with a preliminary SOO to serve as the basis for the one-on-one meetings. (Do not equate "industry leaders" with "large businesses," as there are many very capable small businesses in the service industry.)

Step 2: Develop a Statement of Objectives and Identify Constraints

Developing a statement of objectives and identifying constraints is also part of the normal process in that the results of market research are used to develop a description of the requirement suitable for a solicitation. In this case the authors stress: "Whenever possible, the objectives should be 'grounded' in the plans and objectives found in agency strategic performance plans, program authorization documents, and budget and investment documents."

Steps 1 and 2 are not distinctly separate processes. As a result of the market research, a final SOO, including the necessary constraints, is developed. It should be noted here that steps 1 and 2 are the same as those used when developing an SOW or PWS for a standard services acquisition, except that instead of an initial SOO at the last stages of market research, a draft SOW/PWS or RFP could be used, and as a result of the market research a final SOW/PWS would be developed and the RFP issued.

Steps 3 and 4, even while based on FAR 15.201 and 15.202 as the authors suggest, would require an adjustment to the typical approach to the presolicitation phase of an acquisition.

Step 3: Conduct Initial "Competition"

The authors suggest an "initial competition" based on FAR 15.202, which permits an advisory multi-step process:

FAR 15.202(a) The agency may publish a presolicitation notice (see 5.204) that provides a general description of the scope or purpose of the acquisition and invites potential offerors to submit information that allows the Government to advise the offerors about their potential to be viable competitors. The presolicitation notice should identify the information that must be submitted and the criteria that will be used in making the initial evaluation. Information sought may be limited to a statement of qualifications and other appropriate information (e.g., proposed technical concept, past performance, and limited pricing information). At a minimum, the notice shall contain sufficient information to permit a potential offeror to make an informed decision about whether to participate in the acquisition. This process should not be used for multi-step acquisitions where it would result in offerors being required to submit identical information in response to the notice and in response to the initial step of the acquisition.

(b) The agency shall evaluate all responses in accordance with the criteria stated in the notice, and shall advise each respondent in writing that it will be invited to participate in the resultant acquisition or, based on the information submitted, that it is unlikely to be a viable competitor. The agency shall advise respondents considered not to be viable competitors of the general basis for that opinion. The agency shall inform all respondents that, notwithstanding the advice provided by the Government in response to their submissions, they may participate in the resultant acquisition.

The authors maintain that this initial competition is needed to give potential offerors "the time to understand the agency's objectives, constraints, and history of performance, so they can craft an approach and solution to the agency's needs." They also note that "the advisory multi-step process is not like a competitive range decision: the choice is the contractor's whether to continue to compete."

The use of the term "initial competition," even when explained, is likely to generate protests as lawyers for those not considered "competitive" seek any means to interrupt the procurement process. A better term might be "advisory process" to coincide with the FAR language.

A somewhat similar process, using "sources sought" synopses, has been in use for some time in the R&D community. Sources sought synopses are used to seek out firms capable of performing particular R&D efforts. The synopsis describes the project purpose and invites interested firms to submit their qualifications to perform the work. They are informed that there is no guarantee that a solicitation will ever be issued and proposals will not be accepted. Firms that fail to submit adequate qualifications are informed that they lack the requisite qualifications and would probably not be selected for award should they respond to any resulting solicitation, but they may request a copy of any resulting solicitation. This process works well and is still in use in the R&D community.

The advisory multi-step process is not in widespread government use and would require training for procurement personnel to ensure that they do it right, as a preliminary step to the "due diligence" phase.

Step 4: Support Contractors during the "Due Diligence" Phase

This step, called "due diligence," will require a major adjustment in the approach to service contracting. Due diligence is used in acquisition to describe the period and process during which competitors take the time and make the effort to become knowledgeable about an agency's needs in order to propose a competitive solution. Lawyers understand this term, but it is not in general use in the procurement community.

Before the FAR 15 Rewrite, there was concern about revealing advance procurement information that might provide a contractor with an unfair competitive advantage. Contracting officers were advised to be careful about what specific information was released prior to issuing the RFP. Generally, the "if you tell one you must tell all" process was followed. This led to the use of sources sought synopses and draft SOWs where procurement information was revealed to all interested parties and they were encouraged to respond, but there would be no dialogue between the government and individual contractors about their responses.

The FAR 15 Rewrite changed all that. The term "advance procurement information" is no longer in the FAR. The FAR now states:

> 15.201(a) Exchanges of information among all interested parties, from the earliest identification of a requirement through receipt of proposals, are encouraged.
>
> 15.201(c) Agencies are encouraged to promote early exchanges of information about future acquisitions. An early exchange of information among industry and program manager, contracting officer, and other participants in the acquisition process can identify and resolve concerns regarding acquisition strategy, including proposed contract type, terms and conditions, and acquisition planning schedules; the feasibility of the requirement, including performance requirements, statements of work, and data requirements; the suitability of the proposal instructions and evaluation criteria, including the approach for assessing past performance information; the availability of reference documents; and any other industry concerns or questions. Some techniques to promote early exchanges of information are—
>
> (1) Industry or small business conferences;
>
> (2) Public hearings;

(3) Market research, as described in Part 10;

(4) One-on-one meetings with potential offerors (any that are substantially involved with potential contract terms and conditions should include the contracting officer; also see paragraph (f) of this section regarding restrictions on disclosure of information);

(5) Presolicitation notices;

(6) Draft RFPs;

(7) RFIs;

(8) Presolicitation or preproposal conferences; and

(9) Site visits.

This FAR citation dramatically changes the presolicitation process and is tailor-made for the use of an SOO. The SOO provides only broad information about the government requirement. Potential offerors are going to need a significant amount of additional information if they are to present a competitive, performance-based proposal. Now everything is open for discussion. This is where the fourth step comes into play. The authors describe the due diligence process as follows:

> There is a simple truth. The more an offeror understands about an agency's objectives, problems, and constraints, the more likely that offeror is to provide a superior solution. The due diligence period provides offerors that opportunity.
>
> In concept, due diligence allows the competitors full and open access to the government to ask questions, inspect actual conditions, and better understand the problem to be solved and the conditions under which they must work. The amount of time to be spent in due diligence

should be commensurate with the size and complexity of the program. For major programs, this could be six weeks or more. Whenever possible, the agency should seek, during the due diligence phase, to provide complete and unfettered access to both managers and sites to verify conditions. Again, it is to the agency's advantage to have offerors who really understand the objectives and use that information to craft superior solutions.

The authors' due diligence concept makes sense and should lead to better proposals. There are some potential problems, however.

The first problem is getting program personnel to devote the necessary time to deal with contractor visits and questions. The service industry is very competitive, and there will likely be a number of potential offerors wanting attention. For program personnel this could involve a significant amount of time away from their duties. The prospect of entertaining multiple contractor visits and questions may cause program managers to seek more conventional acquisition approaches.

Second, attempts to limit the number of potential offerors wanting their turn at due diligence could lead to protests; even if a contractor has been told that it is unlikely to be a viable competitor, the contractor can still choose to participate. Limiting this right to participate would be a mistake. While the government is permitted to limit the number of offerors in the competitive range, this right applies only after receipt of proposals.

Finally, whether the FAR intended to or not, the pre-solicitation process outlined in 15.201(c) is going to result in presolicitation negotiations. When government and contractor program personnel meet to talk about a pending or potential acquisition, the conversation will end up with a give-and-take discussion. Astute contractor program personnel will gain insight into the government's preferences with respect to offerors' proposals and possibly be able to influence how the government will evaluate their approach. Is this a bad thing? Not necessarily. It might be bad if the government were writing the PWS, but here the due diligence process is designed to help offerors develop their best proposal, including the PWS, performance metrics and measurement, and a quality assurance plan. Nevertheless, it is likely that there will be protests in this area, and in due course the Comptroller General will address what can or cannot be said during the SOO presolicitation process.

With respect to due diligence, the authors go on to say:

> There is no requirement that due-diligence questions and answers be part of a written process. And, unless the question results in an amendment to the solicitation, there is certainly no rule that says every contractor should know what other contractors are asking and know the answers to those questions as well. However, the "fair and equitable" standard does dictate that, if two contractors ask the same question, they get the same basic information in response...but it doesn't have to be written.

There is a problem here, but only with respect to the "written process." In the event of a protest, the Comptroller General and the courts place a great deal of importance on contemporaneous writings. When it comes down to who said what, the party that has something in writing that dates back to the event in question has a definite advantage. Contracting officers should insist that program personnel keep a written record of what they said to whom. These would be internal memorandums and not generally available to other potential offerors. This information would also be valuable to program personnel to ensure that they are providing consistent information during due diligence.

FAR paragraphs 15.201(a) through (e) address presolicitation activities and generally permit open communication between the government and industry relating to a potential procurement.

FAR 15.201(f) addresses the restrictions on communications after release of the solicitation:

> 15.201(f) General information about agency mission needs and future requirements may be disclosed at any time. After release of the solicitation, the contracting officer must be the focal point of any exchange with potential offerors. When specific information about a proposed acquisition that would be necessary for the preparation of proposals is disclosed to one or more potential offerors, that information must be made available to the public as soon as practicable, but no later than the next general release of information, in order to avoid creating an unfair competitive advantage. Information provided to a potential offeror in response to its request must not be disclosed if doing so would reveal the potential offeror's confidential business strategy and is protected under 3.104 or Subpart 24.2. When conducting a presolicitation or preproposal conference, materials distributed at the conference should be made available to all potential offerors, upon request.

Basically, this FAR citation moves what used to be advance procurement information restrictions from the presolicitation phase to the period between the release of the RFP and the receipt of proposals. Once proposals are received, however, the regular evaluation, negotiation, and best value award processes apply.

Step 5: Conduct Best Value Evaluation and Make Award

The final step is to receive proposals, conduct the evaluation, negotiate with those in the competitive range, and make a best value award. The due diligence phase ends upon receipt of proposals. Any further communications with offerors are governed by FAR 15.306(b), *Communications with offerors before establishment of the competitive range,* which permits communications regarding past performance information and other issues necessary to understand offerors' proposals. Such communications cannot be used to cure proposal deficiencies or material omissions, materially alter the technical or cost elements of the proposal, or otherwise revise the proposal. In short, the government may ask an offeror to clarify something in its proposal, but the clarification is unacceptable if it amounts to a modification to the proposal.

The evaluation and negotiation of competing proposals based on an SOO are more complex than those for standard services solicitations. Acquisition planning must provide for sufficient time for this to be accomplished properly.

Evaluation—Evaluating proposals based on an SOO will be more complex than usual because the proposals may vary widely as the offerors propose their own way of meeting the government's requirements. Generally, the evaluation consists of three steps:

1. Evaluators examine each offeror's PWS, performance metrics and measurements, and quality assurance plan on their own merits to decide if the proposed methods will meet government requirements. Among other things, the evaluators must consider whether the proposed performance metrics and measurements will support performance assessment and provide accurate results. The evaluators must also consider whether the government has sufficient resources to monitor the contractor's performance in accordance with its proposed quality assurance plan. Those proposals found to be unacceptable should be rejected.

2. The evaluators make a comparative assessment between those proposals found acceptable initially, using tradeoff methods that determine the respective values of the differing performance levels, and then score and rank the proposals.

3. The evaluators determine which proposals are the most highly rated and should be recommended for inclusion in

the competitive range. The other proposals should be rejected once the contracting officer establishes the competitive range.

Each evaluation must be fully documented as to the rationale for the scoring, the risk analysis, and the tradeoffs made among the differing proposals to determine which proposals are the most highly rated. This contemporaneous documentation will prove invaluable in the event of a protest.

Negotiation—Contracting officers should plan on extensive negotiations after establishing the competitive range to ensure complete and mutual understanding of each offeror's proposal. First, emphasis should be placed on the technical aspects of the proposals to ensure a mutual understanding of the proposal and that the proposed approach will satisfactorily meet the government's requirements. Even the most highly rated proposals are likely to have deficiencies, significant weaknesses, or other problems that must be resolved. Multiple rounds of negotiations may be required. The emphasis should then be placed on the wording of the proposals to ensure that it is contractually acceptable and does not contain ambiguities, inconsistencies, or loopholes that will complicate contract administration. Keep in mind that the winning offeror's proposal will be incorporated into the contract by reference and will be the only contractual requirement the contractor must follow.

Award—It should be noted that making an award based on an SOO must be done on a best value basis. This is the only approach that makes sense when dealing with multiple approaches to the same requirement. The lowest–priced, technically acceptable source selection is not viable because the government cannot reasonably establish acceptable standards based on an SOO that provides only minimal information. Making an award based on price alone is an obvious nonstarter.

As with the evaluation, the source selection decision must be fully documented. Source selection decisions must be made in accordance with FAR 15.308, which requires that the decision documentation include the rationale for any business judgments and tradeoffs made or relied on by the source selection authority, including the benefits associated with additional costs. While the FAR does not require that tradeoff decisions be quantified, Comptroller General protest decisions indicate that the tradeoff rationale regarding each offeror must be explained sufficiently to justify the decisions made. This applies particularly to competitions using an SOO where differing approaches are proposed, and the award decision must be based on both technical and cost tradeoffs.

Awarding on the basis of an SOO brings forth a potential problem. The contractor has proposed how it would do the work. The government has incorporated the proposal into the contract by reference, making it the contractual requirement. To what extent would the changes clauses apply? Does the government have the right to unilaterally change the description of the services that the contractor designed? Even though the contractor has a right to an equitable adjustment, would a unilateral change be a good idea? Probably not. Any needed changes to a contract based on an SOO should be bilateral because the contractor's input will be critical to ensuring that the contractor can perform to the proposed change.

Releasing Funding Information

The presolicitation activities related to the use of an SOO require some new approaches with respect to providing information to potential offerors, primarily because the SOO provides only a limited overview of the government's objectives. In a standard performance-based services acquisition, the PWS provides sufficient information to the offeror to judge the size of the requirement and to price its proposal accordingly. But this information is lacking in an SOO. Would the due diligence process provide sufficient information? Maybe, but maybe not—it depends on the questions posed by each offeror. However, one thing you want to avoid is having offerors guessing wrong about the size or scope of your requirement and delivering proposals that offer too much or too little and fail to meet your objectives.

It is important that potential offerors understand the scope of your requirement. It would not be appropriate to indicate in your SOO the number of bodies, hours, or other resource requirements because this might inhibit offerors' responses. You may, however, indicate the amount of funding available.

There is no FAR prohibition with respect to the release of funding information (although this is not usually done in standard services acquisitions). However, given the paucity of information provided in the SOO, it would seem appropriate to include some kind of funding information in the SOO. This information could be provided in the scope section or as a constraint that an offeror must observe.

Funding information may be released in many different ways—a specific amount, a dollar range, a minimum or maximum amount, or in some other fashion specifically designed for your requirement. However, when using an SOO, providing an indication of the funding available is the best way to ensure that all proposals are written and priced within the same parameters. This will be critical when evaluating proposals that may have significantly different approaches.

SUMMARY

The SOO concept requires a new look at how to approach the acquisition of services, particularly during the presolicitation phase. This is not a simple process. Market research is a key factor in gathering the information needed to develop the SOO document and will probably require more time and effort than usual. Being open to potential offerors and providing access to all information during the presolicitation phase may prove to be a difficult adjustment for acquisition personnel. Evaluating differing approaches in proposals and making tradeoffs to determine which proposal offers the best value will also prove to be difficult. Training will be required to acquaint government program and contracting personnel with this process. Contractor personnel may also need training on how to word a contractually acceptable proposal that can be incorporated by reference.

Can this concept work? Absolutely. It is a common sense approach to the acquisition of services that, when understood by the parties involved, can produce better and less costly services contracts.

Chapter 5 provides a model SOW format and discusses what kind of information belongs in an SOW, where it goes, and why. This information is applicable to both the PWS and the functional SOW and, as appropriate, to the SOO.

Notes

[1] Department of Defense, Department of Defense Handbook for Preparation of Statement of Work (SOW), MIL-HDBK-245D, 3 April 1996, Section 5-Statement of Objectives (SOO) Method. Online at *https://acc.dau.mil/adl/en-US/46583/file/13871/DODhandbook%20For%20Prep%20of%20SOW.pdf* (accessed February 2012).

[2] An Interagency-Industry Partnership in Performance: Department of Agriculture, Department of Commerce, Department of Defense, Department of the Treasury, General Services Administration, and Acquisitions Solutions, Inc., Seven Steps to Performance-Based Acquisition. Online at *https://www.acquisition.gov/comp/seven_steps/step4.html* (accessed February 2012).

[3] Ibid.

[4] Department of Defense Handbook for Preparation of Statement of Work (SOW), 28.

[5] Seven Steps to Performance-Based Acquisition, "VBA Loan Servicing SOO," September 8, 2000, p.7. Online at *http://www.acquisition.gov/comp/seven_steps/library/VBAsoo.pdf* (accessed February 2012).

[6] Ibid.

[7] Ibid.

[8] Ibid.

[9] "An Innovative Approach to Performance-Based Acquisition Using a SOO." Online at *https://www.acquisition.gov/comp/seven_steps/library/adv0501.pdf* (accessed February 2012). Originally published in Acquisitions Directions™ Advisory, May 2001. Used with permission of Acquisition Solutions, Inc.

5   The SOW Format

It is important to organize the presentation of information in your SOW effectively. One of the common problems with SOWs occurs when different categories of information are mixed, making it difficult to identify the requirements and their relationships.

View the SOW as a large box divided into separate compartments of information pertinent to the description of your requirement. Your job is to sort the information into appropriate compartments, with each compartment containing just one type of information. Organizing the format of your SOW around the types of information to be presented helps ensure that all related information is presented in one place in the SOW.

A sample SOW format is shown in Figure 5-1. It should be noted that this is simply a sample and is not intended to be taken as a standard. The format you use should be customized to best fit the needs and requirements of your project and organization.

The items listed in Figure 5-1, which represent the ten types of information common to most SOWs, fall into three major categories. First is the general information necessary to introduce the requirement to the contractor. Next are the work requirements, which are the most important part of the SOW. Third is the supporting information necessary to complete the description of your requirement.

These categories can be used as your SOW format; they are general enough to fit most requirements. While you must tailor each SOW to its own requirements, your first step should be to separate the information into the appropriate SOW sections. A particular

FIGURE 5-1
Sample Sow Format

Part I: General Information
   A. Introduction
   B. Background
   C. Scope
   D. Applicable Documents
Part II: Work Requirements
   A. Technical Requirements
   B. Deliverables
Part III: Supporting Information
   A. Security
   B. Place of Performance
   C. Period of Performance
   D. Special Considerations

SOW may not require each of these information types, but you should consider each initially to determine if it is applicable.

As noted, the format in Figure 5-1 is just one of many ways to organize your SOW. Any sensible format is acceptable. The specific format used is not as important as ensuring that the SOW information is separated according to the categories of information and presented in a coherent fashion.

Organizing your SOW well makes it easier for the author to write and for everyone else to read. It is easier to write because the basic outline is established—all you have to do is fill in the details. It is easier to read because the information is presented in a coherent fashion. The grouping of similar information into a single section helps avoid confusion and redundancy (although some redundancy may be required) and presents a clear picture of your requirement. This not only enhances the contractor's ability to read and understand the SOW, but also simplifies its review by contracting and higher management personnel.

This chapter describes the SOW contents using the format presented in Figure 5-1. The purpose of each SOW section is described, and comments are provided about what information should be placed in the section. When appropriate, the relationship of the SOW information to the proposal preparation instructions is also addressed.

SOW PART I: GENERAL INFORMATION

The information presented in Part I of the SOW provides a general introduction to the work requirements described in Part II. Part I is introductory in nature, so keep it short and to the point.

The introduction, background, and scope sections may be written as individual sections or combined. The purpose of these sections is to ensure that the contractor understands the purpose and extent of the requirement, and how it relates to the overall program. Do not include specific work-related information in these sections; that information goes in Part II: Work Requirements.

Section A: Introduction

The purpose of the introduction is simply to "title" the SOW. It provides a general description of the requirement, with only enough detail for a contractor to recognize generally what the procurement is about.

The most common problem in writing an introduction is length. Normally no more than two or three sentences are needed. Specific details are not required; they are provided in the technical requirements section. The introduction below is an example of an overly long introduction:

1.0 INTRODUCTION

The JSC NIO SS and Space Station Freedom (SSF) Payload Project Office plans, organizes, manages, and controls those activities required to integrate experiments/facilities into a total payload complement for JSC assigned pressurized module missions and/or flight increments. Pressurized module payloads are generally comprised of experiments and/or facilities from various scientific or technical disciplines within the user community that can be packaged together to share common orbiting vehicle capabilities. In support of this office, the contractor is responsible for providing the manpower and the other resources, as required, to accomplish the tasks identified in this part of the SOW. Applicable functional areas include:

- Payload/program management

- Mission feasibility and design

- Data management

- Support hardware development

- Right operations

- Payload integration management

- Advanced program/planning

The contractor shall develop a task WBS that will satisfy all management cost and technical requirements set forth in Part II of this SOW. The work statement numbers in this SOW shall be used only as a guide and general reference during the performance of all aspects of this contract. The contractor shall support the definition of SLS-2, SLS-3, SLS-4 missions, and future assigned payload integration management activities on SSF.

The purpose of the first two sentences in the last paragraph of this introduction is not clear. There was no other reference to a task WBS in the solicitation. In any event, this is either a work requirement or a solicitation requirement, and it therefore should not be in the introduction. If it is a contractual requirement (something that is developed after contract award), it should be described as such in Part II, in the technical requirements section of the SOW. If it is a solicitation requirement (required for purposes of evaluation), it should be included in the proposal preparation instructions.

The first paragraph of the example is fine if it is intended to combine the introduction and background sections, but if there is to be both an introduction and a background section in this SOW, there are several better alternatives.

Alternative 1
1.0 INTRODUCTION

This requirement is for technical support services for the JCS NIO SS and Space Station Freedom (SSF) Payload Project Office to support the definition of SLS-2, SLS-3, SLS-4 missions and future assigned payload integration management activities on SSF. Support is to be provided in a number of functional areas, including:

- Payload/program management
- Mission feasibility and design
- Data management
- Support hardware development

- Right operations

- Payload integration management

- Advanced program/planning

Alternative 1 simplifies the introduction by using only the third sentence of the first paragraph and the third sentence of the second paragraph as introductory information. The other information in the first paragraph is background information, and the other information in the second paragraph should be in the proposal preparation instructions.

Alternative 2
1.0 INTRODUCTION

This requirement is for technical support services for the JCS NIO SS and Space Station Freedom (SSF) Payload Project Office to support the definition of SLS-2, SLS-3, SLS-4 missions, and future assigned payload integration management activities on SSF.

In addition to the changes made by Alternative 1, Alternative 2 moves the listing of the functional areas to an introductory paragraph in Part II: Work Requirements. When the work requirements consist of multiple tasks, it is a good idea to use an introductory paragraph in Part II to summarize the tasks to be addressed rather than to place this information in the Part I introduction. Otherwise, when the SOW is printed there will be too much physical separation between the summary information and the details of the work requirement.

Alternative 3
1.0 INTRODUCTION

This requirement is for technical support services for the JCS NIO SS and Space Shuttle Freedom (SSF) Payload Project Office in a number of functional areas.

In addition to the changes made by Alternatives 1 and 2, Alternative 3 reduces the introduction to its absolute minimum by omitting the information on the definition of particular missions and future assignments. Instead, that information is placed in the introductory paragraph in Part II: Work Requirements.

Clearly, there are a number of ways to present the introduction. The key is that the introduction should not contain information relating to specific requirements or information better placed elsewhere in the SOW.

Section B: Background

The purpose of the background section is to describe how the requirement evolved and its relationship to the project it supports. This information helps the contractor understand the overall project environment and how the proposed work relates to it.

For example, if the requirement is for an IT system or software, the problems with the existing system or software that the new requirement is to correct should be identified. If the contractor understands where the current requirement comes from and where the project is headed, it is in a better position to offer ideas that will help attain these goals. The background is particularly important when you are seeking innovations and state-of-the-art effort.

The background is usually described in two or three paragraphs; however, there are exceptions. For example, the SOW for the management of a breeding and experimental facility for woodchucks (for research purposes) contained a four-page background section. It outlined the history and results of studies of progressive hepatic diseases and their relationship to the woodchuck facility where such studies are conducted. This background information, although long, provided significant information related to the purpose of the facility and the associated research.

The background section provides the historical information the contractor needs to understand the current requirement. Generally, this section is short and concise, but its purpose is to provide necessary information, not to save paper. The problem with long background sections is that current requirement may be addressed in this section, rather than in the work requirements section where it belongs. This misplaced requirement can cause confusion and adversely affect your project. (In the woodchuck facility example, there was no reference at all to the current requirement.)

When writing your background section, identify related research, studies, or other efforts that contribute to the contractor's understanding of the requirement. Reference these as background information, but explain the specific relationships as part of the appropriate task descriptions in the technical requirements section in Part II. For example, if a series of studies led to the current requirement, describe the studies (briefly) in the background section. Then include the details of how the studies support the current requirement in the appropriate task descriptions in the technical requirements section.

Technical problems that have occurred in past contracts for the same or similar effort should be identified to help avoid the same problems in the current contract. Mention the problems as part of the background, but reserve their specific description for the appropriate task description in the technical requirements section of Part II. This keeps the problems in context with the work requirement.

A common writing problem occurs when details of a work requirement are mentioned in the background section and then later in the technical requirements section, but with different wording, so that there appears to be two different work requirements. Avoid this problem by paying careful attention to the purpose of each section and limiting each SOW section to a specific kind of information.

Section C: Scope

The purpose of the scope section is to describe the overall project purpose and specific objectives of the requirement to help the contractor understand the size or magnitude of the anticipated effort. You do not want the contractor to propose a major R&D effort, for example, when all you are seeking is a simple study or analytic effort.

State the project purpose and specific objectives of the requirement in terms that indicate the relative size or magnitude of the effort. For example:

> The overall project purpose is to develop and acquire automatic stamping machines for all agency depots, tailored to the needs of each particular depot. The specific objective of this contract is to develop and acquire automatic stamping machines for the agency's seven (7) southwestern depots.

In labor-intensive requirements, you may also express the scope in terms of the estimated number of work hours, work days, or work months required for contract performance. This may be done by task, as an overall figure, or broken down by labor category, as long as it contributes to contractor understanding of the scope of the effort. For example:

The estimated level of effort is as follows:

Labor category	Hours
Principal investigator	1,872
Co-investigators	2,309
Research support	16,224
Animal technicians	6,552
Clerical/administrative support	4,992

Some agencies, when contracting for services, use locally developed level-of-effort clauses to express the estimated level of effort required by each labor category. In such instances, draw the contractor's attention to the clause by referencing it in the scope section. For example:

> The estimated level of effort for this requirement is set forth in section F of the RFP, in clause F.3, Level-of-Effort—Cost-Reimbursement Term Contract.

As noted earlier, specific resource requirements are not necessarily appropriate for a PWS used in performance-based contracting (see Chapter 3) or in a statement of objectives (SOO) (see Chapter 4).

Generally, you should not indicate the scope in terms of the amount of funds available. Contractors accept a work-hour estimate as an indicator of the magnitude of the effort, but a dollar amount tends to be viewed as a goal. When dollar amounts are used, contractors may structure their proposals around the dollars available rather than the actual requirements, particularly if the procurement is sole source.

In some industries, however, such as construction and advertising, dollar figures are commonly used to indicate project scope. In such instances, indicate the scope by dollar ranges or not-to-exceed figures, but do not reveal the government's estimate or level of funding. When using an SOO, however, it may be appropriate to indicate the level of funding (see Chapter 4) because the contractor will be proposing the complete SOW and must show that the requirement will be met in an efficient and effective manner.

Section D: Applicable Documents

The purpose of this section is to provide the contractor a consolidated listing of all documents cited in the SOW as part of the work requirement. The listing helps ensure that the contractor does not overlook a pertinent document that might affect how the contractor develops its proposal or performs the work. These documents include government directives, formal government or commercial specifications and standards, and other documents specifically cited in the SOW as applicable to the work effort. Documents that are mentioned in the SOW but not cited as part of the work requirement, such as illustrations or examples, should not be included.

The listing of applicable documents is placed early in the SOW to ensure that the contractor reads it. If you place it at the end of the SOW, or include it as an attachment, it is more likely to be overlooked. This information is important and needs to be prominently displayed. If the contractor fails to include the requirements of a cited document in the end product, it may adversely affect contract performance.

When writing this section, be sure to identify each document by title, number (if applicable), and date of the pertinent edition or revision. For example, if the SOW required the contractor to prepare a report using Microsoft Word, the citation in the Applicable Documents section might read:

Microsoft Word Users Guide, Version ____, Dated ____

A complete reference for each document, particularly the edition or date, is important. It establishes the legal relationship of the cited document to the work requirement. If a cited document is revised after contract award, the revision does not apply to the contract unless the contract is modified accordingly.

Do not use language that attempts to hold the contractor responsible for keeping up with changes to cited documents. This is generally unenforceable because the government is responsible for defining its requirements and updating them as necessary.

Review each document carefully to ensure that only the pertinent portions are referenced. If a document is referenced only by its title, the entire document becomes part of your SOW. This may create a problem if the referenced document contains requirements that conflict with other SOW or contract requirements. If only part of a document applies, reference only the applicable portions, down to the paragraph or sentence level if necessary. In addition, any allowable deviations should be identified either by direct citation or by reference to the appropriate SOW paragraph. For example:

> Specification Practices, MIL-STD-490, dated 30 Oct 1968. Limited to the Sections set forth in Paragraph 5.1.2 of the SOW.

or

> Specification Practices, MIL-STD-490, dated 30 Oct 1968. Limited to the Sections set forth in Paragraph 5.1.2 of the SOW and with the deviations permitted by SOW paragraph 5.6.3.

As part of the citation for each document, it is important to indicate if the document is attached to the SOW by using the phrase "see attachment __." If the cited document is not provided with the SOW, provide the name and address of the entity or the web address/URL where the document can be obtained. If the document is not available to the contractor because it is classified or otherwise restricted, inform the contractor where the document may be viewed and how to obtain any necessary permission.

Ask the contracting officer if a contract clause will be used to provide the required direction with respect to referenced documents. If a clause will be used, you need only indicate that the clause provides the required direction. For example, four standard FAR clauses are available for use when federal or military specifications are involved:

- 52.211-1, *Availability of Specifications Listed in the GSA Index of Federal Specifications, Standards and Commercial Item Descriptions, FPMR Part 101-29*, which describes how to obtain federal specifications, standards, and commercial item descriptions

- 52.211-2, *Availability of Specifications, Standards, and Data Item Descriptions Listed in the Acquisition Streamlining and Standardization Information System (ASSIST)*, which describes how to obtain military specifications and standards

- 52.211-3, *Availability of Specifications Not Listed in the GSA Index of Federal Specifications, Standards and Commercial Item Descriptions,* which describes how to obtain specifications, standards, and commercial item descriptions that are not available through GSA

- 52.211-4, *Availability for Examination of Specifications Not Listed in the GSA Index of Federal Specifications, Standards and Commercial Item Descriptions,* which describes how to go about examining specifications, standards, and commercial item descriptions that are not available for distribution.

The FAR clauses may be used as examples for the development of local clauses when the cited documents are not federal or military specifications, standards, or commercial item descriptions.

The related SOW paragraph should be referenced for each entry, unless doing so would be unnecessarily confusing, such as when each entry requires multiple references. This might happen, for example, when a cited document applies to a number of different tasks. In such instances it is better not to include any references, as a long list of referenced SOW paragraphs makes for difficult reading.

If the SOW does not reference other documents as part of the requirement, this section is not needed.

SOW PART II: WORK REQUIREMENTS

Section A of the work requirements addresses technical requirements and Section B addresses deliverables.

Section A: Technical Requirements

The purpose of Part II, Section A, is to describe the contractual work requirements. This is the most important part of the SOW. This section contains all of the technical details related to the work requirement. You must describe the work requirements, the required end products, and any special considerations or restraints that apply. In addition, you must provide the criteria that will be used in determining whether the requirements are met.

It is important to note that the SOW applies only to actions taken after contract award. Do not include any material related to the contractor's proposal or other matters pertaining to the solicitation or source selection process.

Describe the Work Requirements

Your description of the work requirement must be definitive enough to serve as the basis for the contractor's technical, management, and pricing proposals. If the contractor responds to your solicitation with questions seeking to clarify your requirement, you have failed to express that requirement adequately.

Your description of the work requirement should reflect the results of the market research conducted to determine what the commercial marketplace has to offer, its capabilities and practices, how it describes its work outputs or products (such as performance indicators, performance standards, and acceptable quality levels), and if there have been technological or other changes in the products or services required that would affect how the requirement is described.

You should carefully consider the ramifications of your description. For example, your requirement is for a contractor to run a soil testing program, and you describe the requirement by saying, "the contractor shall test all soil samples." What are you testing for, and why? What kinds of tests must the contractor conduct? How many tests are required? When and where shall the contractor conduct these tests? These are just a few of the questions that will go unanswered if you oversimplify or generalize the description of your work requirement.

You must explicitly state your requirements in the initial SOW or require the contractor to provide the necessary detail in its proposal for incorporation in the final SOW (except when using an SOO). If you do not, you may get exactly what you asked for rather than the required end product. The following steps can help guide you in describing your work requirements.

1. Divide the Work into Tasks

Divide the work into separate tasks and related subtasks, if possible, and describe each one separately. Make each task description stand alone. Describe the work related to each task, including the criteria for determining whether the requirements are met. When writing a PWS, the criteria for determining whether the requirements are met would be expressed as performance indicators, performance standards, and the AQL, and placed at the end of the applicable task or subtask description.

Reference other tasks as necessary to establish relationships and avoid redundancies. For example, if part of the requirement of a particular task is to be performed in the same manner as in an earlier task, simply indicate that the work is to be performed as in the earlier task rather than repeating the requirement:

> The statistical sampling methodology used for this Task shall be the same as set forth in Task 1.

Be careful, however, about how you use references. Do not reference references. If you have three tasks and each task requires the use of the same statistical sampling methodology, reference the sampling requirements of the first task in each of the following tasks. If Task 2 simply references Task 1, do not reference the sampling requirements of Task 2 when describing Task 3. For example, if Task 1 establishes a requirement for the use of a specific statistical sampling methodology, the same requirement in Task 2 would be expressed by referencing the requirement in Task 1. The same requirement in Task 3 would also be expressed by referencing the requirement in Task 1.

Multiple references make a task description difficult to read and can cause misunderstandings. For example:

> In a multi-tasked requirement, Task 1 requires the use of a particular statistical sampling methodology and establishes certain testing procedures. Task 2 requires the use of the Task 1 sampling methodology but different testing procedures. Task 3 requires the use of the Task 1 sampling methodology and Task 2 testing procedures and establishes a particular quality assurance requirement. Task 4 requires the use of the Task 2 testing procedures, the Task 1 sampling methodology, and the Task 3 quality assurance requirement.

If you used references in each of the cases in this example, the contractor would have to be searching back and forth continually to figure out what is to be done. It is better in such instances simply to repeat the requirements in full. The SOW must effectively communicate your requirements; clarity is more important than saving paper.

2. Use Functional Descriptions or Performance-Based Descriptions

Describe each task and subtask as a functional or performance-based requirement. Use design parameters only as necessary to ensure that the end product will meet your requirements. Describe the key technical requirements that must be accomplished to produce the desired results. Identify what needs to be done, who will do it, and when. Describe each task completely. Describe what each product is expected to do or accomplish in terms that establish performance objectives and set design parameters for that product.

As appropriate, relate the product's major critical characteristics to categories, such as performance, operational suitability, standardization, and interfaces. Require the submission of drafts when the interim or end product is a report. Indicate the required time frames for review, approval, and revisions of the drafts.

3. Define Requirements

Define the project requirements as precisely as possible within the context of a functional or performance-based description. Keep in mind that the description must focus on what is to be accomplished, not provide the details of how to do the work.

In an R&D effort, for example, describe any major scientific or technical breakthroughs required. If you require the solution of a specific research problem, define the problem so that it stands out from any collateral or peripheral research requirements. In effect, make sure that your SOW aims the contractor in the direction you intend. Regardless of the nature of your requirement, when there is associated effort to be performed, make sure that your SOW describes the relative importance of each part of your requirement.

To the extent possible, describe the relationships among requirements, systems, and subsystems, as well as with other projects. For example, if the requirement involves the development of computer software, describe its operating environment (i.e., the hardware and software, such as operating systems, database management systems, and utility software) to the extent possible. This description will help ensure that the contractor will provide software compatible with the environment in which it must operate.

Do not assume that the contractor will intuitively understand the performance requirements. This is particularly important when developing an SOW for a sole-source procurement. As noted earlier, there is a tendency in sole-source procurements to write SOWs based on discussions with the contractor rather than the actual government requirement. This can result in unwritten requirements that you and the contractor have already discussed and agreed to. Be careful that you do not overlook such requirements; they must be described in the SOW.

4. Describe All Work Elements

Describe all specific work elements, including documentation and data requirements; phasing requirements; quality, reliability, and maintainability requirements; fabrication requirements; testing requirements; and installation requirements. Do not overlook work elements that occur at the end of the contract, such as training and maintenance. If you are uncertain about some work elements, use the proposal preparation instructions to require the contractor to discuss the specific work elements and then incorporate any added information into the final SOW.

The following excerpt from an SOW for the presentation of training courses illustrates the need to define all work elements fully:

> 3.2.11 Prepare final exams and quizzes as appropriate to evaluate each class.
>
> 3.2.14 Attendance and, where specified, grades must be recorded and submitted to the COTR within two (2) weeks after the class is completed.

The problem is not what is stated in this example but what is not stated. Testing requirements are not mentioned anywhere else in the SOW, not even in the descriptions of the courses to be presented. This leaves the question of testing up to the contractor. The development and maintenance of tests is a time-consuming and expensive task, if done properly. In this instance, the contractor could decide not to use any testing at all (to lower contract costs) and still fully meet the stated contract requirements. If testing is part of the requirement, it must be explicitly described as such.

In another instance, an RFP for a specific training course failed to say anything about textbooks. The contractor proposed to teach from the applicable Navy directives (not creating a textbook lowered the contract price significantly) and was awarded the contract. Later, the COTR complained about the lack of textbooks. The contractor pointed to the RFP and contract, saying there was no such requirement. End of story.

Do not generalize the work elements with statements such as, "the contractor shall provide all necessary supporting documentation." This permits the contractor to decide what supporting documentation is necessary, and you may not be happy with the results. For example:

- **Manufactured items.** When procuring a manufactured item (such as a drill press), items of supporting documentation (such as operating and maintenance manuals and spare parts listings) are usually required. These items should be identified as part of your work requirement, both in this section and in the deliverables section.

- **Training.** Training courses should be documented by training plans, training outlines, handouts, and manuals. If you do not state a requirement for supporting documentation, the contractor is not required to provide it.

- **Computer software.** A requirement for the development of computer software should specifically identify the supporting documentation required. This includes such items as user's manuals, programmer's guide for code, diagnostic and error documentation, and applicable test plans. If these items cannot be specifically identified initially, the specific types of documentation that will be required should be identified, and the SOW should specify a point in time when such decisions will be made.

5. Describe Pertinent Previous Efforts

Reference any previous effort that might be helpful in meeting the current requirement. This includes efforts with negative results that established that a particular solution or course of action will not work as well as efforts with positive results. This information is similar to, but not the same as, the information provided in the background section of the SOW. The information in the background section refers to the project as a whole. The information here refers to the particular task.

Identify the results of related research, studies, or other efforts that will contribute to the contractor's understanding of the task requirement. The contractor must understand the project relationships and related research to plan and perform the task requirements properly. For example, previous effort would be pertinent if the task is a continuation of previous effort or is based on previous studies or similar effort.

6. Describe Known Risks

Describe the uncertainties related to contract performance when the effort goes beyond the state-of-the-art, requires use of new or untried techniques, or successful performance otherwise bears a significant risk. Ensure that task descriptions clearly identify technical, design, or other problems anticipated during contract performance. For example, in a requirement for the development of ink used in printing currency, the known problems related to such development (such as the chemical composition and hazardous materials) were identified to ensure that prospective contractors understood the risks involved. Identify the risks involved and use the proposal preparation instructions to require contractors to discuss how they would resolve such problems.

In particular, describe problems that were not resolved in previous contracts of a similar nature. Do not conceal knowledge of previous problems; to do so is to invite a repetition of such problems.

7. Ensure That Descriptions Are Consistent

Ensure that the descriptions are consistent and use the same terminology throughout. Calling a requirement a report in one task and later referring to it as a study can cause confusion and lead the contractor to believe that these are different requirements. Do not make up your own terminology; this will confuse the contractors and those who review your work. Use commonly understood terms, events, and documents. If it is necessary to use a number of project management terms and government acronyms, consider producing a tailored glossary to be attached to your SOW.

8. Use the Proposal Preparation Instructions

In some instances, the requirement itself is so complex or innovative that you cannot define it fully. If this is the case, describe the requirement as clearly as possible in the initial SOW and use the proposal preparation instructions to require the contractor to provide the performance details. The details in the successful proposal can then, if appropriate, be incorporated into the SOW prior to award.

Even if the requirement cannot be fully described, do not leave the contractor free to pursue its own approach unchecked. Require the use of control processes, such as design or milestone reviews, to oversee the contractor's actions whenever a choice or decision must be left to the contractor's discretion.

9. Describe the Tasks in Sequence

Whenever possible, describe the tasks in the sequence in which they occur. Ensure that the descriptions flow in an orderly manner, both within the task and from one task to another. This makes it easier for both the contractor and the government to understand and monitor the flow of work.

Be careful about the use of a concurrent effort that requires the contractor to perform multiple tasks at the same time. Concurrent effort is difficult to manage effectively and leads to interdependency, in which a technical problem in one effort adversely affects the other effort.

For example, as part of your requirement, the contractor must develop and build two instruments. These instruments have different functions but must be compatible. You can direct the contractor to develop and test one of the instruments and then the other, using the specifications of the first instrument to ensure the compatibility of the second. This is a safe approach, but it takes time. Your other choice is to direct the contractor to develop and build the instruments concurrently. This approach is faster, but there is a risk that once built, the instruments will not be compatible because of unanticipated technical problems. Lack of compatibility often cannot be detected until the instruments are tested together.

When project needs dictate the use of concurrent effort, ensure that each task references the other effort and, as appropriate, explains the interrelationships. Consider using planning software to help develop the task assignments and monitor concurrent effort during contract performance.

10. Describe Project Phasing

Complex projects are often divided into phases, such as a study phase, design phase, prototype phase, etc., so that the overall project can be managed more effectively. Government approval is usually required to move from one phase to the next. This government oversight provides greater control over the progress of the project than would otherwise be the case. The price you pay for the greater control is the added time for the government review and approval process.

If the requirement is divided into phases, describe the required phasing of the effort so that the interrelationship of the phases is clearly defined (that is, so that each phase clarifies and defines the remaining phases). Each phase may contain a single task or multiple tasks. Describe the tasks and the phases in the sequence in which they occur. Identify the specific requirements of each phase. Describe how the contractor obtains approval to continue from one phase to another. For example, a phase may end with a specific milestone or a specific event such as a design review; government approval of the completion of the phase signals the start of the next phase. When government approval is required, describe the review and approval process and the time allotted for the review and the resulting revision process.

Describe the Contract Management Requirements

In addition to describing your technical requirements, the SOW must describe the contract management requirements, such as reports and other management control systems that you require the contractor to maintain. Management reports (e.g., progress reports) provide information necessary for you to manage and monitor contract performance. Management control systems, such as a computer-based schedule planner and manager or a quality assurance program, are systems run by the contractor. These systems provide project visibility and help ensure conformance to contract requirements.

When describing management reporting requirements, it is important to describe the purpose of the report required, the specific areas to be addressed, and the frequency of submission. Do not over specify your requirements; permit the contractors to use their own existing reporting systems as long as they will yield the required information. Describe what the reports are to accomplish in the initial SOW and use the proposal preparation instructions to require each contractor to fill in the details. Negotiate the details and incorporate the contractor's proposed reporting system into the final SOW before award.

Minimize your information requirements. Do not require any information that you are not going to read and act upon when it is received. Report preparation is expensive and time-consuming. Asking for information that is "nice to have" clutters up the reports and adds unnecessary costs.

Specify reporting formats in the initial SOW only when a particular format is necessary for project purposes. For example, if you manage the project using a particular computer-based schedule planner and manager, you will need a report from the contractor in a format that facilitates the input of the data to your system. As an alternative, you may want to require the contractor to manage its work using the same software. In most instances, however, it is best simply to identify your information requirements and let the contractor use its own format.

Do not require the submission of frequent written reports. Assess the frequency of reporting on the basis of the complexity of the work and how you plan to manage the contract. Normally, reports submitted more frequently than monthly are a waste of time and money because they cannot be read and acted upon effectively. In addition, frequent reporting diverts the contractor's time and energy from productive effort. If you must monitor contract performance closely, use telephone calls, impromptu meetings, and site visits instead of frequent written reports.

To ensure the timeliness of the information reported, establish reporting periods that are realistic. Use the proposal preparation instructions to require the contractor to indicate how it prepares its reports and how long it takes. Contractors, like the government, have their own bureaucracy, and written reports are not generated overnight. For example, a contractor's accounting system may produce its reports on the tenth of each month, with data effective as of the first of the month, and it takes four days to develop and submit its report to the government. If you require your report on the first of each month, the most current financial data will not be available.

Take the time to find out how the contractor generates its reports and adjust the reporting periods in the final SOW accordingly. There will always be a lag in the timeliness of the information provided, but if you know what the time lag is, you can minimize its impact.

At a minimum, require the contractor to report on the progress of the contract. Progress reports are used to monitor the contractor's technical progress toward completion of the contract. Require the contractor to address the status of the work (usually in terms of milestones, percentage of completion, or some other measure that is mutually understood), problems encountered and their solutions, progress predictions (including potential problems and possible solutions), and the contractor's plans for the next reporting period. Progress reports are generally submitted in letter form.

Progress reports may also be used to monitor the status of contractual expenditures (i.e., financial progress), but only in cost-reimbursement, time-and-materials, and labor-hour contracts. Financial progress reports usually include the costs incurred during the reporting period by cost element or labor category, the cumulative costs incurred for the contract to date, and the funds remaining on the contract. When financial progress reports are required, they are usually made a part of the technical progress report.

Avoid asking the contractor to report anticipatory costs—costs expected to be incurred during the next reporting period. The use of anticipatory costs can cause problems when actual costs vary from the estimated costs. Concern about the difference between actual and estimated costs diverts attention from the technical problem causing the cost variance. In most instances, resolving the technical problem is much more important than worrying about the contractor's estimating ability. If it is necessary to track anticipatory costs, require the contractor to report any significant expenditures anticipated rather than the total anticipated costs.

Require the use of specific management control systems, such as cost/schedule control system criteria (C/SCSC), as used by DoD, or a computer-based schedule planner and manager, but only when necessary for project purposes. If you require the use of a specific system and the contractor does not already use that system, you will incur added costs—the contractor's costs for training and maintenance of a new system as well as the costs and problems associated with integrating a new system into its existing management system. Balance the value of the use of the specified system against the added costs.

Balancing the value is particularly important with respect to progress and financial information because you will require the contractor to manage and maintain two sets of books—one set in the format of the contractor's existing management system, and the other using the same information but in your specified format. Such duplication can create problems during contract performance.

Use the proposal preparation instructions to find out how the contractor proposes to manage the contract. To the extent possible, use the contractor's existing management systems as long as they will yield the required information and provide the required level of management control.

Identify Government Responsibilities and Interfaces with Third Parties

The primary purpose of the SOW is to describe your requirements clearly and establish the contractor's responsibilities in contract performance. However, the government's responsibilities must also be described, including responsibility for such activities as government reviews and approvals, government-conducted testing, and any other actions taken by government personnel that are directly related to the contractor's performance. Address these responsibilities as part of the related task description rather than as a separate subject in another part of the SOW.

There are other government responsibilities that are not directly related to the contractor's performance, such as government-furnished property and key personnel requirements. These are addressed in the "other considerations" section of the SOW.

When describing government responsibilities that affect contract performance, it is important to indicate their impact on the schedule. For example, when reviews and approvals are required, indicate how long it will take to conduct the review and provide the approvals or comments. Also describe the contractor's actions upon completion of the review and approval process, such as correction and re-submittal. Be sure to allow sufficient time for both government and contractor actions.

Describe any known interfaces among the government, the contractor, and third parties. Interfaces are instances when third-party actions will affect contract performance, such as when a third party will develop hardware, software, or information needed by the contractor to continue performance. If the third-party action is not completed on time, the contractor's performance will be adversely affected.

Identify the respective interface responsibilities and, if known, the timing involved. If you know that an interface will occur but you cannot describe the details, provide as much information as possible, even if it is only the fact that there will be an interface. Indicate, if possible, how and when the interface will be fully defined. Interface actions require planning and coordination; putting even minimal interface information in the SOW helps focus both contractor and government management attention on this requirement.

Provide for Performance Schedules

Avoid establishing fixed performance schedules or milestones in the initial SOW, except when project needs dictate performance by specified dates. A fixed schedule in the initial SOW inhibits the contractor's ability to plan its proposed effort. Establish only an overall schedule. Use the proposal preparation instructions to require the contractor to define the milestones or specific work schedule (i.e., a critical path schedule) in its proposal. Negotiating the schedule and milestone details generally results in a more workable plan. Once agreement is reached, incorporate the plan in the SOW.

If for some reason it is not feasible to finalize performance schedules or milestones before award, require the delivery of such a schedule shortly after award. This could happen, for example, when a study or an analytic effort is required before the remaining effort can be defined sufficiently to establish a schedule. At a minimum, the schedule should identify the contractor's key activities or milestones and provide a time frame (schedule) for attainment. Provide time for the review and approval of the schedule and for its periodic review and update.

The final SOW may contain two schedules: a performance schedule (related to the performance progress) in the technical requirements section and a delivery schedule (related to the delivery of specified products) in the deliverables section. A performance schedule is not always necessary; a delivery schedule is always required.

Consider Using Work Plans

Consider putting a work plan in your final SOW, but not in the initial SOW. A work plan identifies the key work elements and provides a schedule that demonstrates how the work will be accomplished within the project time frame. The work plan may also address the methodology to be used and how known problems will be resolved. Work plans are most appropriate for studies, analytic efforts, and R&D but can be used effectively in other efforts as well.

In many instances, as part of your procurement planning, you will have developed a work plan to demonstrate to your management that the project is feasible. This is your concept of how the work should be done. It is the contractor, however, who must perform the work, and the contractor's concept may differ from yours.

The most effective work plans usually result from negotiations. Directing the use of a particular work plan in the initial SOW inhibits the contractor's flexibility and use of innovative techniques. Generally, the initial SOW is silent on the subject of work plans. You may use a task description to identify specific analytic techniques or methodologies that you do (or do not) want used. However, do this only when the use or non-use of a specific analytic technique or methodology is necessary to achieve desired results.

Use the proposal preparation instructions to require the contractor to propose a work plan. This gets the contractor involved and generally leads to a more workable plan. Negotiate the details and incorporate that part of the contractor's proposal in the final SOW before award.

If at all possible, do not make the development of a work plan and methodology the first task in the SOW. It is important to ensure agreement on the work plan, schedule, and methodology *before* contract award. Otherwise you will have to resolve any disagreements on government time and at government expense.

Do not pay for something under the contract that can be obtained for less cost during the solicitation process.

In some circumstances, the work plan, schedule, and methodology must be developed during contract performance (as in a complicated R&D project), but this is the exception rather than the rule. In such instances, the development of the work plan is usually set forth as a separate task in the SOW, with the work plan as the deliverable item.

Provide for a Final Report

Many contracts require the submission of a final report. Describe the subjects to be addressed in the final report. Make the description specific enough to ensure that all the topics of interest are addressed, but leave room for creativity on the part of the contractor. Use a general description rather than a detailed description. Formats for final reports vary, but the following subjects are usually addressed:

- **Executive Summary.** An executive summary highlights the salient features of the final report. Use an executive summary only when it adds value to the report, such as facilitating upper management review. An executive summary is usually used for long, complex reports. If the report is short and simple, require an introduction instead. Consider limiting the executive summary to relatively few pages.

- **Background.** The background relates the history of the contract performance, including any modifications. When appropriate, as in R&D, it also traces the progress of the research that led to successful contract completion, summarizing the work performed, problems encountered, and solutions developed.

- **Scope.** The scope describes the extent of the effort expended. Require a scope paragraph that cites the size or extent of the technical effort in terms of the technical effort covered, not the work effort expended (i.e., what was accomplished, not how many hours it took to do the work).

- **Work Performed and Results.** Require a detailed description of the work performed, including both the positive and negative results of the work.

- **Problems Encountered and Resolutions.** Require a discussion of the technical problems encountered during contract performance and how they were resolved. If the problems were not resolved, require an explanation and a discussion of the impact of the unresolved problem on the project.

- **Future Direction.** When appropriate, require recommendations regarding follow-on effort or the direction of future research. This is usually used only when the contractor will clearly be in a sole-source position for any future effort resulting from the contract.

You do not want to be surprised by the structure and content of the final report. Require the submission of a draft final report for your review and approval. This helps ensure that the final report will contain the information required. Allow sufficient time for review and approval of the draft as well as its final correction and revision before the required delivery date of the final report.

Assess the review requirement objectively. Consider how many people will be involved in the review and how much time will be required to get responses from all the reviewers. Consider the nature of the report (complexity, length, etc.) and the nature of the comments likely to be received from the reviewers. Consider whether a review of the revised report will be required (e.g., if numerous reviewer comments are anticipated). Be realistic in your assessment and adjust the overall project schedule accordingly.

These guidelines also apply to interim deliverables. Any document submitted by the contractor should first be submitted and reviewed in draft form.

Describe the Contract Work Products

Describe all work products, including those produced during contract performance rather than at the end of it. Work products are deliverable evidence of compliance with SOW requirements. The contractor is required to deliver only those work products explicitly described as such in the SOW.

All interim and end products for each task should be identified as part of the task description. An interim product is anything, other than the end product, that is physically delivered during contract performance, such as draft documents, interim reports, designs, and test results. A deliverable that signals the completion of a task or milestone event is usually an interim product. An end product is the deliverable that signifies contract completion.

For R&D efforts, interim products include such things as designs, reports, or breadboard models, usually delivered in conjunction with the attainment of a contract milestone. The end product is a final report, a prototype, or an operating item, depending on the purpose of the contract.

For studies and analytic efforts, interim products are usually draft copies of the final report but may also be separate reports that demonstrate progress or completion of a part of the overall project. The end product is normally a final report.

For IT software efforts, interim products range from interim documentation to software packages that demonstrate only a part of the overall system. The end products are the operating software and the supporting documentation.

For general services efforts, such as janitorial services or transportation services, the services are provided on a daily basis. It is usually not possible to define a specific deliverable in such instances.

For technical support services, which are usually ordered on a work order or task order basis, the deliverables are defined in each order rather than in the basic contract.

The purpose of describing the contract work products is to relate the technical effort to the desired results. The physical characteristics of the interim and end products are described in the deliverables section of the SOW.

Describe Any Special Considerations That Apply

Special considerations, in this context, are those details that uniquely characterize your requirement and can make the difference between a successful and an unsuccessful contract. The following discusses how special considerations might be addressed in different kinds of acquisitions.

Studies and Research Efforts—Consider stating study or research requirements as a series of questions to be answered or areas of interest to be addressed. In most cases the purpose of the study or research effort is to answer questions or develop information about specific areas of interest. If your SOW is generalized or otherwise incomplete in this respect, the contractor must use its own discretion in setting the direction of the work. If the contractor does not view the requirement as you do and goes off on a tangent, you may not achieve your contract goal.

Establishing the questions or areas of interest in the SOW sets the direction of the work effort and helps keep the contractor within the boundaries of the requirement. It also establishes a quality standard for your use in assessing the contractor's compliance with the SOW requirements.

For example, if your requirement is to conduct a study to determine the feasibility of relocating certain field offices to another location for purposes of consolidation, what questions must be answered? The following are just a few of the possible questions:

- Are adequate facilities available at the new location?
- How much will the move cost?
- How much will the move save, both in dollars and efficiency?
- What are the economic implications of the move for both the areas where the offices were and the area of relocation?
- How many employees will be affected by the move?
- How will the move affect current employees?
- How many employees are likely to move to the new location?
- Can the employees who do not move be placed elsewhere in the federal government?
- What programs can be established to obtain employment retraining for those employees who do not move?
- Are qualified personnel available at the new location to replace those who do not move?
- What is the cost of living at the new location? Is this likely to affect how many employees will move?
- Is housing available at the new location? What are the housing costs? Will this affect the number of employees who will move?

These are only some of the questions that must be answered to determine if a move is feasible. If these and other questions are not stated in the SOW, the contractor may consider other questions more important and not provide the results you anticipate.

If you cannot identify the questions or areas in the initial SOW, you can use the proposal preparation instructions to require the contractor to propose them. You should negotiate the details, making sure that you and the contractor understand the direction and emphasis of the contractual effort, and incorporate the questions or areas of interest into the SOW before award. Ensure that the final SOW clearly establishes the direction of the contractual effort.

Data Collection—Collecting data is often the first step in a study, analytic, or R&D effort. It is important to address data collection in the SOW because, unless you clearly define this step, it can go on forever.

You should first identify the kinds of data to be collected, such as technical or scientific data about a specific subject, or economic data about a specific product, industry, or country. Then identify the data sources, such as technical and scientific journals, trade publications, newspapers, periodicals, or interviews with certain people or types of people. You will also need to indicate who will provide or obtain the data (government, contractor, or both).

If the government will provide all or part of the data, the SOW must describe when the data will be provided and its form. Be definitive; it is not appropriate simply to indicate that "pertinent data" will be provided or that the data will be provided "as necessary." Specific identification of each data item is not necessary, but you must describe the types or categories of data to be provided and when.

The form of the data is also important (e.g., hardcopy, digital media) because the data may have to be manipulated before it is usable. For example, if your data is in hardcopy, some printed and some handwritten, the contractor may have to convert the data to digital media to make it usable.

If the contractor will be responsible for data collection, the SOW must provide some means to control the extent of the data collection effort. Data collection is a time-consuming and expensive task if not controlled properly because it is often difficult to determine when enough data has been collected. You can control this effort somewhat by specifying the kinds of data to be collected and restricting the sources to be used, but doing so inhibits the contractor's use of innovative approaches. You can also restrict the amount of time allotted for data collection, but this not only inhibits the contractor's approach but also presupposes that you know the optimum amount of time required for this effort.

The contractor exercises primary control over the amount of time spent for data collection. Accordingly, the contractor should be involved in this determination. Use the proposal preparation instructions to require the contractor to provide details of its proposed data collection effort. At a minimum, require the contractor to describe how the data will be collected, the sources to be used, and the schedule of the data collection effort.

The data collection details should be negotiated and that part of the contractor's proposal should be incorporated into the final SOW. This makes the details of the data collection effort a part of the contractual requirement. The contractor is more likely to comply with a plan it developed than one arbitrarily mandated by the government.

If data collection is the initial step in the work requirement, it must be defined in the SOW before contract award. When the government provides the data, the data collection requirement is usually defined in the initial SOW. When the contractor is responsible for data collection, the effort is usually defined in the final SOW by incorporating the contractor's proposed data collection process. In some instances the data collection effort cannot be defined at all, because it will occur later in contract performance and is dependent on the results of the initial work efforts. If so, the SOW should provide a requirement for the definition of the data collection effort before it starts.

IT Systems and Software—Many projects involve developing IT systems or software. Before initiating a contract for developing a new IT system or new software, consider what other options are available. These include incrementally improving all or part of the existing system or software or purchasing commercial off-the-shelf systems or software. Making incremental improvements takes longer but reduces risks. Using commercially available systems or software also reduces risks but may generate integration problems when used with existing systems.

Engineering a completely new product should be a last resort. If a new product is the only way to meet your requirement, initiate your planning well in advance of your need for the product. In addition to the usual planning and procurement lead time, be sure to allow sufficient time for acceptance testing, training, and debugging or fine-tuning the end product.

When developing an SOW, particularly for IT systems or software, you are not expected to do everything yourself. Ensure that you have sufficient resources available to define the procurement objective and technical specifications. Sufficient resources and facilities should also be available to manage and support the contractor's activities and to review and critique the contractor's interim and end products.

It is often helpful to check with others who have had the same or similar problems. Find out what they have done and request assistance from those who have appropriate expertise. As a last resort, hire a contractor to assist in the planning and SOW development. Be careful, however, when using contractor assistance: a contractor who helps develop the SOW must be precluded from competing for the actual requirement.

Both management and users should be involved in acquisition planning, SOW development, evaluation of technical proposals, and monitoring and review of contractor efforts. User involvement is particularly important. Ensure that the user understands and concurs with the requirements of the SOW and participates in proposal evaluation and the testing and acceptance of the end product. The user is your customer; if the end product does not meet the user's requirements, your project will not meet its goals.

Describe IT system or software requirements clearly and in detail, including the applications area and the specific need and function the system or the software is to satisfy. You should focus on your objectives and the end product, using functional terms when possible. Define the standards to be used, and cite the applicable federal standards (unless they are clearly not applicable).

When the requirement involves the development of software, describe the operating environment (i.e., the hardware and software, such as operating systems, database management systems, and utility software) to the extent possible. Describe how files are to be prepared, including sufficient detail to preclude delivery of files that cannot be used. The level of the operating system, the release level of commercial software for data files, the target machine, and other equipment on which the software is to work or be compatible with should also be described. Specifically identify the supporting deliverables associated with the software deliverable, such as user documentation, programmer's guide for code, appropriate diagnostic and error documentation, and applicable test plans and criteria.

If your project is not structured as a formal project with the checks and balances of formal systems acquisition, you must provide for ongoing review of the technical effort. Describe the review requirements as part of the appropriate task effort. Review requirements include providing for periodic reviews of the estimates for hardware capacity and reviewing the planned use of software development tools, database management systems, and other technical resources. System conformance to security, privacy, and internal controls should be assessed periodically, and end products should be reviewed for appropriateness, technical integrity, and conformance standards.

Quality control at the point of acceptance is the key to ensuring product conformance. Ensure that the delivered product does not contain hidden additional costs in the form of high maintenance costs caused by errors in logic or deviations from standards. To ensure quality, you must provide a clear definition of the expected quality, usually in terms of what the system or software is to do or accomplish in the operating environment.

Define the methodology (acceptance criteria) for measuring compliance for both interim and end products. If the effort is divided into phases, define the acceptance criteria for each phase. Conduct comprehensive testing of interim and end products, preferably by the actual users. Use testing procedures that clearly demonstrate that the products produce exactly the required results in a real-world operating environment. Ensure that interim and end products are prepared according to the required standards (to ensure maintainability) and that the effort is fully documented. Establish a period of time during which the contractor is required to maintain the system or software and correct any latent defects.

Commercial Items—The FAR[1] states that, to the maximum extent practicable, SOWs should be written in terms that enable contractors to supply commercial items or nondevelopmental items in response to agency solicitations. The FAR goes on to say that prime contractors and subcontractors at all tiers should be required to incorporate commercial or nondevelopmental items as components of items to be supplied to the agency. The FAR[2] indicates that this policy includes, as appropriate, the modification of current requirements to ensure that the requirements can be met by commercial or nondevelopmental items.

A commercial item is a product or service customarily sold in the commercial marketplace but that can be used for government purposes as is or with minor modifications. This includes items under development that are not currently available in the commercial marketplace but will be available in time to satisfy current delivery requirements.

A nondevelopmental item is a previously developed item of supply used exclusively for government purposes by federal, state, or local governments that can be used as is or with minor modifications. This includes items being produced that are not yet in use.

When acquiring commercial items or services or nondevelopmental items, the SOW description of the requirement must contain sufficient detail for potential contractors to know which commercial items or services may be suitable. The SOW should describe the type of product or services required and explain their intended use in terms of the functions to be performed, the performance requirements, or the physical characteristics.

When acquiring commercial services, it is important to focus on the specific services the contractor is expected to perform. Provide sufficient detail to ensure that the contractor will understand and be able to price the extent of the services required. If you are not sure how to describe a commercial-type service, check to see how the same or similar services were described in past contracts. Be careful, however, *never* to use the language of a previous SOW without first finding out how well it worked in practice. You do not want to repeat someone else's mistakes.

You should also conduct market research on commercial services to determine whether there are published industry procedures or standards that establish how the services are performed in the commercial marketplace. For example, for grounds keeping services, there are established standards as to how grass is to be cut and sidewalks edged; for janitorial services, there are established standards for how rooms are to be cleaned. Referencing such procedures or standards in the SOW will help minimize the length of the SOW and avoid the problem of having your requirements at variance with how such work is normally performed. Keep in mind that the people actually doing the work will not have seen the SOW and generally will perform your work in the same way that they perform the same work for other customers.

Commercial products are generally described in terms of the salient physical or performance characteristics of the product required. The primary source of such information is brochures or other descriptive literature published by manufacturers or dealers, which can be obtained during market research.

The characteristics of commercial products are often described in a manner that only the manufacturer can meet. Be careful that you do not inadvertently create a restrictive requirement by copying directly from commercial literature. Examine commercial literature objectively and select only those characteristics that are necessary to ensure that the product will meet your needs and that can be met by more than one manufacturer.

Manufactured Products—A functional description of a requirement for a manufactured product must concentrate on the physical characteristics and functions that describe what the end product will do or how it will operate. When describing numerical requirements (e.g., height, weight, dimensions), use ranges or minimums and maximums rather than specific numbers (except as necessary to meet project requirements) to avoid creating a restrictive description. Using restrictive descriptions and excess requirements may lead to protests from unsuccessful contractors. Only your minimum requirements should be described; do not ask for anything that cannot be justified as an actual requirement. When describing a requirement for manufactured items, you should consider the following:

- **Power.** What are the power requirements? This includes such things as input power to run the equipment and output power in terms of production.

- **Capacity.** What kind of load must the equipment handle? This could range from production capacity (as in IT equipment) to lifting capacity (as in a forklift).

- **Accuracy.** What accuracy level is required? This could range from error rates to the accuracy of measurements.

- **Reliability.** What reliability level is required? This includes mean-time-between-failures, failure rates, and repair rates.

- **Physical Restrictions.** What restrictions or physical characteristics apply? This includes an item's size, dimensions, weight, and configuration.

- **Ruggedness.** What operational environment considerations apply? This could range from an item's ruggedness (ability to withstand vibration or shock) to its ability to operate under extreme conditions (heat, cold, moist, dry, or saltwater).

- **Environment.** Must the equipment meet, or be protected from, environmental or health and safety constraints? These include devices to protect operators and the public from hazards produced by or used with the item, such as hazardous materials, electromagnetic radiation, toxic products, and other pollutants. They also include requirements to protect the item from damage from such hazards.

- **Materials.** Are special materials required? This usually applies only when project needs dictate the use of special materials, such as particular chemicals or a special grade of steel or other construction materials.

- **Interchangeability.** Are there interchangeability requirements? These address the ability to interchange parts or components within the item or between the item and other specified items.

- **Compatibility.** Are there compatibility requirements? These address the need for the item to operate in conjunction with other items; for example, pieces of equipment operating in tandem must be able to plug into each other. Compatibility also addresses the ability of the item to fit in with other items, such as a requirement that a replacement laboratory table be the same height as the adjoining table.

- **Transportation and Storage.** Are there special requirements related to transportation and storage? These include any special characteristics that must be built into the item, such as hooks and handles, and requirements for skids or pallets.

- **Installation.** Are there special installation requirements? These could range from a need for a crane to lift an item to the third floor of a building, to a need to construct special foundations for the item where it is to be placed.

Some of these items are performance (functional) requirements and some are design requirements. Most product descriptions are a combination of functional and design requirements. In addition, many agencies have directives that place specific requirements on the procurement of manufactured products. These must also be considered when describing your work requirement.

Formal Technical Meetings—Include any requirements for formal technical meetings to be held after contract award as part of the applicable task description. These are meetings at which technical progress and technical problems, rather than administrative matters, will be discussed. Such meetings are usually conducted in conjunction with a specific task or milestone set forth in the SOW, such as preliminary design reviews and critical design reviews. The contractor needs information about such meetings to plan and price its proposal; both parties need the information to manage and monitor contract performance.

If the meeting is to be conducted at a government facility, the SOW must describe the purpose of the meeting, when and where it will be held, who will conduct the meeting, and the anticipated duration. Indicate the number of participants and, when appropriate, the classification level and access procedures. If the contractor will make a presentation, the SOW must describe any documentation requirements, such as handouts or briefing papers. It should also indicate what equipment, such as audiovisual equipment, whiteboards, and overhead projectors, will be available for the contractor's use.

If the meeting or briefing is to be held at the contractor's facility, describe its purpose, when it will be held, the number of government participants, any documentation requirements, and, as appropriate, the classification level. Use the proposal preparation instructions to require the contractor to discuss any other details deemed necessary.

If you feel that formal technical meetings are necessary but do not want to dictate the details, you can also use the proposal preparation instructions to require the contractor to propose the details. Indicate the requirement for the meeting and its purpose in the initial SOW. Negotiate the details proposed by the contractor in its proposal and incorporate the results in the final SOW.

Incorporation of Other Documents—You may incorporate the requirements of other documents into the SOW when necessary to describe the work requirements completely. Documents that may be incorporated include government documents or publications; federal, military, or commercial specifications or standards; and documents published by other agencies or commercial concerns.

For example, an SOW required compliance with the National Electric Code (NEC) in a construction contract, stating that junction boxes shall be provided as indicated on the drawings and where required by the NEC. The contractor submitted a claim for additional work for the installation of a particular junction box, claiming that the drawings did not indicate a junction box at that location. The contractor lost because, based on how the contractor performed the work, the NEC required installation of the junction box.

In this instance the drawings did not show the junction box requirement, but the contractor was required to perform as specified by both the drawings and the NEC. If the SOW had not made reference to the NEC, the government might have had to bear the extra cost.

You must exercise care when incorporating the requirements of other documents in your SOW. If you simply cite the title of the document, you are making the entire document a part of your work requirement. Other documents, such as formal specifications and standards, often include coverage that may not be applicable to your requirement or may even be contrary to what you want, particularly if the document has not been revised in some time. Revisions to published documents rarely keep up with technological changes.

Each document should be reviewed carefully and tailored to your requirement, incorporating only those parts pertinent to your requirement in the SOW. For example, if you want the work performed in accordance with Chapter 4 of XYZ standard, but the rest of the standard does not apply, you should state in the SOW that the work is to be performed in accordance with Chapter 4 of the XYZ standard; do not cite the entire standard. Tailoring must be specific, down to the sentence level, if necessary. Ensure that all documents incorporated as part of the work requirements are also listed in the applicable documents section of the SOW and that the listing reflects the tailoring of the documents.

Technical Data Requirements—Technical data is recorded information of a scientific or technical nature other than computer software and administrative data, such as financial and management reports. Technical data requirements, such as reports, usually result from the completion of a task or attainment of a milestone and should be described as such.

Describe the format and content of the technical data requirements for each task as part of the task description. The physical characteristics of the technical data, such as the number of copies and the media, however, should be described in the deliverables section of the SOW.

Require delivery only of technical data that you intend to use. The preparation of technical data for delivery is expensive and time-consuming. Excessive data requirements (including nice-to-have rather than need-to-have data requirements) increase contract costs without adding significant value to the results.

One way to avoid over-specification is to describe in the SOW what technical data is required and why, and then in the proposal preparation instructions require the contractor to propose the specific data to be provided and its format. Negotiate the details and incorporate the results into the SOW before award.

Some agencies use the Contract Data Requirements List (CDRL), DD Form 1423, to order data and prepare the Data Item Description (DID), in plain paper format, as shown in MIL-STD-963B, to describe data. If your agency uses these forms, you should not describe the data and data delivery requirements in the text of the SOW. Instead, make reference to the forms in the SOW and use the forms to describe the details. When using these forms, make sure that you double-check the details on the forms with the text of the final SOW and any related documents, particularly with respect to delivery times.

Describe the Criteria for Determining Whether Requirements Are Met

Each task, as well as the contract as a whole, must have a product or an event that demonstrates successful completion. You must, therefore, develop a way to measure contractor achievement and determine if the contractor's performance is successful, at both the task and contract level. This is done by establishing quality requirements in the SOW and, when appropriate, testing to ensure that the requirements are met.

Quality Requirements in Functional SOWs—To describe quality requirements in a functional SOW, you must determine the attributes of contract performance and how these attributes can be measured. Quality attributes are the characteristics or features of contract performance that signify successful performance.

Indicate how the attributes are to be measured by describing how satisfactory quality will be determined. Describing quality requirements helps ensure that the end product is usable and establishes a standard for measurement of the contractor's performance. When appropriate, you should describe how products will be tested or demonstrated to verify compliance with technical requirements.

When buying standard commercial items, describe quality attributes in terms of the essential physical and functional characteristics of the required items. Use criteria such as the kinds of material, dimensions, size, capacity, principle of operation, restrictive environmental conditions, essential operating conditions, and other pertinent information that further describes the item required. Use attributes that can be measured through inspection or testing of the end product.

When buying technical hardware such as electronic or scientific equipment, describe quality attributes in terms of the performance or configuration of the end product. Use criteria such as weight, dimensions, power, speed, accuracy, processing rate, error rate, ease of operation, or other measurements that indicate the contractor's degree of success. Use attributes that can be measured through inspection or testing of the end product.

When buying studies or analytic efforts, describe quality attributes that indicate the contractor has successfully met the goals of the contract. Use attributes such as how well specified questions or areas of interest are addressed, how well results are documented or otherwise substantiated, and whether appropriate emphasis is provided. Describe these attributes as part of task performance; this helps relate the quality requirements to the performance requirements. These attributes can be measured by inspecting the end product.

When buying support services (these can range from janitorial services to technical support services), describe quality attributes in terms of the adequacy of the services provided. Use attributes such as responsiveness, on-time performance, the amount of service provided, the rate of rework required, or some other term related to the quality of the services performed.

You need to be careful not to overspecify quality attributes—doing so may interfere with contract performance by setting unrealistic goals that inhibit the contractor's flexibility in managing its own effort. A common example is when the SOW requires unrealistic response times, such as "the contractor must provide the technical support within thirty minutes of notification...." This response time might be appropriate for emergency services, but not for normal technical support. Ask yourself how long it would take the government to respond in a similar situation. Keep in mind that you will have to pay for any unusual requirements; be sure that they will be worth the extra cost.

Determining quality attributes for technical support services is particularly difficult because it is often hard to pinpoint a particular feature of contract performance that signals successful performance. In many instances performance of the work is the only deliverable, and it is provided on a daily basis. It may be better to generalize the quality attributes in the SOW and to rely on the monitoring of contract performance to control performance quality. This decision must be made on a case-by-case basis.

Establishing quality attributes is also difficult when buying R&D efforts because it is often not possible to specify the end product. It is hard to establish a quality level for a product you are not sure can even be made. R&D encompasses a wide range of efforts, including elements of any of the situations described above. Quality requirements are often established as the project progresses through the R&D process, using project management techniques such as design and milestone reviews. If your contract is for an R&D project, use the project management approach to control your quality requirements. If your contract is in support of a project, use the techniques discussed.

The quality attributes discussed relate to the condition of the end product and should not be confused with quality assurance

(QA) programs such as ISO 9000, 9002, or 9003 or a contractor's internally developed QA program. Contractor QA programs are concerned with developing or maintaining quality work during contract performance and are designed to ensure that required quality attributes are met. Generally, the government relies on the contractor's QA program, but you may direct the use of a particular QA program in your SOW when necessary.

Quality Requirements in Performance-Based Service Contracting SOWs—The process of developing quality requirements for the performance work statement (PWS) used in performance-based service contracting (PBSC) is more exacting than that needed for the development of quality requirements for a functional SOW. A functional SOW for services usually describes the quality requirements in general terms and does not establish specific measurable performance standards. As noted in Chapter 3, however, the description of the quality requirements in a PWS requires that the expected work outputs be expressed in terms of objective, measurable performance standards. This requires a job analysis of each task and significant subtask to define the services in terms of the expected results, the development of performance indicators, performance standards, acceptable quality levels, and a quality assurance plan. This is significantly greater detail than that required for a functional SOW.

Testing Requirements—Testing must be addressed in the SOW if interim or end products will be tested to determine the contractor's compliance with SOW requirements. How test requirements are described depends on the circumstances of your project. For example, in many R&D projects testing requirements cannot be established initially because the end product cannot be fully defined. In such instances, testing can only be described as a requirement to be defined during contract performance through the submission of a test plan by the contractor. However, there are instances in which you know what the end product should be able to do, such as in the development of software to perform a particular function. When this is the case, the final SOW must be more specific about the testing requirements.

When you can determine the testing requirements in advance, you should develop an objective method of verifying compliance with the SOW requirements. The contractor cannot be held to the SOW requirements if there is no method to verify compliance. If there are varying methods and you do not specify one, the contractor may make the selection. This is not always desirable. The most common methods of verification are modeling, technical analysis, demonstrations, and testing. When describing testing requirements, address the following (these also apply to the other methods of verification):

- **Indicate who is to conduct the testing.** Testing may be conducted by the government, the contractor, or a third party.

- **State when the tests will be conducted.** The timing of tests is usually described in terms of a milestone or other attainment within the task. Do not use calendar dates. Ensure that sufficient time is allowed. Include time for installation and setup, conducting the test, documenting and analyzing the test results, government review and approval, and any resulting contractor actions.

- **Describe the test.** At a minimum, indicate what the test is, how it is to be conducted, what the test is to accomplish (what you are testing for), and how the results are to be documented.

- **Describe the form and condition necessary** to make the test item ready for testing to ensure that the contractor's item is delivered in a test-ready condition.

- **Describe how the test results are to be documented and analyzed** and describe the contractor's action when the government review and approval process is completed, such as correction, revision, or replacement. Indicate the time frames for this process.

When the contractor will conduct the testing, it is usually a good idea to get contractor input before completing your testing approach. In the initial SOW, indicate that there is a test requirement, describe what the test is to accomplish, and specify how it is to be documented. Use the proposal preparation instructions to require the contractor to propose a test plan. Negotiate the details and incorporate that part of the contractor's proposal in the final SOW before award.

Section B: Deliverables

The purpose of this section is to separate the description of the physical characteristics and the delivery schedule for interim and end products from the description of the technical requirements. This separation is necessary to avoid confusing work requirements with delivery requirements. The work requirements are described in the technical requirements section; the products of the work requirements and scheduled delivery are described in the deliverables section.

What Is a Deliverable?

A deliverable can be a prototype or other manufactured product, a design, a report, computer software, or anything else that can be physically delivered. This definition includes interim deliverables, such as reports, draft documents, interim findings, and test results and analyses, as well as end products. A deliverable usually signals the end of a task or the accomplishment of a milestone and is used to measure successful performance.

There are exceptions to the requirement that a deliverable be a physical item. The presentation of a formal training session, for example, is usually treated as a deliverable. Meetings, however, are not usually considered deliverables. Meetings can be described as deliverables when they signal completion of a task or the meeting of a milestone, but this is the exception rather than the rule. Most meetings are held in connection with a specific task and are described as part of the task rather than as a product of the task. A report that summarizes the results of the meeting is a deliverable item, but the meeting itself is not.

Describing Deliverables

Describe all deliverable items, the quantity (or number of copies), and the delivery time. Avoid using specific calendar dates, if possible. Express the delivery time in terms of a period of time after contract award or after a specific event, such as the completion of a task or attainment of a significant milestone. Ensure that each deliverable is identified with the associated task by specific cross-reference or by narrative discussion. Deliverables may include:

Manufactured Products—If the deliverable is a manufactured product, identify the item, the deliverable quantity, and when delivery is due. If testing is to be conducted upon delivery, reference the testing requirement and indicate that the item must be delivered in a test-ready condition.

Written Material—If the deliverable is written material, such as a report or a design, identify the item, the number of copies required, and when delivery is due. If your intention is to duplicate and further distribute the deliverable, indicate that a reproducible copy is required.

Digital Media—If the deliverable is on digital media (i.e., a compact disc, USB flash drive, or removal storage device that digital data can be stored on, hereafter referred to as a "disc") containing a computer program or data (such as a report), you should pay particular attention to the description of the disc. The description must be sufficient to ensure that the information is usable upon receipt. For example, indicate the size and format of the disc and describe how the files are to be prepared and named. Describe the files in sufficient detail to preclude delivery of files that cannot be used. As appropriate, describe the version of the operating system, the release version of commercial software for data files, the type and model of machine, and other equipment with which the software is to be compatible.

If the deliverable is a disc that contains a software program rather than data (e.g., a report), consider requiring several copies of the disc. At least two working copies of each disc, plus an archive copy, should be delivered to ensure there is a usable backup if there are problems with one of the discs.

If the primary deliverable is a disc, indicate if a hardcopy is required and, if so, how many copies. At least one hardcopy is usually required when the disc contains information, such as a report. Hardcopies are not usually required when the disc contains a program.

Identify supporting deliverables separately. These include user documentation, programmer's guide for code, appropriate diagnostic and error documentation, and applicable test plans and criteria associated with the software deliverable. Supporting deliverables may be delivered on disc(s), in hardcopy, or both, depending on what they contain and how they will be used.

Review your description of the IT operating environment in the technical requirements section of the SOW. That description should be repeated in this section, if necessary, to ensure the contractor understands what is required. In this instance, redundancy is a good thing and can help avoid future problems.

Packing, Packaging, and Marking Requirements

Do not overlook the packing, packaging, and marking requirements necessary to prevent deterioration and damage during shipping, handling, and storage. Items such as electronic equipment, IT equipment, and hazardous materials require special attention. Marking requirements are particularly important with respect to hazardous materials. Check for environmental constraints, such as sensitivity to heat, cold, or humidity, that will affect how the item is packed and shipped. If the item is going into storage after delivery, check to see if any special packing, packaging, or preservation requirements apply.

Most agencies have locally produced contract clauses to cover the typical packing, packaging, and marking requirements. The FAR does not address these issues to any great extent. Put your requirements in the initial SOW, and then consult with your contracting officer to determine if some of these issues are covered by local or FAR clauses. It will be easier for the contracting officer to provide the appropriate advice if your requirements are in writing.

SOW PART III: SUPPORTING INFORMATION

Part III of the SOW sets forth supporting information that applies to contract performance but does not fit anywhere else in the SOW format. Typically, these considerations are in support of, rather than part of, the work requirement. They include information related to security issues, the place and period of performance, government-furnished property or information, key personnel considerations, rights in technical data or computer software, or other contractual requirements unique to the specific procurement.

Section A: Security

Security issues must be considered in all contracts, even those that are unclassified, and early consideration of these issues is critical. Security issues can affect the timing of the procurement, particularly with respect to obtaining personnel and facilities clearances. Consider the time required to obtain personnel and facilities clearances in terms of the release of your SOW and timing of the initial contractual effort.

Security issues also affect the place of performance if classified work is required and the potential contractors do not have the appropriate clearances to perform classified work at their own facilities. If a number of the potential contractors do not have the appropriate facilities clearances and timeframes are short, you may have to consider having the classified work performed at a government facility.

If the contractor will use its own computers for classified work, you must determine the appropriate sanitization requirements for the contractor's IT and word processing equipment. If contractor personnel will be using government computers, you must ensure that they have the necessary clearances to view any other information that might be on the computers they will be using. These requirements must be set forth in the SOW.

You will need to check with your security officer to determine if your requirement involves any security issues. You may have to explain the clearance processes in the SOW to ensure that the potential contractors understand these requirements.

Section B: Place of Performance

Contract performance may take place at the contractor's facility, a government facility, a third party facility, or any combination thereof. While there are solicitation provisions that require the contractor to identify its specific place of performance, identifying the place of performance in the SOW helps make the SOW a complete document and also indicates the government's preference in this matter.

Section C: Period of Performance

The period of performance is the term of the contract, i.e., how long the contract will be in effect, and not the length or scope of the work effort. Express the period of performance as a time period after award rather than a specific date. Use specific dates only if the dates are critical, such as when the contract is to expire at the end of a fiscal year.

The performance period is usually longer than the estimated scope of the effort. For example, a performance period of four to five months should be used when the scope of effort is estimated to be three work months. This is necessary to give the contractor some flexibility. It is not realistic to expect contractor personnel to devote 100 percent of their time to a single contract, particularly if the contractor is small. In addition, contractor personnel, like government personnel, have other demands on their time, such as corporate meetings, emergencies, training, and administrative responsibilities.

The term of performance must be compatible with the other time periods in the SOW. Check the contract term against the delivery times in the deliverables section, the estimated scope of effort in the scope section, and, when incorporated in the SOW, the contractor's work plan. In addition, check to ensure that the period of performance is compatible with any contract clauses used in other parts of the contract.

Do not put the contractor's back to the wall with contractual timing unless the timing is critical to project success. The typical result of tight schedules is lower quality because contractors cut corners to meet the schedule, or they deliver late. If the schedule is too tight, the contractor may do both. Contractors are well aware that the government rarely defaults a contract on the basis of late delivery. The period of performance must be realistic.

Section D: Government-Furnished Property

The identification of government-furnished property and when it will be furnished is usually addressed as supporting information. Government property clauses in the FAR describe the rights and obligations of the parties with respect to government-furnished property. The applicable clause depends on the type of contract used and is selected by the contracting officer for placement in Section I of the contract.

Government property clauses require that specific identification of the property and when it will be provided be set forth in the contract schedule or specifications. Government-furnished property is addressed in three places in the contract: (1) the fact that the government will furnish government property or data is part of the work requirement addressed in the technical requirements section of the SOW; (2) the supporting information (identification and delivery) is set forth in the supporting information section of the SOW; and (3) the related clauses are set forth in either Section F or Section I of the contract. If a significant amount of property is involved, the property should be listed in an attachment and a reference made to it in this section.

Section E: Qualifications of Key Personnel

Many contracts, particularly those for technical support services, use locally developed key personnel clauses[3] to identify and control the use of the contractor's key personnel (such requirements are usually not appropriate for use in a PWS or SOO). A key personnel clause requires that the contractor propose its key personnel by name. After award, the clause requires that substitutions of key personnel be made only after (1) advance notification to the contracting officer, and (2) a determination by the contracting officer that the substitute meets the requisite qualifications for that position. It is necessary, therefore, to describe the requisite qualifications and reference the clause in the SOW.

Use key personnel requirements sparingly. Each position identified as a key personnel position carries with it the administrative burden of reviewing each personnel change in that position for the life of the contract. If it is necessary to use a key personnel clause, only the top managerial and technical positions should be named as key personnel positions. Designate lower-level positions as key positions only when specific levels of expertise are required.

Describe the qualifications required for each key position. Specify the level of expertise and the educational or experience background required. Use the proposal preparation instructions to require the contractor to identify its key personnel and demonstrate how they meet the requisite qualifications. Permit the contractor to provide and explain equivalent education or experience levels as a substitute for those specified. You are not required to accept the contractor's equivalency contentions, but doing so helps avoid problems when there are equivalent educational or experience levels of which you were not aware. If exceptions are made, the SOW should be modified accordingly before award.

If appropriate, indicate the percentage of time the key personnel are expected to devote to the contract. If you do not want to dictate the degree of participation, you can use the proposal preparation instructions to require the contractor to provide this information and incorporate the information into the SOW. This might be appropriate, for example, in an R&D contract with a university when you want to ensure significant participation by the specified key person rather than his or her assistants.

Give some thought, however, to the effect that a specific description of the qualifications of key personnel might have on an offeror's response. Describing specific qualifications may inhibit the offeror's ability to provide an innovative solution that uses personnel with different qualifications. For example, the FAR[4] states that when acquiring information technology services, the solicitation must not describe any minimum experience or educational requirement for proposed contractor personnel unless the contracting officer determines that: (1) the needs of the agency cannot be met without that requirement, or (2) the use of other than a performance-based contract is required.

You do not necessarily need to use a key personnel clause. Use the proposal preparation instructions to require potential contractors to identify those persons they consider key personnel and describe their qualifications. Even though you have not mandated certain personnel qualifications, you may evaluate the cited qualifications as a function of how well the offeror understands the requirement. You may also consider the cited qualifications in a comparative assessment of offerors' key personnel when determining the most highly rated proposals. This technique does have an elevated risk of protest; however, if you document a rational justification for your evaluation and can show this in your debriefing of the unsuccessful offerors, you should be able to avoid a protest.

SOWS FOR SEALED BIDDING

The nature of sealed bidding requires particular attention to how the requirement is described. The FAR[5] states that sealed bidding may be used only if:

- Time permits the solicitation, submission, and evaluation of sealed bids.

- The award will be made on the basis of price and other price-related factors.

- It is not necessary to conduct discussions with the responding offerors about their bids.

- There is a reasonable expectation of receiving more than one sealed bid.

The use of sealed bidding is appropriate only if *all* of these conditions are met. Otherwise the use of competitive proposals (negotiation) is required.

How the Differences between Sealed Bidding and Negotiation Affect the SOW

In sealed bidding, award must be made on the basis of price (i.e., a fixed-price contract), no discussions may be held, and the bids may not be changed after bid opening. In negotiation, any appropriate pricing arrangement may be used, discussions may be held with offerors after the receipt of proposals, and the proposals may be changed to reflect these discussions. These differences affect SOW preparation for sealed bidding in two ways:

- **The SOW must be particularly definitive.** If a contractor must offer a fixed price, the SOW must be so definitive that the contractor can price the effort accurately based solely on the SOW presented in the solicitation. Under a fixed-price contract, the contractor guarantees performance, even if it is at the contractor's own expense. This makes the accuracy of the contractor's pricing an important factor both in the contractor's willingness to compete and later in the contractor's performance. A contractor working at a loss is going to be more interested in minimizing the loss than in maximizing the quality of the contract product.

- **The SOW must stand on its own.** In the sealed bidding process, the bidder submits its bid price, the bid price and any designated price-related factors are evaluated, and award is made to the lowest bidder. There is no opportunity to discuss the technical aspects of the bid with the bidder and no opportunity to use the proposal preparation instructions to obtain additional information to refine or clarify your SOW. The SOW must completely describe the requirement the first time. Your SOW must be good enough that you are willing to take the contractor's word that it can perform the work successfully without any discussions or supporting information at all.

Under these circumstances, sealed bidding should be used only when the requirement can be described so clearly that a contractor proposal is not required to determine if the contractor can do the work. This is why the use of sealed bidding is usually restricted to requirements for commercial or commercial-type supplies and services.

Techniques to Support the SOW

Several techniques are available to support your SOW when sealed bidding is appropriate but a fully definitive SOW is not possible due to the nature of the product being procured.

Bid Samples

The FAR[6] permits the use of a bid sample requirement only when characteristics of the product cannot be described adequately in the specification or purchase description but are important to the acceptability of the bid. A bid sample is a sample of the actual product to be furnished by the bidder to demonstrate the characteristics of the product offered. These characteristics include balance, facility of use, feel, color, pattern, or other characteristics that cannot otherwise be described in writing. If you have to see, feel, touch, or test an item to determine if it will meet your requirement, you should obtain a bid sample.

The SOW must indicate the number and size of the samples and otherwise fully describe the samples required. All characteristics for which the samples will be examined must be identified. If the bid sample is to be tested, describe what tests will be used and ensure that the description of the samples is such that the items will be delivered in a test-ready condition.

Note, however, that the FAR[7] states that when more than a minor portion of the characteristics of the product cannot be adequately described in the specification, products should be procured by two-step sealed bidding or negotiation, as appropriate. Two-step sealed bidding or negotiation offers the contractor more flexibility in the submission and testing of samples.

Descriptive Literature

The FAR[8] permits a requirement for descriptive literature only when it is necessary to determine, before award, that the products offered meet the specifications and to establish exactly what the bidder proposes to furnish. Descriptive literature is information such as cuts, illustrations, drawings, and brochures that show the characteristics or construction of a product or explain its operation.

The SOW must describe what descriptive literature is to be furnished and the purpose for which it is required. This is usually accomplished by describing the salient characteristics of the product that the literature must demonstrate. Salient characteristics may include design, materials, components, performance characteristics, and methods of manufacture, assembly, construction, or operation.

When using a descriptive literature requirement, ensure that the listed salient characteristics are limited to those characteristics that are necessary to determine the acceptability of the product. Do not include information related to the qualifications of the bidder or for use in operating or maintaining equipment.

Brand Name or Equal

The FAR[9] permits the use of brand name or equal purchase descriptions for products readily available in the commercial marketplace when an adequate specification or more detailed purchase description cannot feasibly be made available in time for the acquisition. A brand name or equal description identifies the required item by brand name and model number or other description that serves to specifically identify the required item. The description must clearly state that either the brand name product or an equal product shall be provided.

To support the submission of an "or equal" product, the description must also identify the salient characteristics of the brand name product that the "or equal" product must meet. Contractors submitting an "or equal" product must submit descriptive literature demonstrating that their product meets all the salient characteristics listed.

Two-Step Sealed Bidding

Two-step sealed bidding is a combination of negotiation and sealed bidding used to obtain the benefits of sealed bidding when a description of the requirement suitable for sealed bidding is not available but all other conditions for sealed bidding apply.

Step 1 is a negotiated process in which technical proposals are submitted and evaluated, and, when necessary, discussions are conducted to clarify questions relating to the technical proposals. No pricing information is provided in this step. Step 1 is completed when all proposals have been evaluated and found to be either technically acceptable or technically unacceptable. The technically unacceptable proposals are rejected.

Step 2 is sealed bidding. The offerors who submitted technically acceptable proposals in Step 1 are invited to submit priced bids for their own technical proposals in Step 2. All the rules for sealed bidding apply. Award is made to the lowest evaluated price.

Even though discussions are permitted in Step 1 of the two-step process, the SOW still must be as definitive and stand-alone as possible. The SOW must set forth the technical requirements definitively; the discussions in Step 1 are only to determine the proposal's conformity with the technical requirements in the SOW. The SOW will not be revised as a result of the information provided in the proposals and nothing will be incorporated by reference.

The two-step process is most appropriately used when there is a definitive requirement but the requirement could be performed in a number of ways and the government does not want to restrict competition by dictating the manner of performance.

SUMMARY

A well-written SOW answers the "what, why, where, when, and how" questions. *What* you want to buy is addressed in the introduction and scope sections. *Why* you want it is explained in the background section. *Where* the work is to be done is covered in the place of performance section. *When* the work is to be done is covered in the period of performance section. *How* the work is to be done is set forth in the technical requirements and delivery sections, supported by the applicable documents and supporting information sections.

The purpose of the SOW format is to compartmentalize the information about your requirement so that the SOW communicates your requirement effectively and facilitates your management of the contract. Conduct market research to determine what the marketplace has to offer and incorporate this information into the description of your requirement. Market research notwithstanding, it may be necessary to obtain specific contractor input before issuing your final SOW. This is done by issuing an initial SOW supplemented by proposal preparation instructions that require the contractor to provide specific kinds of information. This information is made part of the final SOW by incorporating all or part of the contractor's proposal by reference. The final SOW becomes the contractual requirement at the time of contract award.

Chapter 6 addresses common problems in writing SOWs. This information is designed to help you avoid problems when writing an SOW and to help you ensure that any contractor-provided information that is to be incorporated by reference does not contain loopholes or ambiguities that will make contract administration difficult.

Notes

[1] FAR 12.101.
[2] FAR 11.002(a)(2)(v).
[3] The FAR does not provide a key personnel clause.
[4] FAR 39.104.
[5] FAR 6.401.
[6] FAR 14.202-4.
[7] FAR 14.202-4(b).
[8] FAR 14.202-5.
[9] FAR 11.104.

6 Common Problems in Writing SOWs

Writing an SOW can be difficult. Even if you have developed an outline, getting the first words down on paper can be a problem. One way to start is to write the first draft concentrating only on expressing your ideas of what needs to be done. Focus on describing your requirement without worrying about the format or the language—simply get your ideas down on paper. If you concentrate initially on format and language, you may forget some of your ideas, and the ideas are the important element.

After describing your requirement, you can go back and refine the draft concentrating on the format and language you use. The finished SOW has to describe clearly what is to be accomplished, not how to do it. Detailed "how to" instructions should be used only as necessary to ensure that the contractor is headed in the right direction.

It is important to have someone review and edit your SOW objectively. A review and edit by one of your peers may identify problems that have escaped your attention. Your goal is to produce an SOW that can be processed into an effective contract with little or no change. If the contracting officer has to ask for SOW revisions, the processing of your requirement will be delayed significantly.

GENERAL WRITING GUIDELINES

As you revise the rough draft, organize your thoughts. Ensure that there is a logical flow from sentence to sentence and from paragraph to paragraph. Introduce the topic of each paragraph in the paragraph's first sentence. Ideally, each paragraph (or subparagraph) should be limited to a single topic. You can check your organization by reading just the first sentence of each paragraph and subparagraph. If these make up a coherent outline of what you want to say, you probably have organized your SOW well.

Within reason, your sentences should be short and concise. Avoid long sentences that must be read several times to determine the meaning. Keep in mind, however, that a string of short, choppy sentences is equally difficult to read.

Readability is usually measured in terms of the sentence length and the number of syllables per word or number of multi-syllable words. The typical readability standard (used by most newspapers and magazines) is an average of 17 words per sentence and an average of 147 syllables per 100 words. This standard, however, is geared for readers with an eighth-grade education. Given the technical nature of many government requirements, it may be difficult to write at that level and still describe your requirement adequately.

A reasonable writing standard for government SOWs ranges from the eighth-grade standard to an average sentence length of 25 words and an average of 167 syllables per 100 words (college level). The lower standard applies to SOWs for standard commercial supplies or services, and the higher standard applies to more complex requirements, such as R&D and technical support services. (These standards are not a reflection on the education of the readers of the SOW but on the complexity of what you have to describe.)

Number your SOW paragraphs using any numbering system that makes sense. A numbering system facilitates the organization of your SOW and the referencing and cross-referencing of SOW information. The number of subparagraphs and lower divisions should be kept to a minimum. If you find that you have a number of divisions below the subparagraph level, you are probably not expressing yourself well. Subparagraph references like 5.2.3.4.1 and 5.A.1.(a)(2)(iii) are too complicated and may cause your readers problems. In addition, use bullets sparingly; they are difficult to reference.

Give some thought to what your SOW will look like when printed. You should make the document as readable as possible by presenting the SOW in a rational format. When considering the font type and size to use, check with your contracting officer to find out what font type and size will be used for the rest of the contract. You do not have to be compatible (the SOW is usually an attachment to the RFP), but your font size should not be smaller than that used in the RFP.

Margins are also important; a tightly typed, single-spaced document that goes from one side of the page to the other is difficult to read. Judicious use of white space can improve the readability of your document. While the printing tools available on your word processor can be effective, you should be careful how frequently you use bold face, italics, and underlining. Overuse can reduce their effectiveness.

COMMON AMBIGUITIES IN SOWS

Ambiguities arise when the SOW is written so that the meaning or intent of the requirement is uncertain, leaving the contractor in doubt about what is required. These ambiguities often result in differing interpretations of the requirements. Ambiguities can make even a simple contract difficult because they obscure the intent of the contract. Unfortunately, the resulting problems usually do not show up until well into contract performance.

Correcting such problems after award is an expensive and time-consuming process and sometimes results in a dispute that must be resolved by a board of contract appeals or a federal court. The boards and courts generally favor the contractor's interpretation of an ambiguity, as long as it is reasonable, because a contract is usually interpreted against the party who drafted the ambiguous language.

Ordinarily, a contractor enters into a contract with the intent to provide a quality product. This is how the contractor stays in business. However, when faced with an ambiguous SOW, the contractor must make its own interpretations of the requirement. These interpretations are influenced by a number of factors, such as the contractor's technical competence, its financial status, corporate or individual goals, and the contract schedule. The contractor's interpretation may produce a result contrary to what you intended.

Contractors are charged with the responsibility to question obvious ambiguities before award, and the government must respond with clear-cut answers. Often, however, ambiguities are not recognized as such initially, and the contractor proceeds based on its own understanding of the requirement. This is why problems with ambiguities usually do not show up until the contract is nearing completion.

The following are some of the ambiguities commonly found in SOWs.

Inconsistency of Requirements

Ambiguities are usually the result of careless writing that causes inconsistencies in the SOW requirements. These inconsistencies occur, for example, when work requirements are set forth throughout the SOW instead of being concentrated in the technical requirements section. Fragmenting the requirement throughout the SOW often results in contradictory (and thus ambiguous) requirements in different places in the SOW. For example:

On page 13 of an SOW:

> It is the intent of the government to have individual post(s) in the Part III, Section J, Exhibit I, manned by the same guard on a normal weekly basis, not to exceed a total of 10 hours per day.

On page 17 of the same SOW:

> It is the intent of the government to have individual post(s) in Part III, Section J, Exhibit I, manned by the same guard on a normal weekly basis, not to exceed a total of 12 hours per day.

If overlooked, this error could have a significant effect on the pricing and staffing proposed by the contractor.

Calling a Requirement by Different Names

Ambiguities also occur when the same requirement is called by different names at different places in the SOW, making it difficult to determine if the description is one or two requirements. For example, the following was found in an SOW for guard services.

> (2) Roving Patrol Posts. Make patrols in accordance with routes and schedules established in the Guard Post Assignment. Record and immediately correct security violations and initiate all necessary reports.
>
> (10) Unauthorized Access. Discover and detain persons attempting to gain unauthorized access to property through independent aggressive patrol or through operation of security systems.

It is not clear whether the reference to independent aggressive patrol in (10) refers to the roving patrol in (2) or represents another, unexpressed requirement. The term "independent aggressive patrol" does not fit well with a roving patrol following established schedules and routes. A contractor could easily interpret this to mean a requirement for two different kinds of patrols.

Conflicting or Unreasonable Schedules

Ambiguities are often created when schedules conflict or are not reasonable. For example, an RFP for multiple presentations of 11 different procurement training courses was issued on June 3, with proposals due on July 3. The SOW stated that the contractor was to review and update the existing course materials and begin presentations the first week of October. Course presentations were to be ordered individually through the issuance of delivery orders. The contractor was to price the effort on the basis of a fixed price per delivery order. The last paragraph of the SOW, titled "Contract Schedule" stated:

> Contractor is to provide revised course materials to the COTR within 45 calendar days after receipt of initial delivery order. The COTR will coordinate with Government contracting subject matter experts, who will review the course materials and provide approval of required materials to the contractor within 30 days after submission. If changes are made by the Government, the contractor will be given 15 days to implement the changes before resubmitting for final approval.

There are a number of problems with the scheduling in this example. The wording of the SOW indicates that the contractor must begin the review and revision process immediately after award in order to be ready for October presentations (there was no schedule for individual presentations). However, the first sentence of the "Contract Schedule" paragraph could be interpreted to mean that the review and revision process begins when the contractor receives the first delivery order for a course. It could also mean that the revision process is on a per-course basis and starts with the first delivery order for each course.

Furthermore, the schedule is unrealistic. The "Contract Schedule" paragraph provides for a 90-day review and revision process after award; however, there are only 90 days between the due date for proposals and the presentation of the first courses in October. When you consider that the proposals must be evaluated, discussions held, and award made, at best there will be not more than 60 days left after award before the first presentations are due.

This means that the contractor has only 15 days to accomplish the initial review and revisions because the government gets 30 days to review and approve the revised materials, and the contractor gets 15 days to implement any required changes. This does not include the time the government will take to review the contractor's changes and provide final approval. Also not included is the time it will take the contractor to have the revised course material printed and shipped to where the courses are to be presented.

This schedule clearly will not work. The government would either have to revise the schedule for the initial course presentations or permit the contractor to print and provide the old course materials for the initial courses and print the revised materials later when the revisions are approved. Students in the initial courses will be provided obsolete materials—hardly a goal for a training requirement.

This schedule may also affect the quality of the review and revision process. If the contractor is to meet the schedule, it must expedite the revision process. This is likely to reduce the quality of the revision effort in favor of getting it done in a hurry. This also is not an appropriate goal for a training requirement.

Schedules are a critical factor in any contract. Timing requirements occur both in the description of the work requirements and the description of the delivery requirements. These requirements must be objectively reviewed to ensure that they make sense and do not conflict.

Incomplete Description of Requirement

Ambiguities also occur when the SOW writer assumes that the prospective contractor will, or should, "intuitively understand" a requirement and therefore does not describe it fully. It is a mistake to rely on the contractor's intuitive understanding, whether it is a sole-source SOW or a competitive procurement.

For example, the first task in an SOW called for the review and revision of eight procurement training courses, stating, "The contractor shall review a sample text of each course and revise course material with new DoD and Navy regulations."

Federal procurement is first governed by the FAR, then by agency regulations (DoD), and finally by component regulations (Navy). The wording of the SOW indicates that only changes to DoD and Navy regulations are to be considered when revising course materials. FAR changes, unless they require implementation instructions at a lower level, are not reflected in the lower level regulations. In addition, there is usually a time lag between the issuance of FAR changes and implementing instructions at the lower levels. Since the wording in this SOW does not require any revisions resulting from FAR changes, following these instructions might result in inadequate and misleading material.

You might be tempted to assume that any competent contractor would understand what is meant here, and you would be right. However, if a prospective contractor was not all that competent and its proposal did not reflect an intent to ignore FAR changes, you could end up with a contractor who met all the contractual requirements yet produced an inadequate product.

In competitive procurements, some SOW writers leave out parts of a requirement purposefully, on the basis that "any qualified contractor should know this." In effect, the SOW writer is using the incomplete SOW as an evaluation factor to test the offeror's competency. If an offeror does not question the missing material and does not address it in its proposal, this indicates that the offeror is not sufficiently qualified to do the work. This is a mistake—understanding a poorly worded SOW should not be a criterion in determining an offeror's competency.

A contractor is required to do only what is written into the contract. If a requirement is not spelled out in the SOW or a contract clause, it is not a contractual requirement and cannot be enforced without a contract modification and (usually) additional funding. Although there are exceptions to the requirement that everything must be in writing (such as a subtask that is inherently part of the primary task), you cannot count on legal technicalities to rescue you from the results of careless writing.

Vagueness and Generalized Language

Ambiguities often result from vagueness in the SOW—when activities are alluded to but not clearly described, or when passive or indefinite wording is used. Phrases or sentences that are not clearly expressed (or perceived or identified) lack the preciseness needed in a good SOW. For example, the following describes a requirement in a fixed-price SOW for training services:

> The contractor shall prepare textbooks and training materials for, and present, the eight (8) different courses at CONUS activities and locations outside the Continental United States, i.e., Europe, Japan, Korea, and Hawaii.

The SOW did not provide any information on specific locations or the number of overseas training courses (the SOW did provide information on the aggregate of the previous year presentations, but not with respect to where the training was conducted).

Vagueness such as this presents significant problems for a contractor who must estimate shipping and travel costs in developing a fixed price for such an effort. In this case the problem could have been resolved by providing for shipping by the government, at government expense, and for instructor travel to be on a cost-reimbursable basis. This would have leveled the competitive playing field and resulted in lower costs to the government.

The major problem with such ambiguities is that they must be corrected before the procurement can proceed. Correction takes time and can have a ripple effect throughout the SOW when correction of one part of the SOW requires correction of other parts. For example, correction of a vague work requirement often requires correction of delivery schedules.

Another example of vague wording:

> Substitute materials may include, but are not limited to, those otherwise provided under the bill of materials for specification ....

Who decides the "but not limited to"? This wording permits the contractor to decide what substitute materials to provide. What does "otherwise provided" mean? Assumptions can be made about the interpretation of this sentence, but they will only lead to problems.

Some ambiguities are difficult to detect on review. These usually occur when the SOW writer is unsure how to describe the requirement and uses generalized language. Since a reviewer would probably have the same difficulty describing the requirement, he or she might not recognize the ambiguity. If not detected on review, generalization can (among other things) make it difficult to distinguish between an LOE and a completion SOW. Generalizations can cause the contracting officer to use inappropriate contract clauses or incorrect funding procedures and possibly cause problems with personal versus nonpersonal services.

For example, in a study or analytic effort, a contractor is told to review a number of general areas, but the SOW does not provide any specificity or indicate the relative importance of each area to the final results. The contractor will probably focus on those areas it knows best and minimize coverage of those areas in which it is less competent. As a result, the contractor may fail to focus on those areas of most interest to the government.

In a similar situation, the results may intentionally or unintentionally reflect the contractor's point of view rather than the objective analysis intended because of the lack of specific direction. This can be a particular problem when dealing with academics who often espouse a particular point of view as part of their academic credentials.

In another example, in a contract for software development, the SOW is not clear regarding the documentation to be provided. If the preparation of complete documentation is expensive or time-consuming, the contractor may choose to provide only the minimum documentation based on the vague definition of what is required. Or, if the contractor is not familiar with the government's documentation requirements, it may simply fail to understand what is actually required. In either event, the government will get less than what was anticipated.

Vague or generalized language can lead to delays in the procurement when caught and corrected before award; however, correction after award can lead to serious problems in contract administration, ranging from performance delays and increased costs to end products that do not meet the contract requirements. Many contractors (who often know more about how the requirement should be performed than the government) will simply ignore the language problems and perform the contract properly. However, you cannot, and should not, count on the contractor to fix your mistakes. Legally, vague or generalized language gives the contractor the right to interpret the requirements in its favor, and this may not be to the benefit of the government.

Use of Abstractions

Abstractions that are little more than sweeping ideas or fancy concepts that cannot be defined can cause problems. For example:

> The requirements for preventive maintenance must ensure optimum system availability for continuous use....

"Optimum system availability"? "Continuous use"? Who decides what these terms mean? Optimum means the best or most favorable. Continuous means continuing to do something without ceasing or without a break. Does this mean that the preventive maintenance must ensure (make certain) the most favorable system availability for use without a break? Abstractions sound good, but they produce problems when it becomes necessary to enforce them.

Unnecessary Comments

Unnecessary comments or nonessential statements can cause confusion. These most often occur when you try to "fill out" paragraphs that you think are too short. For example:

> Several papers published by the Bureau of Mines bear witness to this problem and may represent useful guidelines for analysis.

What papers? The SOW didn't identify them further. What does "useful guidelines" mean? Does the use of the word "may" indicate that maybe they will not represent useful guidelines? This kind of sentence causes more problems than it resolves.

Poor Sentence Construction

Poorly constructed sentences are always a problem. Have a competent editor or peer review your work. The following is an example of a statement that obviously was never reviewed:

> The appropriate work to be done, as specified herein and periodically referenced throughout, reflects the immensely understated needs of known cost-effective requirements for solution.

There isn't anything right about this sentence, except perhaps the spelling. The following is a little better, but still must be read several times before you are reasonably sure of the meaning:

> Discover and detain persons attempting to gain unauthorized access to property through independent aggressive patrol or through operation of security systems.

On first reading, the phrase, "through independent aggressive patrol" appears to relate to "gaining unauthorized access." But this doesn't make sense, so on the second reading you would probably conclude that the phrase relates to "discover and detain." You are creating potential problems whenever you write a sentence that must be read twice to be understood.

Typos or Missing Text

Typos and missing lines of text can occur in any document. However, as the language in an SOW carries the weight of the contract, it is especially important that this type of mistake be removed from the document before it causes confusion. For example:

> These rules and regulations are posted in all buildings under the charge and control of the entering in or on such property.

This is clearly a typo, with one or more lines of text missing, and would be caught by a careful review by someone not involved in the writing of the SOW. (This is the kind of typo that the SOW author might miss because the author, knowing what should be there, will read right through it.) If this is not caught before award, the contractor will either have to seek clarification or hope that the missing words are not important.

Improper punctuation can also create problems. For example:

> Make patrols in accordance with routes and schedules established in the Guard Post Assignment Record and immediately correct, security violations and initiate all necessary reports.

The comma after "correct" appears to be a typo. But it could also indicate a missing word. Most readers would assume the comma is incorrect because the sentence reads well without it. If, however, the comma is correct and wording is missing, this assumption could result in a failure to ask the right questions and thus overlook a significant requirement.

Overly Complicated Vocabulary

It is essential that you do not get carried away with your linguistic abilities. Using big words or technical terminology may demonstrate your educational attainments but does little for effective communication. For example:

> The orifice-penetrating device requires an aperture opening of sufficient size that can be placed equidistantly between the upper and lower dimensional limits of the in-place safety shield.

Anything this complicated has no place in an SOW. There is probably a simple way to explain this requirement. Again, if you have to read a sentence twice to figure out its meaning, the sentence needs rewriting.

Excessively Long Sentences

Writing excessively long sentences is a common writing problem. Check the length of your sentences when you review your first draft. Rewrite your sentences if they exceed 32 words (this is the number used by many editing programs to signal that a sentence is too long). When your sentences get too long, your thoughts tend to wander too. The result is rambling sentences that are often next to impossible to decipher. For example, the following sentence was found in a contract for the construction of a nuclear plant:

> The project, hereinafter referred to as the "project," is an installation of one generating unit, as referenced above, designated a Power Generating Station Unit No. 4, designed to support continuous base load operation, comply with applicable laws, codes, and regulations, to be integrated with existing standards and practices, and, as stated elsewhere, is intended to be a replicate, except where affected by interfaces with site-unique facilities, of the existing Power Generating Station Unit No. 1 with a replicate structure, facilities, and equipment.

By the time you are done reading this sentence, you have forgotten what the subject was. Think of this sentence whenever you are tempted to shrug off and not correct an excessively long sentence.

CONFLICTS BETWEEN THE SOW AND CONTRACT CLAUSES

Problems with ambiguities are not restricted to the SOW itself. It is important to check the entire RFP and contract to ensure that the clauses and provisions used do not conflict with what is in the SOW. The following example is from a two-part training requirement; the first part was for course development, and the second part was for course presentation.

The SOW

> The SOW called for the development and presentation of a training course. There would be four presentations of the course over a period of two years. The first course was to be

presented 90 days after award. The timing of the rest of the courses was not established; they would be ordered as the need arose. Pricing was on the basis of a fixed price for course development and, priced separately, a fixed price per course presentation.

The SOW called for the course text and supporting materials to be provided to the government for review 60 days after award. The government would complete the review within 10 days, and the contractor would be required to make any changes resulting from the review by the time of the first presentation.

Section B

In Section B of the RFP, *Supplies or Services and Price/Costs,* the contracting officer indicated that the first two courses were the contract's minimum quantity, and the second two courses were option quantities; however, this was not reflected in the SOW.

The contracting officer also placed an ordering clause in Section B. This clause identified the ordering office and indicated that oral orders could be issued, to be followed up by written orders. The clause did not indicate when the orders would be issued or who was authorized to issue them.

Section H

The contracting officer placed a key personnel clause in Section H, *Special Contract Requirements.* This clause required the identification of the contractor's key personnel and stated that no substitutions (within the contractor's control) could be made during the first 90 days of the contract. Thereafter, the contractor must provide at least 15 days' advance notice of a substitution, and the government would provide a response within 15 days.

The contracting officer also put a clause in Section H that required a post-award conference to be held 20 days after contract award.

Section I

The contracting officer also placed a delivery-order limitation clause in Section I, *Contract Clauses*. This clause stated that the minimum order would be two courses (this is what the government must order), and the maximum order would be four courses (this is the most the government can order at the contract price).

Do these clauses create an ambiguity? Yes, they do. In the first place, the SOW indicated a requirement for four course presentations. There was no indication that two of the presentations were option quantities. The difference is that the government is not obligated to order the option quantity. Thus we have an SOW that indicates a firm requirement for four presentations and a requirement in Section B that indicates a firm requirement for only two courses. So what is the real requirement?

The ordering clause in Section B also creates uncertainty. The authorization for the use of oral orders indicates that there may be very little lead time between the ordering of a course and its presentation (oral orders are used only when there is not sufficient time to provide a written order). The contractor is committed to presenting the courses, at a fixed price, over a period of two years, whenever the courses are ordered. This affects the contractor's allocation of its resources because the contractor is committed to make its instructor resources available with possibly very little notice.

Your better contractors are likely to decline to commit their resources to compete for a requirement with this type of uncertainty. They may decide that their resources are better employed competing for requirements that promise a greater return than two to possibly four courses over a two-year period. Revising the ordering clause to indicate that the government will issue its delivery orders in writing, at least 30 days in advance of a requirement for a course presentation, could alleviate the resource allocation problem. But first you must realize that the wording of the ordering clause creates a problem.

There is also a potential conflict between the ordering clause and the key personnel clause. The contractor must provide at least 15 days' notice of a substitution, but this assumes that the contractor gets at least 15 days' notice of the requirement for a course presentation. This probably would not be the case if an oral order were to be issued.

The prohibition against key personnel substitutions during the first 90 days of the contract may also create an ambiguity since the first presentation is not scheduled until 90 days after contract award. This holds the key personnel involved with course development in place but does not affect instructor personnel unless there is a need to substitute key instructor personnel before the first course presentation. This prohibition does not make sense—the government always has the right to disapprove a substitution. If the purpose of a clause is not clear, it should be changed; otherwise, you are creating problems for yourself.

The post-award conference requirement is puzzling. The purpose of a post-award conference is to ensure that both the government and the contractor understand the requirements. Post-award conferences are normally held immediately after contract award, before the contractor begins substantial performance, so that there is no wasted effort if problems arise. In this instance, the contractor has 60 days to develop the course material, but the post-award conference will not be held until one-third of the development time has passed. By this time the contractor should be well into the development effort. In a training effort any post-award misunderstandings are more likely to involve the development effort than course presentation. Holding the post-award conference 20 days after award would require a change order to correct problems that could have been avoided if the conference had been held right after award. A change order will cost needless time and money.

As author of the SOW, you are often also responsible for the technical administration of the contract. Problems that occur during contract performance are your problems. You should, therefore, be concerned with the quality of the entire RFP and contract, not just the SOW. Ambiguities caused by conflicts between the contract clauses and the SOW are just as much a problem as ambiguities caused by a poorly written SOW.

The bulk of the contract itself is put together by the contracting officer based primarily on the type of contract used, but there are a number of clauses that are directly related to the type of effort called for in the SOW. The fact that the contracting officer is responsible for the bulk of the contract does not, however, relieve you of the responsibility to ensure that the wording of the contract does not create problems. Once the contract is awarded, you will be responsible for administering the entire contract.

It is critical that you review the entire RFP before issuing it. You need to pay particular attention to the clauses and provisions that are set forth in full text. In the contract example used above, the contracting officer used two different option clauses, both in full text. A review of the contract would have raised the question of why there were two different clauses. A closer look would have revealed that one of the clauses, FAR clause 52.217-8, Option to Extend Services, was not the right clause—this clause is for continuing services (training courses are not continuing services) and has a six-month limitation on the extension of services. The appropriate clause would have been FAR 52.217-9, Option to Extend the Term of the Contract, which permits extensions in increments of one year each. The other option clause used, FAR 52.217-7, Option for Increased Quantity—Separately Priced Line Item, is not authorized for use in service contracts. So if a review had been done, it would have revealed that both option clauses were inappropriate for use.

So what is the problem? None, unless the contractor wanted out of the second year of the contract. Neither of the clauses used could have been exercised over the contractor's objections because they were not applicable to a training contract. If the government does not use the right clauses, the mistake can be corrected only by a bilateral modification to the contract (there are some exceptions to this, but they do not apply here). In this particular case, the contractor would not have to agree to a contract modification (the contract ends after the first year) or would have to receive some consideration (usually money) from the government for its agreement. In any event, the mistake would cause the government to expend unnecessary time and effort to correct a problem that should have been corrected before issuance of the RFP.

Examine the clauses set forth in full text closely. These are locally developed clauses, agency or FAR clauses that have blanks to be filled in by the offeror, or FAR clauses that are deemed important enough to be set forth in full text. Check them against the requirements of the SOW to ensure that there are no conflicts.

Clauses that are incorporated by reference are usually FAR clauses, and your ability to review them depends on how much research you want to do. You should at least read the titles of these clauses—most are self-explanatory—and ask the contracting officer to explain those that you do not understand.

OBTAINING CONTRACTOR COMMENTS

It is your responsibility, as well as the contracting officer's, to ensure that the SOW is clear, concise, and free of ambiguity. As noted, you can minimize ambiguities by asking one of your peers to review your SOW. You may also obtain contractor comments by requesting a review of your SOW prior to issuance of the RFP or shortly thereafter.

Draft Solicitations

A draft solicitation is a process in which prospective contractors are asked to review a draft of the RFP before it is issued and to provide comments on anything they think should be changed or clarified. The contractors are told that the draft RFP is not a formal solicitation, and there is no guarantee that a formal solicitation will ever be issued. They are also told that the government will review their comments, and any changes resulting from their comments will be reflected in the formal solicitation, if one is issued. In addition, they are told that their comments will not be revealed to other potential contractors.

The draft solicitation process is an effective means of obtaining contractor comments because the contractors are assured that their comments will be held in confidence. Contractors are much more likely to be candid if they know that their competitors will not see their comments. The FAR[1] now allows for an early exchange of information about a requirement, including consideration of the feasibility of the SOW. This would allow the government to address the contractor's concerns to ensure a mutual understanding. While a draft SOW alone could also be used, it is usually more effective to permit prospective contractors to see the entire RFP.

This process helps clean up the SOW (and the rest of the RFP) because the prospective contractors will look at the SOW from a contractor's perspective of "how would I do this?" and see problems that may not have been evident from the government's perspective.

Preproposal Conference

A preproposal conference is a meeting of prospective contractors held shortly after the RFP has been issued and the contractors have had an opportunity to review the RFP requirements. At the conference, the contractors are briefed on the government requirement and encouraged to ask questions. If the questions cannot be answered on the spot, answers are provided in writing at a later date, when a transcript of the conference, including all questions and answers, is provided. All prospective contractors, including those that did not attend the conference, are provided a copy of the transcript.

This process is less effective than the draft solicitation process, in terms of candid responses, because participants will be reluctant to talk about their firm's innovations or unique capabilities, or their technical approach, in the presence of their competitors. However, with respect to SOW problems, such meetings can reveal weaknesses in the SOW because participants are not reluctant to point out such problems (unless they plan to take advantage of the weaknesses if they receive the contract award). Preproposal conferences are also administratively burdensome because of the need to transcribe the questions and answers and provide the transcript to all interested parties.

Proposal Preparation Instructions

Ambiguities can also be minimized as an offshoot of the use of proposal preparation instructions. These instructions are used to request work plans, schedules, procedural details, and other information that helps in evaluating the contractor's understanding of the requirement. However, if a contractor's proposal indicates a lack of understanding, this may be more of a reflection of your SOW writing than of the contractor's expertise, particularly if the contractor has a known expertise in the subject matter. This possibility should be explored and any necessary corrections made before contract award.

Despite the fact that amendments to the RFP will delay award, it is far less expensive in terms of time and money to fix an SOW problem before award than after it.

GUIDELINES RELATED TO THE USE OF WORDS

The following guidelines can help you exercise care in your choice of words when writing an SOW:

- **Use the word "shall" to express an action by the contractor.** The SOW contains what are essentially commands to the contractor. Using the imperative ensures that there is no misunderstanding of the contractor's responsibilities.

- **Use the word "will" to express an action by the government.** Do not use "will" in conjunction with contractor actions because the word does not expressly require the contractor to take action. The consistent use of "shall" for contractor actions and "will" for government actions makes it easier to distinguish contractor responsibilities from government responsibilities.

- **Avoid words that are vague or inexact.** Words such as "similar," "type," "average," and "about" create uncertainties and make it difficult to determine how well the contractor has performed.

- **Avoid the use of colloquialisms, buzz words, jargon, and in-house or trade terminology that may not have a common meaning to all readers.** The meaning of such terms often varies by geographical area and segments of industry.

- **Use words consistently.** For example, do not refer to a requirement for a "brace" at one point and later refer to it as a "support." This causes confusion as to the real meaning and could lead the contractor to provide both a brace and a support. Problems like this are not likely to become evident until after award.

- **Use the active rather than the passive voice.** Avoid use of the words "should" or "may" when describing contractor actions. For example: "The contractor should establish a program" creates uncertainty as to whether the program is required or desired, in effect permitting the contractor to make the decision. Use the active voice ("The contractor shall establish a program") to ensure that the action is taken. The passive voice does not specify who is acting.

- **Use simple words and phrases when possible.** Given the technical nature of many government requirements, any reduction of multi-syllable words will improve the SOW's readability. When possible, use the active work words from the list in Figure 6-1[2] to describe contractor actions. This list contains some of the more commonly accepted active work words for use in SOWs. The listing is not intended to be all-inclusive, and its use is optional.

GUIDELINES RELATED TO THE USE OF PHRASES AND TERMS

The following guidelines related to the use of phrases and terms may prove useful in writing a clear, effective SOW:

- **Minimize use of the terms "as shown" and "as specified herein"** or other terms that inexactly or only generally reference other parts of the SOW, the contract, or another document. Make your references explicit, citing the page or paragraph number of the referenced item.

- **Avoid use of the phrases "as required," "as applicable," and "as necessary."** These phrases are not sufficiently definitive and leave the action to be taken to the contractor's discretion. If one of these phrases must be used, explain the specific circumstances under which an action would be "required," "applicable," or "necessary."

- **Do not use qualifying phrases to modify the actions of the contractor.** SOW requirements must be definitive and clearly stated. The following are examples of qualifying phrases that tend to create ambiguity and misunderstanding:

    "as approved by"   "to the satisfaction of"

    "in the best judgment   "insofar as possible"
    (or opinion) of"

FIGURE 6-1
Active Work Words

Work Word	Definition	Work Word	Definition
analyze	solve by analysis	institute	set up, establish, begin
annotate	provide with comments	integrate	combine parts to make a whole
ascertain	find out with certainty	interpret	explain the meaning of
attend	be present at	investigate	search into, examine closely
audit	officially examine	judge	decide, form an estimate of
build	make by putting together	make	cause to come into being
calculate	find out by computation	manufacture	fabricate from raw materials
compare	find out by likeness or differences	notice	comment on, review
consider	think about, decide	observe	inspect, watch
construct	put together, build	organize	integrate, arrange in a coherent way
contribute	give along with others	originate	initiate, give rise to
control	direct, regulate	perform	do, carry out, accomplish
create	cause to be, make	probe	investigate thoroughly
define	make clear, set limits	produce	give birth to or rise to
design	make original plans, sketch an outline for	pursue	seek, obtain, or accomplish
determine	resolve, settle, decide	reason	think, influence another's act
develop	bring into being	recommend	advise, attract favor of

continues

**FIGURE 6-1
Active Work Words**
continued

differentiate	make a distinction between	record	set down in writing, electronic reproduction of communications
erect	put together, set upright	resolve	reduce by analysis, clear up
establish	set up, settle, prove beyond dispute	review	inspect, examine, evaluate
estimate	judge approximate value or amount	scan	look through hastily
evaluate	find or fix the value	search	examine to find something
evolve	develop gradually, work out	seek	try to discover, make an attempt
examine	look at closely, test quality	solve	find an answer
explore	examine, discover	study	carefully examine or analyze
extract	take out, deduce, select	trace	copy or find by searching
fabricate	build, manufacture, invent	track	observe or pilot the path of
form	give shape to, establish	update	bring up to date
formulate	put together and express	utilize	use, find a use for
generate	produce, cause to be	validate	make valid, confirm
inquire	ask, make a search of	verify	check the truth or correctness of
inspect	examine carefully or officially	warrant	prove or guarantee
install	place, put into position		

"at the discretion of"   "to all intents and purposes"

"unless otherwise   "pending future development"
directed by"

- **Do not use the term "and/or."** This term is ambiguous when used in a contract and allows the contractor to decide whether to add (and) or substitute (or). If you cannot determine whether to add or substitute, describe the circumstance as a decision point during contract performance and describe how the decision will be made.

- **Be careful about using common phrases that are better explained by a single word.** Their use adds words, but not value, to your SOW:

  "in the event that"   — use "if" instead

  "it is possible that"   — use "may" instead

  "due to the fact that"   — use "because" instead

  "in connection with"   — use "of," "in," or "on" instead

  "in accordance with"   — use "with" or "by" instead

  "the majority of"   — use "most" instead

  "in order to"   — use "to" instead

  "whether or not"   — use "whether" instead

  "in the amount of"   — use "for" instead

- **Avoid using blanket phrases that are of little practical value.** Blanket phrases are ineffective because they cannot be translated into a definitive performance standard. These include:

"best commercial practice"

"good workmanship"

"maximum reliability"

- **Avoid phrases that contribute little to the meaning of the sentence**, such as:

    "as noted"   "at the same time"

    "in connection with"   "on the other hand"

    "with reference to"

- **Do not call for the contractor "to assist" or perform "as directed"** unless the SOW explicitly describes the "assistance" actions or the specific circumstances under which "direction" will be provided. These phrases imply impermissible personal services through detailed supervision of contractor employees and fail to properly define the required effort.

- **Watch out for redundant phrases that use two words instead of one.** The word in parentheses is unnecessary and in some cases will create an ambiguity:

    "adequate (enough)"   "combine (together)"

    "could (possibly)"   "(mutual) cooperation"

    "separate (out)"   "share (together)"

    "(sound) logic"   "(still) continues"

    "(still) remains"   "(still) retains"

"sufficient (enough)"   "(essentially) complete"

"(viable) alternatives"   "(considered) judgment"

- **Use abbreviations and acronyms properly.** Spell the word or phrase out in full the first time used, followed by the abbreviation or acronym in parentheses. Consider spelling the word or phrase out periodically in a long SOW. You may also include a glossary when numerous abbreviations and acronyms are used, but include only those terms used in the SOW.

- **Do not use indefinite phrasing to "flesh out" the SOW and make it "sound" better.** The following phrases lack specific interpretation and can be defined in a number of different ways, creating ambiguity and misunderstanding:

  "a sufficient number of times"

  "meaningful results"

  "selection among significant alternatives"

  "delivery of pertinent data"

  "utilization of optimum alternatives"

  "maximum use of available technologies"

  "ensure optimum system availability for continuous use"

- **Do not use the phrase "may include, but not limited to"** or any similar phrase that generalizes what the contractor is to do. This kind of generalization leaves the interpretation to the contractor. You may not like the contractor's interpretation.

The art of writing has many other guidelines—the guidelines presented in this chapter simply demonstrate some of the more common problems in writing SOWs.

Appendix A shows how to review and revise an SOW.

NOTES

[1] FAR 15.201(c).
[2] Department of Defense, *Department of Defense Handbook for Preparation of Statement of Work (SOW)*, April 3, 1996, p. 33. Online at *https://acc.dau.mil/CommunityBrowser.aspx?id=46583* (accessed February 2012).

7 Managing Changes to the SOW

Regardless of how well the SOW is planned, changes inevitably occur throughout the lifecycle of a project. To allow for these changes, FAR Part 43.201 states:

> Generally, Government contracts contain a changes clause that permits the contracting officer to make unilateral changes, in designated areas, within the general scope of the contract. These are accomplished by issuing written change orders on Standard Form 30, Amendment of Solicitation/Modification of Contract (SF 30), unless otherwise provided (see 43.301).[1]

One of a project manager's main responsibilities is to maintain a balance between the scope, cost, and schedule of a project. These three variables are typically referred to as the *triple constraints* of a project and are often illustrated as an equilateral triangle, as in Figure 7-1. The SOW establishes the initial parameters for the triangle by defining the baseline scope, cost, and scheduled project completion date. When one side of the triangle increases or decreases, it has a direct impact on the other two.

To maintain a balance between these triple constraints, a detailed change management process must be in place. Failing to document and manage changes to any of these constraints prop-

---

This chapter has been adapted with permission from *Delivering Project Excellence with the Statement of Work, Second Edition,* by Michael G. Martin, PMP. ©2010 by Management Concepts, Inc. All rights reserved. www.managementconcepts.com/pubs.

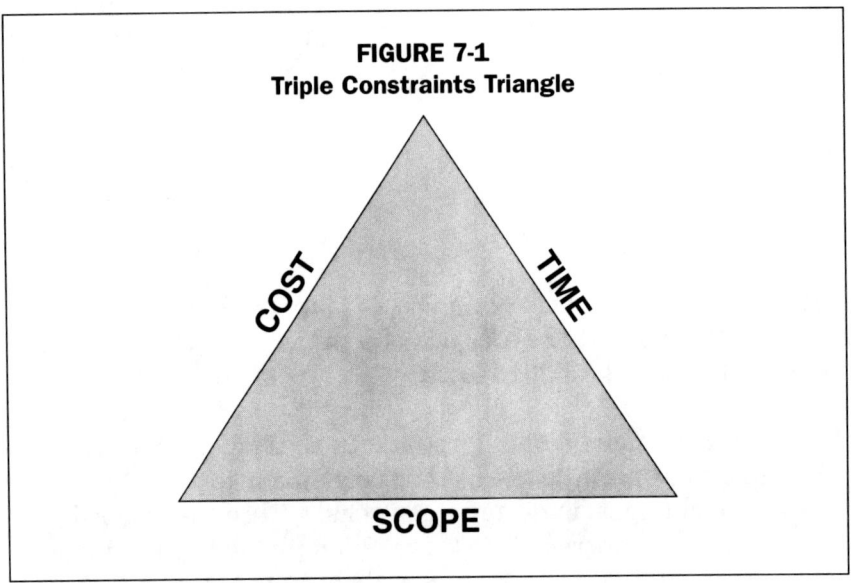

FIGURE 7-1
Triple Constraints Triangle

erly will force the triangle out of balance very quickly. When this happens, the project is heading for trouble.

LEGAL PRECEDENTS BACKING CHANGE MANAGEMENT

Failing to manage project change can lead to a multitude of problems, including scope creep, cost and schedule overruns, poor resource utilization, reduced product quality, and wasted funds. In addition, if either the government or the contractor were to seek retribution for any changes that took place without an approved change order, the probability of winning the suit would be very low.

Several court cases have litigated this very issue. In *Miorelli Engineering v. County of Brevard* (1997), Miorelli Engineering sued Brevard County, Florida, for breach of contract and sought damages for work the company had performed outside the scope of the contract. After going through the trial court and the court of appeals, the case was eventually elevated to the Supreme Court of Florida for a decision. The Supreme Court ruled that Miorelli Engineering could not recover the cost of work it had performed outside the scope of the contract with Brevard County because without a written and approved change order, the county was protected by the sovereign immunity doctrine.[2] This doctrine precludes the institution of a suit against the sovereign (government) without its consent.[3]

In the case of *Choate Construction v. Ideal Electrical Contractors* (2000), Ideal Electrical Contractors sued Choate Construction, arguing that the theory of *quantum meruit* allowed Ideal to recover the reasonable value of services performed outside the scope of the contract.[4] In the law of contracts, the theory of quantum meruit is a doctrine by which the law infers a promise to pay a reasonable amount for labor and materials furnished, even in the absence of a specific legally enforceable agreement between the parties.[5] The agreement between Choate and Ideal specified that Choate would pay Ideal the amount set forth in the subcontract, but both agreed that this amount could increase or decrease to accommodate any changes the parties agreed to in writing. The subcontract further specified that Ideal would not be paid for work performed outside the defined scope unless Choate authorized that work in writing before the work was initiated.

Although Ideal won the case in trial court, Choate appealed the decision to the Court of Appeals of Georgia, which reversed the decision. The appellate court ruled that Ideal had accepted the terms of the subcontract but had not followed the change management process for work performed outside the original scope. Since Ideal did not follow the terms of the contract, it was denied payment for the work under the theory of quantum meruit.

The case of *A.H.A General Contracting v. New York City Housing Authority* (1998) provides yet another example of how not following an agreed-upon change management process can negatively impact an organization.[6] In this case, A.H.A General Contracting was awarded two contracts with the New York City

Housing Authority, one for $2.3 million and the other for $2.4 million. Each contract specifically required A.H.A to submit all claims, along with any supporting documentation, to the Housing Authority in a timely manner. This provision was meant to give the Housing Authority sufficient time to review the claims to ensure that any additional work performed outside the original scope was justified and that public funds were being spent wisely.

Upon completing the work for both contracts, A.H.A submitted two claims for additional work it had performed. A.H.A. claimed an additional $700,513 on the first contract and $205,125 on the second. After reviewing the claims, the Housing Authority recognized only minor adjustments for the additional work and refused to pay the claims in full. A.H.A sued for breach of contract, seeking full payment for the additional work performed.

The trial court and the New York Court of Appeals dismissed A.H.A's claims, ruling that the company had not met the notice of claims and reporting requirements specified in the two contracts. A.H.A lost close to one million dollars in claims on the two contracts, not including legal fees, simply because it did not follow the change management process agreed to in the contract.

These three cases clearly demonstrate the importance of ensuring that change is managed in accordance with the requirements set forth in the contract or the SOW. The companies in these cases wasted millions of dollars on mismanaged projects. Extrapolating these figures across all industry sectors, the impact can easily reach well into the billions or trillions of dollars wasted each year on mismanaged projects.

IDENTIFYING CHANGES

To properly manage project changes, the first step is to identify when a change is proposed or when it occurs. For the purpose of this discussion, *change* is defined as any deviation from the scope agreed to in the SOW (or contract), also referred to as a *cardinal change.*[7] Consider the following three factors when determining whether a change is significant enough to be classified as a cardinal change:[8]

- Has the magnitude of the project work been significantly changed, or will it be?

- Will the change require the procurement of a totally different product or will it alter the quality, character, functionality, or type of work defined in the SOW?

- Does the cost of the proposed change greatly exceed the baseline cost established in the SOW?

If the answer to any of these questions is affirmative, the proposed change can be considered a cardinal change. According to the cardinal change doctrine, contract parties are generally restricted to requesting changes within the general scope defined in the SOW. If a proposed change is determined to be a cardinal change, then the contractor will not be required to implement the change unless specific SOW clauses address how to manage changes of this nature.

The cardinal change doctrine also has legal precedent in the case of *Becho, Inc. v. United States* (2000).[9] In January 1997, the U.S. Army Corps of Engineers contracted Becho to deliver two separate piles of riprap to a quarry in Jackson Hole, Wyoming. The contract required Becho to group the riprap in piles containing materials of dissimilar sizes, in such a way that minimized breakage. The Corps would then pay Becho based on the total number of cubic yards of acceptable material in each pile.

During the course of the project, the Corps determined that some of the material in both piles was unsatisfactory and did not meet the required specifications. The Corps issued a change order that required Becho to remove the unsatisfactory material from the piles and transport it to another location away from the quarry. The change order, however, did not allow for an adjustment in the contract price of the work. Becho agreed to remove the material from the second pile of riprap, but refused to do so for the first pile because the Corps had already accepted and paid for the material.

After removing the material from the second pile, Becho removed its equipment and requested payment for the work. The Corps, however, considered Becho to be in breach of contract because it had not also removed the unsatisfactory material from the first pile. Becho argued in court that the Corps had issued a cardinal change and that Becho was therefore under no obligation to perform the work.

The court recognized the cardinal change doctrine in this case and found in Becho's favor, noting that a cardinal change did not obligate the contractor to perform work outside the general scope of the contract.[10] This issue could have been avoided if the SOW had contained language or a clause specifying how unsatisfactory material was to be handled, including the cost for removal.

Some SOW development teams will choose to identify out-of-scope elements in the SOW. This is essentially a wasted effort that adds no real value to the SOW or the project. A better approach is to make it clear that anything not identified in the SOW is considered out of scope. The project manager or contracting officer's technical representative (COTR) plays a critical role in ensuring that this is clearly communicated to all parties and is adhered to throughout the life of the project. If not, changes on the project can get out of control very quickly. (It should be noted that the COTR's role is specifically to communicate the information to the parties, not to issue the change order. In the federal government, the contracting officer is responsible for issuing any change orders, except when authority is delegated to an administrative contracting officer.[11])

The Big Dig Project, a federal highway project in Boston, Massachusetts, is a great example of what can happen if change is not managed properly. In April 2000, the Federal Highway Administration released an audit report on the project, which identified enormous cost overruns as well as an overall lack of management control. The report concluded that the estimated total cost to complete the project was approximately $14 billion—$11 billion more than the original estimate of $2.6 billion.[12] This was for a single project! Clearly, the additional expenditures caused by the unexpected changes on projects across all industry sectors could easily reach into the trillions of dollars.

MANAGING PROJECT CHANGES

At first glance, the concept of managing change seems simple. So why do so many organizations have such a hard time with it? The reality is that managing change can be one of the most difficult things to do, particularly if your organization has immature project management processes and procedures. The difficulty arises not because the process is technically complex, but rather because of the challenge of getting the project team members to follow the process.

Factors Affecting Change Mismanagement

Factors that contribute to change mismanagement include:

- Lack of a detailed SOW to establish baseline information against which to measure future change

- Lack of a change management section in the SOW that is understood and accepted by all parties involved in the project delivery

- Lack of discipline and rigor among the project team in adhering to and enforcing the change management process

- Poor communications among the project team, causing problems in identifying changes

- Lack of understanding by the project team of what was agreed to in the SOW

- Misinterpretation of changes as not significant enough to warrant or justify a change order.

Each of these factors can easily impede the management of project changes. Thus, it is important to understand what they involve and how they can be avoided on your projects.

Lack of a Detailed SOW

To call a detailed SOW an important factor in managing project change is a tremendous understatement. Without a detailed SOW, it is impossible to determine when a change has occurred and it is impossible to manage the change. It is critical not only to understand when a change occurs, but also to determine how that change is impacting the project's scope, schedule, cost, quality, and manpower.

If an SOW is not in place to establish limits on the project's scope, then essentially all changes are in scope. In this scenario, the scope of the project can quickly grow out of control. Without an SOW to establish a baseline to measure change against, there is no way to manage and quantify the true impact of changes to the project. Having a detailed SOW in place will help establish a baseline to determine when a change has occurred and to measure its impact on the project.

Lack of a Change Management Section in the SOW

Even if a project has an SOW guiding it, there is no guarantee that changes will be managed properly. The SOW can describe the scope of the work in great detail, but if it doesn't address how to identify, review, and approve changes, it could easily contribute to the mismanagement of changes to the project. Having the appropriate change management processes and thresholds in place will help avoid cost overruns.

Lack of Adherence to the Change Management Process

Some projects may have a detailed SOW in place that includes a change management process, but the project team simply isn't following the process defined in the document. This situation is often attributed to a lack of discipline and rigor in the organization, the project manager, or the project team responsible for enforcing the process. If a change process is defined in the SOW, then it must be followed. Otherwise, the team will ignore changes that may drastically increase or decrease the scope of the project. Ignoring the changes also means that no adjustments are being made to the cost, scheduled completion date, or manpower.

If you define a change management process and don't follow it, you set a precedent with the team that managing change is not important. The team will ignore the process, leading to scope creep, cost overruns, schedule slips, poor quality, and poor resource utilization. The change process must be enforced with discipline and rigor to ensure project success. The individual leading the project must not only have strong project management skills, but must also be well-respected by the project team.

Applying the change management process must be an objective driven from the executive leadership of the organization down to the individual team members. Visible support from the top will greatly expedite acceptance of the process at the lower levels of the organization.

Poor Communications

Difficulty in managing change on a project can be amplified by poor communications among the project team members. Lacking mechanisms to ensure that changes are identified and communicated will inhibit the project manager's ability to properly manage changes on the project. To avoid miscommunications, the SOW should address the escalation process that team members should use to identify or request changes. This process will define who can request a change and how to submit it to the appropriate individuals.

Lack of Understanding of the SOW

The project team often lacks an understanding about what was agreed to in the SOW because project managers and organization leaders fail to communicate that information. Some organizations may consider certain information to be confidential and not fully disclose it even to their own personnel. Thus, they either neglect or refuse to provide the project team with a full copy of the SOW. When this occurs, the team goes into the project blind, not knowing what has been agreed to or even what deliverables or services the project is meant to provide.

A simple way to avoid this type of miscommunication is to provide a "cleansed" copy of the approved SOW to each team member, with information specific to their area of responsibility. The cleansed version of the SOW simply omits confidential or proprietary sections as well as information outside the group's area of responsibility.

When team members are aware of what the project is intended to deliver, it is much easier for them to determine when a change or proposed change will impact the agreed-upon SOW. This awareness will help ensure that all changes to the project are captured and properly documented.

Misinterpretation of Changes

Sometimes a proposed change may seem so small or insignificant that it doesn't appear to justify going through the complete change management process. Teams will argue that it will cost more to go through the process than it will to simply document the change. Although this may be true for individual changes, the justification does not hold up against the impact of aggregate changes over time.

A change may seem small or insignificant when proposed, but it may have a cascading impact on other parts of the project. The resulting impact could lead to rework as well as schedule and cost overruns. The cumulative effect of changes could even lead to project failure. Thus, it is imperative that *all* changes be documented and managed according to the agreed-upon change management process, regardless of their size.

TOOLS FOR MANAGING CHANGES

To manage changes properly, standard processes and tools must be in place for documenting and tracking changes to the project. A tool can be defined as a customized template or form used by the project manager to manage change. In addition to the SOW, two primary tools should be used to manage project change: the change order form and the SOW change order tracker.

Change Order Form

The change order form is typically customized to meet an organization's specific change management requirements. The federal government uses Standard Form 30 (SF30), presented in Figure 7-2.[13]

FAR Part 43.301 provides the following guidance regarding the use of the SF30:

> (a)(1) The Standard Form 30 (SF30), Amendment of Solicitation/Modification of Contract, shall (except for the options stated in 43.301(a)(2) or actions processed under Part 15) be used for:
>
> (i) Any amendment to a solicitation;
>
> (ii) Change orders issued under the Changes clause of the contract;
>
> (iii) Any other unilateral contract modification issued under a contract clause authorizing such modification without the consent of the contractor;

FIGURE 7-2
Standard Form 30

AMENDMENT OF SOLICITATION/MODIFICATION OF CONTRACT	1. CONTRACT ID CODE	PAGE OF PAGES

2. AMENDMENT/MODIFICATION NO.	3. EFFECTIVE DATE	4. REQUISITION/PURCHASE REQ. NO.	5. PROJECT NO. *(If applicable)*

6. ISSUED BY	CODE	7. ADMINISTERED BY *(If other than Item 6)*	CODE

8. NAME AND ADDRESS OF CONTRACTOR *(No., street, county, State and ZIP Code)*	(X)	9A. AMENDMENT OF SOLICITATION NO.
		9B. DATED *(SEE ITEM 11)*
		10A. MODIFICATION OF CONTRACT/ORDER NO.
		10B. DATED *(SEE ITEM 13)*

CODE	FACILITY CODE

11. THIS ITEM ONLY APPLIES TO AMENDMENTS OF SOLICITATIONS

☐ The above numbered solicitation is amended as set forth in Item 14. The hour and date specified for receipt of Offers ☐ is extended, ☐ is not extended.

Offers must acknowledge receipt of this amendment prior to the hour and date specified in the solicitation or as amended, by one of the following methods:
(a) By completing items 8 and 15, and returning _____ copies of the amendment; (b) By acknowledging receipt of this amendment on each copy of the offer submitted; or (c) By separate letter or telegram which includes a reference to the solicitation and amendment numbers. FAILURE OF YOUR ACKNOWLEDGMENT TO BE RECEIVED AT THE PLACE DESIGNATED FOR THE RECEIPT OF OFFERS PRIOR TO THE HOUR AND DATE SPECIFIED MAY RESULT IN REJECTION OF YOUR OFFER. If by virtue of this amendment your desire to change an offer already submitted, such change may be made by telegram or letter, provided each telegram or letter makes reference to the solicitation and this amendment, and is received prior to the opening hour and date specified.

12. ACCOUNTING AND APPROPRIATION DATA *(If required)*

**13. THIS ITEM ONLY APPLIES TO MODIFICATION OF CONTRACTS/ORDERS.
IT MODIFIES THE CONTRACT/ORDER NO. AS DESCRIBED IN ITEM 14.**

CHECK ONE	
☐	A. THIS CHANGE ORDER IS ISSUED PURSUANT TO: *(Specify authority)* THE CHANGES SET FORTH IN ITEM 14 ARE MADE IN THE CONTRACT ORDER NO. IN ITEM 10A.
☐	B. THE ABOVE NUMBERED CONTRACT/ORDER IS MODIFIED TO REFLECT THE ADMINISTRATIVE CHANGES *(such as changes in paying office, appropriation date, etc.)* SET FORTH IN ITEM 14, PURSUANT TO THE AUTHORITY OF FAR 43.103(b).
☐	C. THIS SUPPLEMENTAL AGREEMENT IS ENTERED INTO PURSUANT TO AUTHORITY OF:
☐	D. OTHER *(Specify type of modification and authority)*

E. **IMPORTANT:** Contractor ☐ is not, ☐ is required to sign this document and return _____ copies to the issuing office.

14. DESCRIPTION OF AMENDMENT/MODIFICATION *(Organized by UCF section headings, including solicitation/contract subject matter where feasible.)*

Except as provided herein, all terms and conditions of the document referenced in Item 9A or 10A, as heretofore changed, remains unchanged and in full force and effect.

15A. NAME AND TITLE OF SIGNER *(Type or print)*	16A. NAME AND TITLE OF CONTRACTING OFFICER *(Type or print)*
15B. CONTRACTOR/OFFEROR	15C. DATE SIGNED	16B. UNITED STATES OF AMERICA	16C. DATE SIGNED
(Signature of person authorized to sign)		*(Signature of Contracting Officer)*	

NSN 7540-01-152-8070
Previous edition unusable

STANDARD FORM 30 (REV. 10-83)
Prescribed by GSA FAR (48 CFR) 53.243

FIGURE 7-2
Standard Form 30 (continued)

INSTRUCTIONS

Instructions for items other than those that are self-explanatory, are as follows:

(a) Item 1 (Contract ID Code). Insert the contract type identification code that appears in the title block of the contract being modified.

(b) Item 3 (Effective date).

    (1) For a solicitation amendment, change order, or administrative change, the effective date shall be the issue date of the amendment, change order, or administrative change.

    (2) For a supplemental agreement, the effective date shall be the date agreed to by the contracting parties.

    (3) For a modification issued as an initial or confirming notice of termination for the convenience of the Government, the effective date and the modification number of the confirming notice shall be the same as the effective date and modification number of the initial notice.

    (4) For a modification converting a termination for default to a termination for the convenience of the Government, the effective date shall be the same as the effective date of the termination for default.

    (5) For a modification confirming the contacting officer's determination of the amount due in settlement of a contract termination, the effective date shall be the same as the effective date of the initial decision.

(c) Item 6 (Issued By). Insert the name and address of the issuing office. If applicable, insert the appropriate issuing office code in the code block.

(d) Item 8 (Name and Address of Contractor). For modifications to a contract or order, enter the contractor's name, address, and code as shown in the original contract or order, unless changed by this or a previous modification.

(e) Item 9, (Amendment of Solicitation No. - Dated), and 10, (Modification of Contract/Order No. - Dated). Check the appropriate box and in the corresponding blanks insert the number and date of the original solicitation, contract, or order.

(f) Item 12 (Accounting and Appropriation Data). When appropriate, indicate the impact of the modification on each affected accounting classification by inserting one of the following entries:

    (1) Accounting classification
           Net increase $ _____

    (2) Accounting classification
           Net decrease $ _____

NOTE: If there are changes to multiple accounting classifications that cannot be placed in block 12, insert an asterisk and the words "See continuation sheet".

(g) Item 13. Check the appropriate box to indicate the type of modification. Insert in the corresponding blank the authority under which the modification is issued. Check whether or not contractor must sign this document. (See FAR 43.103.)

(h) Item 14 (Description of Amendment/Modification).

    (1) Organize amendments or modifications under the appropriate Uniform Contract Format (UCF) section headings from the applicable solicitation or contract. The UCF table of contents, however, shall not be set forth in this document

    (2) Indicate the impact of the modification on the overall total contract price by inserting one of the following entries:

        (i) Total contract price increased by $ _____

        (ii) Total contract price decreased by $ _____

        (iii) Total contract price unchanged.

    (3) State reason for modification.

    (4) When removing, reinstating, or adding funds, identify the contract items and accounting classifications.

    (5) When the SF 30 is used to reflect a determination by the contracting officer of the amount due in settlement of a contract terminated for the convenience of the Government, the entry in Item 14 of the modification may be limited to --

        (i) A reference to the letter determination; and

        (ii) A statement of the net amount determined to be due in settlement of the contract.

    (6) Include subject matter or short title of solicitation/contract where feasible.

(i) Item 16B. The contracting officer's signature is not required on solicitation amendments. The contracting officer's signature is normally affixed last on supplemental agreements.

STANDARD FORM 30 (REV. 10-83) **BACK**

(iv) Administrative changes such as the correction of typographical mistakes, changes in the paying office, and changes in accounting and appropriation data;

(v) Supplemental agreements (see 43.103); and

(vi) Removal, reinstatement, or addition of funds to a contract.

(2) The SF 30 may be used for:

(i) Modifications that change the price of contracts for the acquisition of petroleum as a result of economic price adjustment;

(ii) Termination notices; and

(iii) Purchase order modifications as specified in 13.302-3.

(3) If it is anticipated that a change will result in a price change, the estimated amount of the price change shall not be shown on copies of SF 30 furnished to the contractor.

(b) The Optional Form 336 (OF336), Continuation Sheet, or a blank sheet of paper, may be used as a continuation sheet for a contract modification.[14]

SOW Change Order Tracker

How does a project get to be a year behind schedule? One day at a time!

—*Anonymous*

This quote speaks volumes on the importance of tracking changes on projects. From the perspective of the project manager, it's easy to get wrapped up in day-to-day management activities and focus exclusively on the day's most urgent issue. But a day-to-day perspective can cause problems for the project over the long run.

Along with SF30, the SOW change order tracker plays an important role in managing project change. This tool assists in tracking all approved and unapproved changes to the project by capturing them in one comprehensive document. Having this information in one place provides a powerful perspective to anyone reviewing the evolution of a project's scope, cost, schedule, and staffing from its original baseline estimates to its completion.

The change order tracker provides several benefits to both the government and the contractor. First, having all the information in one location allows anyone to quickly audit the project to ensure that the final cost is equal to the baseline estimate plus all cost increases attributed to approved change orders. This will confirm that all additional costs were approved by both the government and the contractor, and that no costs were arbitrarily added to the project without prior approval.

Also, if any disputes about increased costs or schedule slips arise between the government and the contractor, the change order tracker can be referenced to quickly identify specifically when the change occurred and its impact on the project.

Another benefit of the change order tracker is that the government and the contractor can build a detailed knowledge base simply by analyzing and comparing the types of changes that arose on similar projects. The respective parties can then use this information to develop future estimates or proposals for similar work. Applying this information on future projects will make project teams more likely to address these issues during the planning phase, which should lead to fewer change orders during project delivery.

The SOW change order tracker can take many different forms, depending on the needs of the organization responsible for managing changes to the project. Figure 7-3 presents a sample SOW change order tracker. This tracker captures basically the same information as the change order form. The difference is that it

FIGURE 7-3
Sample SOW Change Order Tracker

Project Name:
Baseline Cost ($):
Baseline Scheduled Completion Date:
Baseline Staffing (# of Resources):

CO#	Section in SOW	Change Language in the Section of the SOW		Impact (if applicable)					
				Cost		Schedule Completion		Manpower	
		From	To	From	To	From	To	From	To
1									
2									
3									
4									
5									
6									
7									
8									
9									
10									
11									
12									
13									
14									
15									
16									
17									
18									
19									
20									
21									
22									
23									
24									
25									
26									
27									
28									
29									
30									
31									

also shows the cumulative impact of all approved change orders on project cost, schedule, and staffing in a single document.

A change order tracker typically includes the following information:

- Project name

- Baseline project cost from the approved SOW

- Baseline scheduled completion date from the approved SOW

- Baseline staffing (number of resources) from the approved SOW

- Change or contract order (CO) number

- Section of the SOW impacted by the change

- Impact of the change on the language contained in the approved SOW

- Impact of the change on project cost, scheduled completion date, and staffing.

Because this information is obtained directly from either the SOW itself or an approved change order for the project, the project team will not need to generate any additional information. Regardless of the particular structure or format of the tracker, it should always capture the data elements that correspond to the triple constraints of scope, time, and cost.

The process of managing and tracking changes on a project requires a great deal of discipline and rigor on the part of everyone associated with the project. For organizations with immature project management processes and methodologies, implementing a change management process can be difficult. However, if new processes and tools for managing change allow for data to be transferred easily from one form and process to another, without requiring a great deal of additional effort by the team, then they will be much more likely to be accepted.

Simply having the processes and tools in place to manage project change is a step in the right direction, but if no one uses them or if they are applied incorrectly, the effort it takes to get to this point will be wasted. When introducing or implementing a detailed change process, it is important to consider the organizational transition to and acceptance of the process. Achieving acceptance at both the organizational and individual levels is a major factor in ensuring that project changes are managed appropriately. When they are, projects will benefit tremendously.

NOTES

[1] General Services Administration, Department of Defense, and National Aeronautics and Space Administration, *Federal Acquisition Regulation*, vol. 1–51, March 2005, 43.201. Online at *https://www.acquisition.gov/far/current/pdf/FAR.pdf* (accessed February 2012).

[2] "Lack of Change Order Sinks Damage Claim," *Civil Engineering*, August 1998, Volume 68, Number 8, p. 32.

[3] 'Lectric Law Library, "The 'Lectric Law Library's Lexicon on Sovereign Immunity." Online at *http://www.lectlaw.com/def2/s103.htm* (accessed February 2012).

[4] "Subcontractor Cannot Recover Payment for Work Performed Outside of Contract," *Civil Engineering*, July 2001, p. 78.

[5] Answers.com™ Business and Finance, Law Encyclopedia, "Quantum Meruit." Online at *http://www.answers.com/topic/quantum-meruit* (accessed February 2012).

[6] "Recovery for Unclaimed Work Denied," *Civil Engineering*, March 1999, p. 75.

[7] Loulakis, Michael C., Simon J. Santiago. "Cardinal Change Doctrine Excuses Performance." *Civil Engineering*, September 2001, p. 96.

[8] Ibid.

[9] Ibid.

[10] Ibid.

[11] General Services Administration, Department of Defense, and National Aeronautics and Space Administration, *Federal Acquisition Regulation,* vol. 1–51, March 2005, 43.202. Online at *https://www.acquisition.gov/far/current/pdf/FAR.pdf* (accessed February 2012).

[12] The Associated Press. "Boston must dig deeper to pay for 'Big Dig.'" *USA Today,* 6 April 2000, p. 11A.

[13] General Services Administration, Department of Defense, and National Aeronautics and Space Administration, *Federal Acquisition Regulation,* vol. 1–51, March 2005, 43.201. Online at h*ttps://www.acquisition.gov/far/current/pdf/FAR.pdf* (accessed December 2011). Form can be found online at *http://contacts.gsa.gov/webforms.nsf/0/0B25C456DA47961385256A1F0 05A981D/$file/SF%2030.pdf* (accessed February 2012).

[14] Ibid., 43.301. Online at *https://www.acquisition.gov/far/current/pdf/FAR.pdf* (accessed February 2012).

APPENDIX A
SOW Review

This appendix is divided into three parts:

- Part A is the first draft of an SOW for the development and presentation of a training course. (The pricing portion of the schedule is also included.)

- Part B is a detailed critique of the SOW.

- Part C demonstrates how the SOW might be revised to provide a clear and coherent description of the requirement.

PART A: THE SOW

This is the first draft of an SOW for the development and presentation of a procurement training course for technical personnel who have to develop contract requirements and manage contracts, or are otherwise involved in the procurement process.

As you read Part A, make notes of your critique of this document. Then match your notes with the critique in Part B. Depending on your background, you may find more or less to critique than will be found in Part B. Parts A and B demonstrate how to analyze an SOW critically to determine how well the SOW describes the work requirement.

SOW FOR ACQUISITION TRAINING FOR MAR PROJECT MANAGERS

SECTION B—SUPPLIES OR SERVICES AND PRICE/COSTS

B.1 CONSIDERATION AND PAYMENT

MINIMUM QUANTITY

LINE NO.	DESCRIPTION	UIO	NO.	Unit Amount	Grand Total
1	Design, development, production and delivery of course materials	Job	1	$_____	$_____
2	Presentation of course a. Williamsburg, VA b. Philadelphia, PA	 Job Job	 1 1	 $_____ $_____	 $_____ $_____

OPTION QUANTITY

3	Presentation of course a. Gettysburg, PA b. Stroudsburg, PA	 Job Job	 1 1	 $_____ $_____	 $_____ $_____

SECTION C—DESCRIPTION/SPECIFICATION/WORK STATEMENT

C.1 STATEMENT OF WORK

C.1.1 BACKGROUND

The Agency, Mid-Atlantic Region (MAR), comprises offices and sites in the States of Pennsylvania, Maryland, Virginia, and West Virginia with a regional office in Philadelphia, PA. The purpose of the training is to instruct the Mid-Atlantic Regional personnel on the basic methods and processes of acquiring products and services and to outline their respective responsibilities.

The Agency contracting is governed by the Federal Acquisition Regulations (FAR), Departmental Acquisition Regulations (DAR) and Agency Guideline #60. Agency/MAR believes that personnel involved in the acquisition process must have a basic understanding of their role and authority in the process as well as the role and authority of the Contracting Officer.

This four and one-half day course will be attended by Superintendents, Facility Managers, Chiefs of Maintenance, Engineers, Project Managers, Contract Specialists, Purchasing Agents, Division Chiefs and Administrative Officers from the Regional office and all local offices within the region who have, or soon will have, responsibilities for initiating and obtaining a mechanism to acquire products or services and to manage the work called for in the contract. Project manager is another term for the Agency person who manages work accomplished by others through contracts and purchase orders.

Typically, participants in this acquisition course will not have attended prior acquisition training, but will have been responsible for all or part of a project involving a commercial contractor.

The Agency/MAR anticipates that the first course will be conducted in commercial facilities (acquired under separate contract) in Williamsburg, VA approximately 3-4 months after the award of this contract. Other sites include Philadelphia, Gettysburg, and Stroudsburg, PA. It is anticipated that the class will be limited to 25 participants.

C.1.2 OBJECTIVES

The objective of this contract is to acquire the services of a commercial contractor to design and conduct a comprehensive course which includes, but is not limited to the following:

1. Understanding the Acquisition Process and the Role of Personnel in the process;
2. Planning for and describing the requirements;
3. Types of specifications/statements of work;
4. Writing the statement of work/specification;
5. Publicizing the requirement to obtain competition;
6. Socioeconomic programs;
7. Developing evaluation criteria and source selection plans;
8. Establishing the Government cost estimate;
9. Methods of open-market acquisition;
10. Types of contracts and their implications for performance;
11. The solicitation process;
12. Conducting the technical evaluation of proposals, negotiation, and source selection (to include the A/E selection process);
13. Interpreting the contract and preparing for the job of COR;
14. Monitoring the contractor's work;
15. Solving problems in contract administration;
16. Remedies for nonperformance;
17. Identifying and dealing with fraud, waste, and abuse;

18. Closing out the contract;

19. Procurement integrity;

20. Role of COR vs. Project Inspection; and

21. Conduction of preconstruction/post award conferences.

C.1.3 TASKS TO BE ACCOMPLISHED

C.1.3.1 The contractor shall design, reproduce, and furnish copies of a student course book for all participants in appropriate-sized three-ring binders identified with the Agency logo and title cover art. One camera-ready copy shall be furnished to the Contracting Officer (CO). Thirty copies will be required prior to commencement of the first course. Additional copies will be required at the commencement of subsequent courses. The Contractor shall be required to submit two (2) draft copies of the student course book for review by Agency/MAR personnel prior to final printing. The Contractor shall also be required to meet with Agency/MAR personnel in Philadelphia, PA two (2) times for a period of 2 consecutive days prior to the final approval of the student handbook.

C.1.3.2 The Contractor shall provide qualified instructor personnel to teach the 4 1/2 day course. The training sessions shall commence promptly at 8:00 a.m. and conclude at 4:00 p.m. The contractor's instructor personnel shall be responsible for understanding the course materials, be knowledgeable in Federal, Departmental, and Agency contracting regulations, and be qualified to conduct the course to classes up to 25 adult participants.

C.1.3.3 The Contractor shall deliver all course materials to the designated Agency/MAR training facility in respective locations prior to the start of each training session, set up the training facility, arrange furniture, as necessary, lay out participant materials, and prepare equipment and instructor aids. During the training sessions, the Contractor shall account for participant attendance by assuring the completion of Agency registration forms. At the commencement of each course, the instructor shall inform the participants that the requirements for receiving a Course Completion Certificate are as follows:

1. Three-fourths or more of the course must be attended and completed.

2. A course evaluation questionnaire must be completed and provided to the instructor at the conclusion of the course.

Immediately following each session, the Contractor's instructor personnel shall leave the training facility neat without trash, including used flip chart sheets stowed in the trash cans and any extra student materials boxed and returned to the Contractor's office. Location for temporary storage or delivery of excess student materials shall be determined by the COR prior to completion of each session.

C.1.3.4 Evaluation Questionnaire

C.1.3.4.1 The Contractor shall prepare a course evaluation questionnaire to be completed by all participants at the end of each course. The questionnaire shall be directed toward eliciting participants' comments as to the value of the material taught, changes and additions recommended, and the quality of the instructor personnel. The proposed questionnaire shall be furnished to the COR for approval by 30 calendar days prior to the first course, and any changes or revisions directed by the CO shall be incorporated by the Contractor. In addition, any changes or revisions directed by the CO from time to time shall be incorporated for use in subsequent course sessions. These changes will be considered minor or major as defined below.

C.1.3.4.2 The original copy of all participants' questionnaires shall be submitted to the COR within the timeframe called for in the contract after completion of each course session, together with the Contractor's assessment of student comments and recommendations for possible changes and revision to the course, if any.

C.1.3.5 Revision to Course Materials

The Contractor may be required, from time to time, to modify the training materials at the direction of the CO. The Contractor shall be responsible for ensuring that any such modifications are reflected in the course materials provided to the participants. Within 10 calendar days of receiving an order to develop technical changes to the material of the course, the Contractor shall submit a draft version of modified materials to the COR for approval. The Contractor shall provide a final copy of the revised course materials, incorporating comments received, to the COR within 2 business days of receipt of those comments. For purpose of proposal preparation, course materials revisions are quantified as follows:

1. Minor Revisions—The Contractor may be required, from time to time, to provide minor revisions to the training materials upon the request of the COR. During the contract period, it is anticipated that approximately 60 man-hours per year will be required for these revisions. Each revision would affect up to 10 percent of the total course material and it is estimated there would be approximately 2 minor revisions per year. The cost for the minor revisions should be included in the fixed price for course presentation. Note: The estimate of the man-hours reflected for the minor revisions is information which is advisory only and is not to be considered as the sole basis for the development of a proposal. Sufficient detail of the proposed approach to task accomplishment must be reflected in the proposal.

C.1.3.6 Course Materials Masters

At the termination of the contract, the contractor shall furnish to the Agency/MAR a complete master set of all course materials, visual aids, and any original art work such as binder graphics, used during the course of instruction in camera-ready, reproducible form. The Contractor shall also furnish to the Agency/MAR an electronic file of all course materials.

C.2 QUALITY OF PERFORMANCE

C.2.1 Monitoring Performance

C.2.1.1 During the life of the contract, the Contractor shall monitor the training courses pursuant to the requirement of the contract to assure that the quality of instruction and materials used is adequate. The instructor shall as a minimum:

C.2.1.1.1 Maintain control of the learning time so that the presentation of information and exercises remains organized and timely; key points and course objectives are met, and breaks are provided within the overall course schedule; and distractions, such as questions that are of minimal interest to the class as a whole and that can be answered later and/or individually are consistently controlled.

C.2.1.1.2   Observe the effect of the instruction on the class and reasonably attempt to clarify, provide instructions, or in some other way, modify the course to help correct problems and improve the participants' opportunity to learn.

C.2.1.1.3   Involve the participants in sufficient exercise and practice with the subject matter to reinforce the understanding and recall of information.

C.2.1.1.4   Act to improve or later correct errors or other problems that may occur during the training session.

C.2.1.2   The Contractor shall meet with the COR from time to time regarding updating, changes or modifications of instructional materials presented. However, no changes involving additional cost to the Government shall be made except pursuant to the Changes clause of the contract.

C.3   CONTRACTOR-FURNISHED MATERIALS

The COR will review contractor-furnished materials for each course session for quality and accuracy. Should errors occur, such as omissions, incorrect collation, illegibility, and packaging, that are caused by the Contractor, the Agency/MAR will reject the material and the Contractor shall correct all errors prior to the beginning of each course session at no cost to the Government.

The Contractor shall deliver one copy of these materials to the COR for review, 30 days prior to the first day of each course session. The COR will comment on quality and accuracy of the materials no later than five business days before the course session is scheduled to start.

C.4   GOVERNMENT-FURNISHED PROPERTY AND SERVICES

The Government will furnish the following:

1. Training facilities

2. Copy of the Departmental Acquisition Regulations

3. Copy of Agency Guideline #60

4. Training certificates

5. Where portions of course materials include Agency publication, the Agency will furnish copies for duplication, instruction, and inclusion into training manual.

6. Consultation services of Agency subject specialists, as determined necessary by the COR.

C.5 CONTRACTOR-FURNISHED PROPERTY AND SERVICES

The Contractor shall provide the professional services of experts, instructors, lecturers, educators, and related support services to provide training in procurement/acquisition management. The Contractor shall furnish the training materials plus any other reference identified elsewhere in this statement of work.

C.6 MEETINGS AND TRAVEL

The Contractor shall meet with the Agency/MAR COR and CO a minimum of two times and a maximum of four times during the period of the contract regarding updating, changes or modifications of instructional materials presented at the direction of the COR. (Refer to Section C.1.3.5 of the statement of work for additional information pertinent to this requirement.)

C.7 COURSE TIMES AND PLACES

It is anticipated that the first course will be conducted in Williamsburg, VA approximately 3-4 months after award of the contract. Subsequent courses will be held in Philadelphia, Gettysburg, and Stroudsburg, PA; however, no definite dates have been set. For purposes of preparing a proposal, the offeror shall assume that a course will be held in Philadelphia approximately 3-4 months after the one in Williamsburg, VA; the one in Gettysburg 5-6 months after the one in Philadelphia; and the one in Stroudsburg 3-4 months after the one in Gettysburg.

C.8 DELIVERY SCHEDULE

Within 15 calendar days after award of the contract, the Contractor shall submit to the COR (copy to the CO) a delivery schedule of all tasks incorporating all required delivery times stated in this solicitation. The COR will have 15 calendar days for inspection and acceptance.

PART B: SOW CRITIQUE

The following is a critique of the SOW set forth in Part A. For easier reference, the draft SOW paragraphs are repeated, with the critique comments following each paragraph.

SOW FOR ACQUISITION TRAINING FOR MAR PROJECT MANAGERS

SECTION B—SUPPLIES OR SERVICES AND PRICE/COSTS

B.1 CONSIDERATION AND PAYMENT

MINIMUM QUANTITY

LINE NO.	DESCRIPTION	UIO	NO.	Unit Amount	Grand Total
1	Design, development, production and delivery of course materials	Job	1	$_____	$_____
2	Presentation of course a. Williamsburg, VA b. Philadelphia, PA	 Job Job	 1 1	 $_____ $_____	 $_____ $_____

OPTION QUANTITY

| 3 | Presentation of course
a. Gettysburg, PA
b. Stroudsburg, PA |
Job
Job |
1
1 |
$_____
$_____ |
$_____
$_____ |

Comments:

Other clauses in this RFP indicate that the contract will be a fixed-price, indefinite quantity contract. As such the Government is required to order the minimum quantity (line items 1 and 2) and cannot order more than the maximum quantity (line item 3) at the offered price. It is not necessary, therefore to establish item 3 as an option quantity. This requirement should be re-examined.

SECTION C—DESCRIPTION/SPECIFICATION/WORK STATEMENT

C.1 STATEMENT OF WORK

C.1.1 BACKGROUND

The Agency, Mid-Atlantic Region (Agency/MAR), comprises offices and sites in the States of Pennsylvania, Maryland, Virginia, and West Virginia with a regional office in Philadelphia, PA. The purpose of the training is to instruct the Mid-Atlantic Regional personnel on the basic methods and processes of acquiring products and services and to outline their respective responsibilities.

Comments:

The first sentence of this paragraph is background information, but the second sentence is better used as introductory material. An SOW should begin with an introductory statement that explains the nature of the requirement. For example:

INTRODUCTION

This requirement is for the development and presentation of a comprehensive 4 1/2-day procurement training course for Project Managers and other personnel of the Agency/MAR.

The Agency contracting is governed by the Federal Acquisition Regulations (FAR), Departmental Acquisition Regulations (DAR) and Agency Guideline #60. The Agency/MAR believes that personnel involved in the acquisition process must have a basic understanding of their role and authority in the process as well as the role and authority of the Contracting Officer.

Comments:

The Introduction is followed by a Background section that explains how the requirement developed. The Background section should contain only historical information. Do not address the current requirements in the Background section. Current requirements are addressed in the body of the SOW in the section that describes the tasks to be accomplished. For example:

BACKGROUND

The Agency/MAR consists of the offices and sites in the states of Pennsylvania, Maryland, Virginia, and West Virginia, with a regional office in Philadelphia, PA. Agency/MAR procurement requirements encompass the entire spectrum of Federal contracting, including construction contracts. The Agency/MAR believes that personnel involved in the acquisition process must have a basic understanding of their role and authority in the process as well as the role and authority of the Contracting Officer.

The Background section should be as short as possible. Usually no more than two or three paragraphs are necessary to explain the origin of the current requirement. Note that both the Introduction and the Background can be developed from the first two paragraphs of C.1.1.

This four and one-half day course will be attended by Superintendents, Facility Managers, Chiefs of Maintenance, Engineers, Project Managers, Contract Specialists, Purchasing Agents, Division Chiefs and Administrative Officers from the Regional office and all offices within the region who have, or soon will have, responsibilities for initiating and obtaining a mechanism to acquire products or services and to manage the work called for in the contract. Project manager is another term for the Agency person who manages work accomplished by others through contracts and purchase orders.

Comments:

This is not background information. It establishes who will attend the course that is to be developed. This information should be presented as part of the task that describes the course development. Unfortunately, this SOW does not specifically identify course development as a task (see C.1.3), but it should have and that is where this information should be.

Including the Contracting Officer, Contract Specialists, and Purchasing Agents as participants in the proposed course reveals a problem in the approach to this requirement. Procurement training requirements differ depending on the category of personnel involved. Contracting Officers require detailed training in all areas of procurement. The training requirements for Contract Specialists (who write formal contracts) and Purchasing Agents (who deal only with small purchases) are different. An Engineer or Project Manager, acting as a Contracting Officer's Representative (COR), requires detailed training in those areas for which they are responsible, such as developing the SOW, proposal evaluation, and contracts management. Superintendents, Facility Managers, Chiefs of Maintenance, supervisors and other management personnel do not need detailed training. They need to understand the process and its terminology, but not in the same detail as the others. Mixed participation, as suggested here, will leave some participants feeling that there was not enough detail and others feeling that there was too much detail. This requirement for mixed course participation should be re-evaluated.

Typically, participants in this acquisition course will not have attended prior acquisition training, but will have been responsible for all or part of a project involving a commercial contractor.

Comments:

What a strange statement! Taken literally this sentence means that Agency/MAR procurements have been conducted in the past by people with no acquisition training at all. This might be understandable for non-contracting personnel, but this paragraph also included all of the contracting personnel. This kind of statement illustrates the need for an objective review of an SOW before it is published. A revision should be made in this paragraph, or the paragraph referring to the course participants, to remove the implication that the Agency/MAR contracting personnel have never received any acquisition training.

This is not background information. It describes course participants and should be presented as part of the task that describes the course development.

The Agency/MAR anticipates that the first course will be conducted in commercial facilities (acquired under separate contract) in Williamsburg, VA approximately 3-4 months after the award of this contract. Other sites include Philadelphia, Gettysburg, and Stroudsburg, PA. It is anticipated that the class will be limited to 25 participants.

Comments:

This is not background information—it refers to the current requirement. Paragraph C.7 also addresses this information. The first two sentences should be incorporated into C.7, particularly the reference to commercial training facilities. The last sentence relates to course development and presentation and should be included in the appropriate task requirement.

This paragraph appears to be in conflict with paragraph B.1 of the RFP. Paragraph B.1 establishes (for pricing purposes) a requirement for two course presentations with a option for two additional presentations. This paragraph appears to establish a requirement for four presentations. Conflicting requirements create uncertainty as to the real requirement. An SOW should be a stand-alone document. It should provide the what, where, when, and how of contract performance. Each uncertainty introduced by the wording of the SOW is a potential contract problem.

The SOW should differentiate between firm requirements and options. Do not repeat the wording of contract clauses, but in this instance a few sentences would have made the requirement clear and eliminated the need to search the rest of the RFP to determine what the requirement really is.

C.1.2 OBJECTIVES

The objective of this contract is to acquire the services of a commercial contractor to design and conduct a comprehensive course which includes, but is not limited to the following:

1. Understanding the Acquisition Process and the Role of Personnel in the process;
2. Planning for and describing the requirements;
3. Types of specifications/statements of work;
4. Writing the statement of work/specification;
5. Publicizing the requirement to obtain competition;
6. Socioeconomic programs;
7. Developing evaluation criteria and source selection plans;
8. Establishing the Government cost estimate;
9. Methods of open-market acquisition;
10. Types of contracts and their implications for performance;
11. The solicitation process;
12. Conducting the technical evaluation of proposals, negotiation, and source selection (to include the A/E selection process);
13. Interpreting the contract and preparing for the job of COR;
14. Monitoring the contractor's work;
15. Solving problems in contract administration;

16. Remedies for nonperformance;

17. Identifying and dealing with fraud, waste, and abuse;

18. Closing out the contract;

19. Procurement integrity;

20. Role of COR vs. Project Inspection; and

21. Conduction of preconstruction/post award conferences.

Comments:

This SOW is for a fixed-price contract. Your requirements must be definitive. Do not use the phrase, "includes, but is not limited to." This phrase is not definite enough for use with this type contract. This phrase is usually used when you want to provide information, but you do not want to be accountable for its accuracy. If you are going to use a fixed-price contract, however, you are responsible for the accuracy of the information provided. A suggestion as to how this might be resolved is set forth in the discussion of how the SOW was revised, in Part C of this Appendix.

Another problem with listing topics to be addressed is that you must provide a clear description of the topic, one that the contractor can understand. This has not been done well here. For example:

- *Topic 2, Planning for and describing the requirements.* This topic involves discussing the types of specifications/statements of work (Topic 3) and how to write them (Topic 4). Does Topic 2 contemplate something in addition?

- *Topic 9, Methods of open-market acquisition.* Normally a discussion of the types of procurement methods would include a discussion of the solicitation process (Topic 11) related to each method. Is there a reason why they are listed separately?

- *Topic 13, Interpreting the contract and preparing for the job of COR.* It is not clear what is intended here. The COR's responsibilities usually begin during the planning process, but this topic indicates that it is related to the administration of the contract. It is likely that what was intended was a discussion of how to prepare for contract administration, but that is not what is said. Do not use ambiguous wording.

- *Topic 15, Solving problems in contract administration.* This wording is too general. It could include Topics 13, 14, 16, 17, 19, and 20.

- *Topic 18, Closing out the contract.* This topic is primarily a contracting officer matter, and could be dealt with under Topic 10, Types of contracts, if it is needed at all.

- *Topic 20, Role of COR vs Project Inspection.* Unless this refers to construction contracts it is difficult to determine what this topic is to address. Since the Background section did not identify the kinds of procurements made by the Agency/MAR, contractors will have to guess at the meaning of this topic. This is not a clearly stated requirement.

- *Topic 21, Conduction of preconstruction/post award conferences.* Do not invent words. Conduction is a noun meaning transmission or conducting of heat or electricity, etc. It is not a verb. Use proper English. This illustrates another problem. When listing items for a requirement of this nature, it is often assumed that you are listing the requirements in the order you want them presented. This is a subtopic of a discussion of the solicitation process and should be addressed earlier.

When establishing a training requirement, carefully consider the relationship of the number of topics to be addressed and the time allotted for their presentation. This requirement is excessive for a 4 1/2 day presentation. Can a contractor present all of this information in 4 1/2 days? Of course a contractor can do this.

If the instructor talks fast enough, it can be done in 3 1/2 days. The real question is will any learning take place? At the very best this requirement is for a broad overview of the procurement process. There will be little time for effective exercises or other learning reinforcement. As noted earlier, these training requirements differ depending on the part the participants play in the procurement process. Even though courses of this nature are common in the Government, this requirement should be re-evaluated with respect to what you want the participants to learn.

Finally, paragraph C.1.2 should be part of the description of the first task under the contract—develop a training course that addresses the following issues—rather than a contract objective. Course development is an important task under this contract.

C.1.3   TASKS TO BE ACCOMPLISHED

C.1.3.1   The contractor shall design, reproduce, and furnish copies of a student course book for all participants in appropriate-sized three-ring binders identified with the Agency logo and title cover art. One camera-ready copy shall be furnished to the Contracting Officer (CO). Thirty copies will be required prior to commencement of the first course. Additional copies will be required at the commencement of subsequent courses. The Contractor shall be required to submit two (2) draft copies of the student course book for review by Agency/MAR personnel prior to final printing. The Contractor shall also be required to meet with Agency/MAR personnel in Philadelphia, PA two (2) times for a period of 2 consecutive days prior to the final approval of the student handbook.

Comments:

The first and fifth sentences refer to a student course book, the last sentence refers to a student handbook. Wording must be consistent. A handbook and a course book can be two different items.

The second sentence requires a camera-ready copy (student course book) for the CO, but doesn't indicate when or why. Is this a courtesy copy or for review purposes? This is the only instance in this SOW in which a delivery is made directly to the Contracting Officer. It should be explained.

The third sentence states, "Thirty copies (student course book) will be furnished prior to commencement of the first course." Paragraph C.1.3.2 states that class size will not exceed 25 persons. What are the extra books for? In addition, the use of "will" instead of "shall" is inappropriate.

The fourth sentence refers to "additional copies." Is this a requirement for 30 books, as stated in the preceding sentence, or 25 books, as stated in C.1.3.2? In addition, the use of "will" instead of "shall" is inappropriate.

The fifth sentence states, "The Contractor shall be required to submit two (2) draft copies of the student course book for review by Agency/MAR personnel prior to final printing." The phrase, "prior to final printing" indicates that this is intended to be the final copy. Is there a requirement for review and approval? When are these draft copies to be submitted? If this is meant to be the review copy, how long will it take for the review and how much time will the contractor have to revise the material? Why isn't the COR reviewing this? Who are the Agency/ MAR personnel? What is their authority and responsibility?

The fifth and final sentence requires two meetings, but doesn't indicate the purpose of the meetings or when they will be held. "Prior to final approval" is not definite enough; are these meetings to be held before or after submission of the two draft copies? Two times for a period of two days equals a total of four days; what are they going to talk about for four days? The use of the word "also" indicates that the meetings are separate from the review mentioned in the previous sentence. This is grossly unclear. Keep in mind that the contractor must come up with a fixed price for all of this effort.

C.1.3.2 The Contractor shall provide qualified instructor personnel to teach the 4 1/2 day course. The training sessions shall commence promptly at 8:00 a.m. and conclude at 4:00 p.m. The contractor's instructor personnel shall be responsible for understanding the course materials, be knowledgeable in Federal, Departmental, and Agency contracting regulations, and be qualified to conduct the course to classes up to 25 adult participants.

Comments:

This is supposed to be a task, but it does not identify specific work to be accomplished. Instead it provides criteria to be met in two different areas, instructor qualifications and course development. The first sentence requires qualified instructors, and then indicates the course length. The second sentence states the timing of classes (but fails to account for the 1/2 day). The last sentence shifts back to instructor qualifications, and finishes with class size. This is mixing apples and oranges. The description of required instructor qualifications should be separate from the description of the course length, timing, and size. But the major problem with this paragraph is that although it is listed as subparagraph C.1.3.2, under paragraph C.1.3, Tasks to be Accomplished, it does not describe a task to be accomplished. This paragraph should be deleted and the information more appropriately placed in the SOW.

C.1.3.2 The Contractor shall provide qualified instructor personnel to teach the 4 1/2 day course. The training sessions shall commence promptly at 8:00 a.m. and conclude at 4:00 p.m. The contractor's instructor personnel shall be responsible for understanding the course materials, be knowledgeable in Federal, Departmental, and Agency contracting regulations, and be qualified to conduct the course to classes up to 25 adult participants.

C.1.3.3 The Contractor shall deliver all course materials to the designated Agency/MAR training facility in respective locations prior to the start of each training session, set up the training facility, arrange furniture, as necessary, lay out participant materials, and prepare equipment and instructor aids. During the training sessions, the Contractor shall account for participant attendance by assuring the completion of Agency registration forms. At the commencement of each course, the instructor shall inform the participants that the requirements for receiving a Course Completion Certificate are as follows:

1. Three-fourths or more of the course must be attended and completed.
2. A course evaluation questionnaire must be completed and provided to the instructor at the conclusion of the course.

Comments:

The first sentence has to do with the delivery of materials and set-up of the classrooms. The second sentence has to do with registration. The third sentence has to do with informing participants of the course completion requirements. These are mixed requirements and should be separated.

A requirement for 75 percent attendance to earn full credit indicates a lack of dedication to ensuring that participants learn anything. 75 percent equals 1 1/3 days of absence. In a 4 1/2-day course this means missing a lot. In an overview course such as this, any absence of more than 1/2 day means a significant learning loss. This requirement should be reconsidered.

Immediately following each session, the Contractor's instructor personnel shall leave the training facility neat without trash, including used flip chart sheets stowed in the trash cans and any extra student materials boxed and returned to the Contractor's office. Location for temporary storage or delivery of excess student materials shall be determined by the COR prior to completion of each session.

Comments:

The first sentence is so garbled that it has minimal meaning. Where is the instructor supposed to dump the trash, if not in the trash cans? This is probably a valid requirement that would be better explained in two separate sentences.

The second sentence uses the acronym COR, but doesn't explain what it means. All acronyms should be explained the first time they are used. This is important in this SOW because of the unexplained interplay between the CO, COR, and Agency/MAR personnel.

The last sentence uses the phrase, "Location for temporary storage or delivery of excess material"—what does this mean?

Subparagraph C.1.3.3 is supposed to be a task under paragraph C.1.3, Tasks to be Accomplished. This subparagraph, however, addresses three different requirements, delivery of course materials and class set-up, Course Completion Certificates, and classroom clean-up after completion of the course. None of these requirements is a task in and of itself, and describing them together is another case of mixing apples and oranges. These requirements should be discussed separately under the task of course presentation (which is never identified as a task in this SOW).

C.1.3.4   Evaluation Questionnaire

C.1.3.4.1   The Contractor shall prepare a course evaluation questionnaire to be completed by all participants at the end of each course. The questionnaire shall be directed toward eliciting participants' comments as to the value of the material taught, changes and additions recommended, and the quality of the instructor personnel. The proposed questionnaire shall be furnished to the COR for approval by 30 calendar days prior to the first course, and any changes or revisions directed by the CO shall be incorporated by the Contractor. In addition, any changes or revisions directed by the CO from time to time shall be incorporated for use in subsequent course sessions. These changes will be considered minor or major as defined below.

Comments:

The third sentence requires a submission to the COR (COR still not defined) and then talks about changes by the CO. Who is in charge here? The relationship between the CO and COR should be explained. When will the CO-directed changes be provided to the contractor? If changes are made there must be enough time for the contractor to make the changes and print up the requisite number of questionnaires for classroom use.

The fourth sentence talks about further changes, from time to time, but it is not clear what is being changed. Surely the questionnaire will not require continual changes. The last sentence indicates that minor and major changes will be defined below, but no definition of major changes is provided (see paragraph C.1.3.5). Does the SOW contemplate major and minor changes to the questionnaire? This doesn't make much sense.

C.1.3.4.2 The original copy of all participants' questionnaires shall be submitted to the COR within the timeframe called for in the contract after completion of each course session, together with the Contractor's assessment of student comments and recommendations for possible changes and revision to the course, if any.

Comments:

If you are going to reference a requirement elsewhere in the SOW or contract, make a specific reference rather than a general one. Identify the paragraph or clause number, as appropriate.

It should be noted that the SOW does not provide a time frame for after-course submission of the questionnaires and contractor's assessment anywhere else in the SOW. This illustrates one of the problems with making vague references. A failure to follow through with the referenced information is difficult to catch, on review, because of the lack of a specific reference.

C.1.3.5 Revision to Course Materials

The Contractor may be required, from time to time, to modify the training materials at the direction of the CO. The Contractor shall be responsible for ensuring that any such modifications are reflected in the course materials provided to the participants. Within 10 calendar days of receiving an order to develop technical changes to the material of the course, the Contractor shall submit a draft version of modified materials to the COR for approval. The Contractor shall provide a final copy of the revised course materials, incorporating comments received, to the COR within 2 business days of receipt of those comments. For purpose of proposal preparation, course materials revisions are quantified as follows:

1. Minor Revisions—The Contractor may be required, from time to time, to provide minor revisions to the training materials upon the request of the COR. During the contract period, it is anticipated that approximately 60 man-hours per year will be required for these revisions. Each revision would affect up to 10 percent of the total course material and it is estimated there would be approximately 2 minor revisions per year. The cost for the minor revisions should be included in the fixed price for course presentation. Note: The estimate of the man-hours reflected for the minor revisions is information which is advisory only and is not to be considered as the sole basis for the development of a proposal. Sufficient detail of the proposed approach to task accomplishment must be reflected in the proposal.

Comments:

1st paragraph. The relationship of the COR and CO in the modification process is not clear. Does the COR review and the CO approve? If so, this is not clear in the SOW.

1st paragraph. Ten days to draft a change is reasonable, but only if they are working days. Depending on when the change is received, the 10-calendar day period could automatically be reduced to 8 working days or even 6 or 7 depending on holidays (contractor personnel get weekends and holidays off too). Keep your terminology consistent. Do not mix calendar days and work (business) days. The use of calendar days is deceptive, because there appears to be more working time than is actually available. Use either business days or working days.

1st paragraph. How long will the Government take to review the changed material? This could be important if the change is directed shortly before a scheduled course presentation. The contractor must be given enough time to make any required changes and print and deliver the changed material.

1st paragraph. The requirement for a final copy of the revised materials within 2 business days is not reasonable. The contractor must decipher the comments and then make the changes. Even if the comments were explicit word changes, two business days is not enough time. If the comments are of the nature, "add coverage of this," or "explain this," or "add more emphasis here," as is often the case, the contractor is going to need significantly more time. If you put unreasonable time requirements in your SOW, do not be surprised if you get unreasonable results.

2nd paragraph. Paragraph C.1.3.4.1 indicated that minor and major revisions would be defined. The last sentence of the 1st paragraph indicates the same, but the 2nd paragraph only addresses minor revisions. It is questionable, however, that there needs to be a distinction between major and minor changes, particularly given the definition of what constitutes a minor change. A 10 percent change in a textbook can hardly be called a minor modification. This would be the equivalent of a 10-page change in a 100 page text. There also seems to be little basis for the 60 man-hour figure. How can the Government estimate how long it will take to make an unknown change? This might be possible if the buying activity had a lot of experience with procurement training courses, but the SOW indicates that there has not been any previous acquisition training provided to the Agency/MAR personnel.

2nd paragraph. The definition of minor modification presents a real problem regarding the validity of the proposed contract. The concept of pre-pricing undefined changes is not valid in a fixed-price contract. Any change to the scope of work of a fixed-price contract must be accomplished by a supplemental agreement or a change order issued under the Changes clause of the contract. In any case, the price and delivery times are subject to negotiation at that time, not in advance of contract award.

2nd paragraph. The basis for estimating the extent of the "minor revisions" is questionable. In fact, with a training course of this nature, there is little likelihood of any changes being required to the textbook itself. At best, this is a survey, or overview course, and while changes do occur in procurement regulations, few are of such magnitude that they would affect the text of an overview course. Most changes will be such that they can be handled from the podium or by a hand-out. So what effect will this requirement have? It will permit, even require, contractors to increase the price per presentation with little likelihood that there will be significant costs incurred. This could be a windfall for the contractor.

It should also be noted that in the first paragraph changes are directed by the CO and in the second paragraph changes are directed by the COR. It could be that the first paragraph is intended to define major changes and the second paragraph to define minor changes. A good SOW, however, does not require the reader to extrapolate the meaning of the requirement.

The last sentence of the first paragraph and all of the second paragraph do not belong in the SOW. These are proposal preparation instructions and belong in Section L of the RFP. The SOW is a contractual document and should address only those activities that take place after award. While changes take place after award, the thrust of the second paragraph is how the contractor should price changes in its proposal. This information does not belong in the SOW.

Course revisions are not an appropriate task under a fixed-price requirement because the nature and extent of the revisions cannot be accurately described before contract award. A requirement of this nature forces the contractor to use contingency pricing. If the contractor guesses right it gets a windfall; if the contractor guesses wrong, it faces a potential loss. A contractor facing a potential loss under a fixed-price contract must find some way to minimize its losses. This usually has an adverse effect on the quality of contract performance.

C.1.3.6 Course Materials Masters

At the termination of the contract, the contractor shall furnish to the Agency/MAR a complete master set of all course materials, visual aids, and any original art work such as binder graphics, used during the course of instruction in camera-ready, reproducible form. The Contractor shall also furnish to the Agency/MAR an electronic file of all course materials.

Comments:

This requirement could create a problem if a contractor intends to utilize its own copyrighted textbook as the basis for the course material. Textbook development is the largest single cost in a requirement for the development and presentation of a training course. Costs can be substantially reduced if a contractor provides its own generic textbook—there are plenty of such textbooks around. When a contractor provides its own textbook, it usually customizes the textbook through the use an agency logo and title on the cover, but this does not give the agency any rights in the contents of the book. Explanations of local procedures can be handled by hand-out material, rather than a textbook change. This requirement should be re-examined. The only reason for a requirement for masters is if the agency plans to teach the material using its own assets at some later date. Unless the agency has trained *procurement* instructors on its staff, this is not a good idea.

The use of the term "termination" is inappropriate. The appropriate term is "completion."

This is supposed to be the last task under C.1.3, Tasks to be Accomplished. While this could be described as a separate task, it should be addressed as a deliverable in a section of the SOW that identifies all contract deliverables (unfortunately, this SOW does not adequately identify all deliverables).

A final note on section C.1.3, Tasks to be Accomplished. The subparagraphs under C.1.3 should be listing the tasks to be accomplished, however:

- *C.1.3.1* talks about development of student course books and meetings. The real task, however, is the development of the course itself, not just the student course books. This could be a valid task if it were explained better.

- *C.1.3.2* talks about qualified instructors, class length, class timing, and class size. This is not a discrete task.

- *C.1.3.3* talks about classroom set-up, course completion certificates, and classroom clean-up. This is not a discrete task.

- *C.1.3.4* talks about the development and use of evaluation questionnaires. This could be a discrete task, but is really part of the requirement for course development.

- *C.1.3.5* talks about revisions to course materials. This is not an appropriate task for a fixed-price contract.

- *C.1.3.6* talks about the delivery of course materials masters. This could be a discrete task, but is really part of the requirement for course development.

One of the first steps in the development of a clear and concise SOW is to organize your requirement into discrete tasks and present them in chronological order. This has not been done in this SOW.

C.2 QUALITY OF PERFORMANCE

C.2.1 Monitoring Performance

C.2.1.1 During the life of the contract, the Contractor shall monitor the training courses pursuant to the requirement of the contract to assure that the quality of instruction and materials used are adequate. The instructor shall as a minimum:

Comments:

While the SOW should establish the desired level of quality, monitoring the contractor's performance is a Government responsibility. The wording of this paragraph seems to abdicate all performance monitoring to the contractor. This should be reworded to indicate that the Government will monitor contract performance to ensure that the instructors do those things listed in C.2.1.1.1 through C.2.1.1.3.

C.2.1.1.1 Maintain control of the learning time so that the presentation of information and exercises remain organized and timely; key points and course objectives are met, and breaks are provided within the overall course schedule; and distractions, such as questions that are of minimal interest to the class as a whole and that can be answered later and/or individually are consistently controlled.

Comments:

The last part of this paragraph, starting with "and distractions" is in error. To direct an instructor not to answer questions is contrary to good instructional practice. The problems associated with answering questions are significantly less than the problems associated with not answering questions. The perceived problem (questions that are not of general interest) could be resolved by paying more attention to the mix of participants. Mixing people of significantly different backgrounds and interests (see the Background section) is bound to result in questions that are not of interest to some of the participants.

C.2.1.1.2 Observe the effect of the instruction on the class and reasonably attempt to clarify, provide instructions, or in some other way, modify the course to help correct problems and improve the participants' opportunity to learn.

Comments:

Who determines what is a "reasonable" attempt? The sentence would be better if "reasonably" was deleted. "Modify the course" is an unfortunate term since the revision of course material is addressed in C.1.3.5 in a different manner. The proper terminology is "to modify the presentation from the podium" meaning to make oral changes. It is the presentation, not the course, which is modified.

C.2.1.1.3 Involve the participants in sufficient exercise and practice with the subject matter to reinforce the understanding and recall of information.

Comments:

The word "sufficient" lacks precise meaning. The sentence would be better if this word was deleted. As noted earlier, it will be difficult to provide much "exercise and practice" considering all of the material which the course must address.

C.2.1.1.4 Act to improve or later correct errors or other problems that may occur during the training session.

Comments:

"Act to improve errors"? This is poorly worded. It also appears to be similar to the requirement stated in C.2.1.1.2. Since the intent of this subparagraph is unclear, it should be deleted.

C.2.1.2 The Contractor shall meet with the COR from time to time regarding updating, changes or modifications of instructional materials presented. However, no changes involving additional cost to the Government shall be made except pursuant to the Changes clause of the contract.

Comments:

The first sentence is too indefinite for a fixed-price contract. The contractor needs better information than "from time to time." For example, this requirement could be linked with the requirement in C.1.3.5. and C.6, assuming the relationships could be defined.

The second sentence is in error. Contracts may be changed by supplemental agreements as well as by change orders. This erroneously gives the impression that only the Government can suggest changes.

This subparagraph is redundant and probably should be deleted.

C.3 CONTRACTOR-FURNISHED MATERIALS

The COR will review contractor-furnished materials for each course session for quality and accuracy. Should errors occur, such as omissions, incorrect collation, illegibility, and packaging, that are caused by the Contractor, the Agency/MAR will reject the material and the Contractor shall correct all errors prior to the beginning of each course session at no cost to the Government.

Comments:

This paragraph is superfluous, it is covered in the Inspection clause required for fixed-price contracts. There is no need to repeat the wording of clauses, unless necessary to clarify a clause's purpose or implementation.

Is there a difference between "contractor-furnished materials" in this paragraph, "student course book" in paragraph C.3.1.1, and "course materials" in paragraph C.1.3.6? If they are different, a clear definition is needed; if they are the same, use the same terminology.

The COR will review, but the Agency/MAR (who are these people?) will reject. Only the Contracting Officer can reject material. The SOW must correctly identify Government responsibilities.

The Contractor shall deliver one copy of these materials to the COR for review, 30 days prior to the first day of each course session. The COR will comment on quality and accuracy of the materials no later than five business days before the course session is scheduled to start.

Comments:

This paragraph seems to anticipate that course materials will be produced on a per course basis. This is contrary to normal business practices since significant savings can be realized through bulk printing. In the normal course of events, once the course materials are initially approved, the materials would be printed in quantities sufficient to meet the entire requirement. This reduces contractor costs and enables the contractor to offer a lower price.

The last sentence in the second paragraph is unreasonable. Five business days is not sufficient time to make corrections, print the new material, and ship it to the location where the course is to be presented. Your requirements must be reasonable if you are to avoid problems during contract performance.

C.4   GOVERNMENT-FURNISHED PROPERTY AND SERVICES

The Government will furnish the following:

1. Training facilities

2. Copy of the Departmental Acquisition Regulations

3. Copy of Agency Guideline #60

4. Training certificates

5. Where portions of course materials include Agency publication, the Agency will furnish copies for duplication, instruction, and inclusion into training manual.

6. Consultation services of Agency subject specialists, as determined necessary by the COR.

Comments:

This is good except that the training equipment to be provided along with the training facility should be described. The availability of standard training equipment, such as overhead projectors, slide projectors, TVs and VCRs, blackboards and chalk or whiteboards and markers, flipcharts and stands, or other equipment will affect how the presentations are planned. The contractor also needs to know if standard equipment will not be available, because this will affect the cost of presentation if the contractor must obtain needed equipment. Paragraph C.1.1 indicates that commercial facilities will be used for the course presentations. Commercial facilities do not necessarily provide training equipment. This should be addressed in the SOW.

C.5 CONTRACTOR-FURNISHED PROPERTY AND SERVICES

The Contractor shall provide the professional services of experts, instructors, lecturers, educators, and related support services to provide training in procurement/acquisition management. The Contractor shall furnish the training materials plus any other reference identified elsewhere in this statement of work.

Comments:

Paragraph C.5 is not needed. Instructor qualifications are addressed in C.1.3.2 and the training materials in C.1.3.1.

The phrase, "plus any other reference identified elsewhere" doesn't make any sense. If you want to reference something, be specific. Delete this paragraph.

C.6 MEETINGS AND TRAVEL

The Contractor shall meet with the Agency/MAR COR and CO a minimum of two times and a maximum of four times during the period of the contract regarding updating, changes or modifications of instructional materials presented at the direction of the COR. (Refer to Section C.1.3.5 of the statement of work for additional information pertinent to this requirement.)

Comments:

The title is misleading; this paragraph does not address travel.

This is the third time meetings are mentioned in the SOW. The first reference is in C.1.3.1, which states that there will be two meetings of 2 days each in Philadelphia prior to final approval of course materials. The second reference is in C.2.1.2 which indicates that there will be meetings from time to time (location and duration unspecified) to discuss updating, changes or modifications of instructional material (this is the same wording as used in C.6). Spreading a requirement throughout the SOW creates confusion and misunderstandings, particularly when redundant wording is used. If there are to be required meetings they should be addressed in one place and fully defined. This is a fixed-price contract and the SOW should not state requirements in such vague terms.

This paragraph indicates that the Agency/MAR, the COR, and the CO, are different persons. The COR and CO can be identified, but who are the Agency/MAR and what is their authority and responsibility?

C.7 COURSE TIMES AND PLACES

It is anticipated that the first course will be conducted in Williamsburg, VA approximately 3–4 months after award of the contract. Subsequent courses will be held in Philadelphia, Gettysburg, and Stroudsburg, PA; however, no definite dates have been set. For purposes of preparing a proposal, the offeror shall assume that a course will be held in Philadelphia approximately 3–4 months after the one in Williamsburg, VA; the one in Gettysburg 5–6 months after the one in Philadelphia; and the one in Stroudsburg 3–4 months after the one in Gettysburg.

Comments:

This is confusing. Paragraph B.1 indicated that the first two courses were a firm requirement and the last two were options. That is not indicated in the wording of this paragraph. You must clearly state your requirements.

The last subparagraph of C.1.1 indicated that the training would be conducted at commercial facilities to be acquired (presumably by the Government) by separate contract. This information should be included in this paragraph, and should be expanded to include a description of the training equipment to be provided (either here or in paragraph C.4). Commercial training facilities can range from a motel room with no equipment to a fully equipped training center. The contractors need to know this information.

C.8 DELIVERY SCHEDULE

Within 15 calendar days after award of the contract, the Contractor shall submit to the COR (copy to the CO) a delivery schedule of all tasks incorporating all required delivery times stated in this solicitation. The COR will have 15 calendar days for inspection and acceptance.

Comments:

If the Government cannot come up with a schedule for course presentations, how can the Contractor develop a delivery schedule? Note that paragraph C.3 requires deliveries 30 days prior to each course session, but lacking a course schedule, the most a contractor can do is say, "Yes, I'll deliver in accordance with the stated schedule." Does the COR need 15 days to inspect and accept this?

This is another example of spreading information all over the SOW. Deliveries are mentioned nine times in six different places:

- **C.1.3.1** "One camera-ready copy (student course book) shall be furnished to the Contracting Officer."

- **C.1.3.1** "Thirty copies (student course book) will be furnished prior to commencement of the first course."

- **C.1.3.1** "Additional copies (student course book) will be required at the commencement of subsequent courses."

- **C.1.3.1** "The Contractor shall be required to submit two (2) draft copies of the student course book for review by Agency/MAR personnel prior to final printing."

- **C.1.3.4** "The proposed questionnaire shall be furnished to the COR for approval by 30 calendar days prior to the first course..."

- **C.1.3.5** "Within 10 calendar days of receiving an order to develop technical changes to the material of the course, the Contractor shall submit a draft version of modified materials to the COR for approval."

- **C.1.3.6** "At the termination of the contract, the Contractor shall furnish....a complete master set of all course materials, visual aids, and any original art work such as binder graphics...."

- **C.3** "The Contractor shall deliver one copy of these materials (contractor-furnished materials) to the COR for review, 30 days prior to the first day of each course session."

- **C.8** "Within 15 calendar days after award of the contract, the Contractor shall submit to the COR (copy to the CO) a delivery schedule of all tasks incorporating all required delivery times stated in this solicitation."

Delivery requirements should be described as part of the related task, i.e., finish the work and deliver the work product (but as noted earlier, the task descriptions are deficient in this respect). The physical characteristics and delivery times of each deliverable should also be described, together, in a separate section. This ensures that the tasks are fully described and that there is a place to look to determine exactly what is to be delivered. Spreading this information throughout the SOW makes it difficult to bring everything together in a coherent fashion and leads to problems in contract performance.

PART C: REVISED SOW

The following is an example of how the SOW in Part A of the Appendix could be revised to make it more coherent and to eliminate the ambiguities. Immediately following the revised SOW are a set of notes describing exactly how the revision was done.

STATEMENT OF WORK
ACQUISITION TRAINING FOR AGENCY/MAR PROJECT MANAGERS

Part A—General Information

A.1   Introduction

A.2   Background

A.3   Scope of Work

Part B—Background

Technical Requirements

B.1   Task 01 Develop the Course and Course Materials

B.1.1   Course Content

B.1.2   Course Participants

B.1.3   Course Textbook and Related Supporting Materials

B.1.4   Course Evaluation Questionnaire

B.2   Task 02 Course Presentations

B.2.1   Course Times and Places

B.2.2   Instructor Qualifications

B.2.3   Delivery of Course Materials

B.2.4   Course Set-up

B.2.5   Course Presentations

B.2.6   Course Completion

Deliverables

B.3   Deliverable Items

B.3.1   Draft Course Textbook and Support Material

B.3.2   Draft Course Questionnaire

B.3.3   Course Materials

B.3.4   Completed Course Evaluation Questionnaires

B.3.5   Master Set of Course Materials

B.3.6   Electronic file

Part C—Supporting Information

C.1   Place of Performance

C.2   Period of Performance

C.3   Special Considerations

C.3.1   Contractor-Furnished Materials

C.3.2   Government-Furnished Material and Services

C.3.3   Qualifications of Key Personnel

STATEMENT OF WORK
ACQUISITION TRAINING FOR AGENCY/
MAR PROJECT MANAGERS

SOW PART A—GENERAL INFORMATION

A.1 INTRODUCTION

This requirement is for the development and presentation of a comprehensive 4 1/2-day procurement training course for Project Managers and other personnel of the Agency, Mid-Atlantic Region (Agency/MAR).

A.2 BACKGROUND

The Agency/MAR consists of the offices and sites in the states of Pennsylvania, Maryland, Virginia, and West Virginia, with a regional office in Philadelphia, PA. The Agency/MAR procurement requirements encompass the entire spectrum of Federal contracting, including construction contracts. The Agency/MAR believes that personnel involved in the acquisition process must have a basic understanding of their role and authority in the process as well as the role and authority of the Contracting Officer.

A.3 SCOPE OF WORK

The purpose of the course is to instruct Agency/MAR personnel on the basic methods and processes of acquiring products and services and to outline their respective responsibilities.

SOW PART B—WORK REQUIREMENTS

TECHNICAL REQUIREMENTS

B.1 TASK 01 DEVELOP THE COURSE AND COURSE MATERIALS

B.1.1 COURSE CONTENT

B.1.1.1 This course shall provide a comprehensive overview of the acquisition process as practiced by the Agency. Course content shall be governed by the Federal Acquisition Regulations (FAR), the Departmental Acquisition Regulations (DAR), and the Agency Guideline #60.

B.1.1.2. At a minimum, the course shall address the following topics:

- An overview of the Agency acquisition process and the role of Agency personnel in the process (to include the Agency procurement planning process and the implications of the rules concerning Procurement Integrity).

- Procurement methods (to include the related solicitation processes).

- Socioeconomic programs.

- Obtaining competition (to include the requirements for competitive and noncompetitive procurement and publicizing procurements).

- Types of contracts.

- Writing specifications and statements of work.

- Developing evaluation plans and source selection plans.

- Conducting the evaluation of proposals, negotiation, and source selection (to include the architect/engineer selection process).

- Monitoring contractor performance.

- Contract changes.

- Contract completion/termination.

B.1.2   COURSE PARTICIPANTS

The course will be attended by Superintendents, Facility Managers, Chiefs of Maintenance, Engineers, Project Managers (Project Managers are usually the Contracting Officer's Representative (COR) on a contract), supervisors of Project Managers, Division Chiefs and Administrative Officers. These personnel are from the Regional office and all offices within the region and have, or soon will have, responsibilities for the acquisition of products and services to support the Agency/MAR mission. Typically these personnel will not have attended prior acquisition training, but have been responsible for all or part of a project involving a commercial contractor. The course will also be attended by Contracting Officers, Contract Specialists, and Purchasing Agents from within the Region who will act as participants and also provide assistance, as necessary, to explain local implementation of official rules and regulations. Each class will consist of up to 25 participants.

B.1.3   COURSE TEXTBOOK AND RELATED SUPPORTING MATERIALS

The contractor shall provide a course textbook for each participant. The text shall be provided in a three-ring binder identified with the Agency logo and course title. Title cover art is optional. Supporting material such as handouts, slides, vu-graphs, and other instructional material shall also be identified by the Agency logo (in the upper left corner) and course title. The contractor shall submit two (2) draft copies of the course textbook and other supporting materials to the COR at least 30 working days prior to the first course presentation. The course textbook and supporting material will be reviewed and returned to the contractor, with appropriate comments, within 10 working days. Any changes that are required by the review shall be incorporated into the course textbook and related supporting material before the presentation of the first course.

B.1.4   COURSE EVALUATION QUESTIONNAIRE

The Contractor shall prepare a course evaluation questionnaire to be completed by all participants at the end of each course. The questionnaire shall be directed toward eliciting participants' comments as to the values of the material taught, changes and additions recommended, and the quality of the instructor personnel. Two (2) copies of the proposed questionnaire shall be provided to the COR at least 30 working days prior to the first course presentation. The questionnaire will be reviewed and returned to the contractor, with appropriate comments, within 10 working days. Any changes that are required by the review shall be accomplished before the presentation of the first course.

B.2   TASK 02   COURSE PRESENTATIONS

B.2.1   COURSE TIMES AND PLACES

B.2.1.1   This requirement is being procured on the basis of a fixed-price, indefinite delivery contract because the times of course presentations are not known at the time of contracting. Courses will be ordered, by the issuance of delivery orders, when course times are determined. The following is the estimated course schedule:

First presentation	(Williamsburg VA)	90–120 days after contract award
Second presentation	(Philadelphia PA)	90–120 days after first presentation
Third Presentation	(Gettysburg PA)	150–180 days after second presentation
Fourth Presentation	(Stroudsburg PA)	90–120 days after third presentation

B.2.1.2.   Training facilities shall be arranged by the Government by separate contract. The contractor shall be notified of the location of the training facility and provided a contact telephone number at least 30 days before the commencement of each training session.

B.2.2 INSTRUCTOR QUALIFICATIONS

B.2.2.1. The contractor shall provide qualified instructor personnel. Instructor personnel shall be knowledgeable in Federal, Departmental, and Agency contracting regulations and shall have had at least two years instructional experience in teaching procurement training courses.

B.2.2.2. Instructors shall be responsible for assuring the quality of the instructions and materials used. Instructors shall:

- Maintain control of the learning time so that the presentation of information and exercises remain organized and timely, key points and course objectives are met, and breaks are provided within the overall course schedule.

- Observe the effect of the instruction on the class and, as necessary, clarify, provide examples, or in some other way, amplify the course material to help correct problems and improve the participants' opportunity to learn.

- Involve the participants is exercises and practice with the subject matter to reinforce the understanding and recall of information.

- Orally update material as necessary to keep participants aware of the latest changes in procurement law or regulation.

B.2.3 DELIVERY OF COURSE MATERIALS

The contractor shall deliver all course materials to the designated Agency/MAR training facility prior to the start of each training session. Specific locations shall be provided to the contractor by the COR at least 30 working days prior to the start of the course.

B.2.4 COURSE SET-UP

The contractor shall be responsible for setting up the training facility, arranging furniture as necessary, laying out participant materials, and preparing equipment and instructor aids.

B.2.5 COURSE PRESENTATIONS

B.2.5.1. Training sessions shall commence promptly at 8:00 a.m. and conclude at 4:00 p.m. (12:00 a.m. on the 4th day). The contractor shall be responsible for providing appropriate class breaks and lunch periods.

B.2.5.2. During the training sessions, the contractor shall account for participant attendance by assuring the completion of Agency registration forms. At the commencement of each course, the instructor shall inform the participants that the requirements for receiving a Course Completion Certificate are as follows:

- Participants must complete at least 4 days of the 4 1/2 day course.

- Participants must have completed and submitted a course evaluation questionnaire.

B.2.6 COURSE COMPLETION

B.2.6.1. Immediately following each course session, the instructor shall ensure that the classroom is clear of any trash and excess material generated during class.

B.2.6.2. The original copy of each evaluation questionnaire shall be submitted to the COR within 10 working days of the completion of each course. The questionnaires shall be submitted under a cover letter that provides the contractor's assessment of participant comments and recommendations for possible course changes, if any.

DELIVERABLES

B.3. DELIVERABLE ITEMS

The contractor shall deliver the following items to the COR:

B.3.1 Two (2) copies of the course textbook and other supporting material for review and approval, in accordance with SOW paragraph A.1.3. Delivery shall be made at least 30 working days prior to the first course presentation.

B.3.2 Two (2) copies of the proposed course evaluation questionnaire for review and approval, in accordance with SOW paragraph A.1.4. Delivery shall be made at least 30 working days prior to the first course presentation.

B.3.3 Twenty-five (25) copies of the course textbook and all supporting material, in accordance with SOW paragraph A.2.3. Delivery shall be made prior to be beginning of each course presentation.

B.3.4 All completed course questionnaires and instructor comments, in accordance with SOW paragraph A.2.6. Delivery shall be made within 10 working days after the completion of each course presentation.

B.3.5 Upon contract completion, the contractor shall provide the COR with a complete master set of all course materials, visual aids, and any original art work such as binder graphics, used during course presentations. This material shall be provided in camera-ready, reproducible form, 10 working days prior to contract completion.

B.3.6 The contractor shall also provide, with the material required by SOW paragraph B.2, above, an electronic file containing the course textbook and all supporting materials.

SOW PART C—SUPPORTING INFORMATION

C.1   PLACE OF PERFORMANCE

Task 01 shall be performed primarily at the contractor's facility. Task 02 shall be performed at training facilities arranged for by the Government in accordance with SOW paragraphs A.2.1 and A.2.3.

C.2   PERIOD OF PERFORMANCE

The period of performance for this contract shall be two (2) years.

C.3   SPECIAL CONSIDERATIONS

C.3.1   Contractor-Furnished Materials

The contractor shall furnish all materials necessary for course presentation except those identified as Government-furnished material in paragraph C.3.2 below.

C.3.2   Government-Furnished Material And Services

The Government will furnish the following:

- Training facilities and equipment (to be provided by separate contract).

- A copy of the Departmental Acquisition Regulations.

- A copy of Agency Guideline #60.

- Agency registration forms and Training Certificates.

- Agency publications. If the contractor chooses to include Agency publications as part of the course materials, the COR will furnish copies for duplication and inclusion into the course materials.

- Consultation services of Agency/MAR subject specialists. Upon written request, the COR will arrange for consultation with Agency/MAR subject specialists during the development of the course material.

C.3.3   Qualifications of Key Personnel

The contractor shall identify, by name, the key management, technical, and instructor personnel who will work under this contract. Substitutions of key personnel shall be made only as directed by the Key Personnel clause in section H of this contract. Requisite qualifications are as follows:

- Management—College degree and three years experience in the management of educational services contracts.

- Technical—College degree and three years experience in the development of procurement training courses.

- Instructor—College degree and two years experience in teaching procurement training courses.

Note: Four years of related work experience may be substituted for a college degree.

NOTES ON THE SOW REVISION

The SOW in this appendix was revised using, as much as possible, the requirements as set forth in the original SOW. The purpose of this revision is to present the description of the requirement in a coherent fashion. This requires the material to be reorganized so that like information is presented together and ambiguous material is deleted. The following discussion, formatted on the outline of the original SOW, shows how the revisions were made, and why, and makes reference to the paragraphs of the revised SOW.

C.1 Statement of Work

The original SOW did not have an Introduction. An Introduction is needed to provide a quick reference to what the procurement is for. See Paragraph A.1.

C.1.1 BACKGROUND

Most of the information in C.1.1 is better presented as part of the work description rather than as background. The information here was redistributed as shown in the following:

- In the first paragraph, the first sentence was used in paragraph A.2, Background. The second sentence was used in paragraph A.3, Scope of Work (this paragraph was added to the revised SOW). A Scope paragraph describes the purpose or objective of the procurement and, when appropriate, provides details (such as workload estimates) that will help the contractor understand the size or magnitude of the requirement. A workload estimate was not needed in this instance.

- In the second paragraph, the first sentence was used in paragraph B.1.2, Course Times and Places (this information is more appropriate in the description of the course content than as background). The second sentence was used in paragraph A.2, Background.

- The third paragraph, with some rewriting, was used in paragraph B.1.2, Course Participants (this information is more appropriate in the description of the course content than as background). The rewriting was done to remove the contracting personnel from those personnel with no previous procurement training.

- The fourth paragraph was also used in paragraph B.1.2, Course Participants, for the same reason as above.

- The last paragraph (with the exception of the last sentence) was used in paragraph B.2.1, Course Times and Places. Paragraph B.2.1 is a combination of the last paragraph of C.1.1 and paragraph C.7. The last sentence of C.1.1 was placed in SOW paragraph B.1.2, Course Participants.

C.1.2 OBJECTIVES

This information should be part of the work requirements, rather than separately listed as a contract objective.

The information in this paragraph, with some revisions and deletions, was used in subparagraph B.1.1.2, Course Content. The revisions were made to provide a more orderly presentation. The deletions were made to avoid confusion or when the topic was a subset of another topic. One topic, contract changes, was added.

C.1.3 TASKS TO BE ACCOMPLISHED

C.1.3.1 The first and fifth sentences, with some rewording, were used in paragraph B.1.3, Course Textbook and Related Supporting Materials, as part of the description of course content. The third and fourth sentences were used, with some rewording, in paragraph B.2.3, Delivery of Course Materials. The second and sixth sentences were deleted because they were too vague to be a valid requirement. If meetings are to be a formal requirement, the description must include the details (purpose, when, where, who, agenda, etc.) needed for the contractor to estimate the costs.

C.1.3.2 This paragraph was divided between paragraph B.2.2.1, Instructor Qualifications and B.2.5.1, Course Presentations. This was done to separate the qualification requirements from the course presentation requirements.

C.1.3.3 This paragraph was divided between paragraph B.2.3, Delivery of Course Materials, and B.2.4, Course Set-up, B.2.5.2,

Course Presentations, and B.2.6.1, Course Completion. This was done to separate the information into proper categories.

C.1.3.4 The first three sentences of C.1.3.4.1 were used in paragraph B.1.4, Course Evaluation Questionnaire. The last two sentences were deleted for the reasons addressed in the discussion of C.1.3.5, below. C.1.3.4.2 was used in paragraph B.2.6.2, Course Completion, to put the information in the proper perspective.

C.1.3.5 These paragraphs were deleted for several reasons. The primary reason is that it is not proper to try to pre-price changes to a fixed-price contract, particularly when the potential changes are ill-defined. In addition, these paragraphs are so vague with respect to major and minor changes that they defy definition, and given the nature of the requirement, there is some doubt that such changes will be needed at all. Finally, most of the information in the subparagraph on minor changes is proposal preparation information and not appropriate for use in an SOW.

C.1.3.6 This paragraph describes a delivery requirement and was used in paragraphs B.3.5 and B.3.6, in the Deliverables section. The hardcopy and electronic requirements were separated because they are different requirements, requiring different preparations for delivery. The original SOW did not address deliverables in a separate section of the SOW; instead, this information was spread throughout the SOW. This made the delivery requirements difficult to ascertain. The revised SOW contains a specific delivery section (paragraphs B.3.1 through B.3.6) that clearly identifies the deliverable items.

NOTE: Paragraph C.1.3.6 was the last paragraph in C.1.3, Tasks to be Accomplished. As noted in the critique in Part B, this section was not well thought out. The following discussion addresses how the contract work requirements in the SOW in this Appendix were approached.

1. Describe the work requirements in detail. Divide the work into tasks. This requirement has two basis tasks: Develop

the Course and Course Materials, and Present Courses. Describe the tasks using a functional description that describes what is to be accomplished, not how to do it. Identify and describe the key elements of each task.

2. The key elements for the first task, Develop the Course and Course Materials, are:

   (a) a general description of the course and the applicable rules and regulations,

   (b) specific identification of required subjects,

   (c) identification of the course participants,

   (d) development of a course textbook and supporting materials, and,

   (e) development of an evaluation questionnaire.

3. The key elements of the second task, Present Courses, are:

   (a) where and when courses will be presented,

   (b) instructor qualifications,

   (c) delivery of course materials,

   (d) course set-up,

   (e) course completion, cleanup, and excess materials, and

   (f) submission of evaluation questionnaires and comments.

4. Although not part of the SOW, use the Proposal Preparation Instructions to require the contractor to provide information necessary for evaluation of its proposal. For the development and presentation of a training course require,

at a minimum, the submission of an overall Course Outline that describes the units of instruction in the order in which they will be presented. This can be amplified by a requirement for a Lesson Plan and a Lesson Outline for each proposed unit of instruction. The Lesson Outline provides a detailed outline of the topics to be discussed in each unit of instruction. The Lesson Plan describes, for each unit of instruction:

- the lesson objectives and major teaching points,

- teaching techniques, instructional aids, and handouts to be employed,

- textbook reading assignments or other readings related to the material to be covered,

- how the material relates to previous instruction and instruction to follow, and

- the amount of time to be devoted to the unit of instruction.

5. This information can then be used to evaluate the contractor's expertise and understanding of the requirement. It focuses attention on the ultimate purpose of the requirement, which is the presentation of the instruction. The proposed Course Outline, Lesson Plans, and Lesson Outlines can then be incorporated in the SOW before award to ensure that what the contractor proposed is mandated by the contract.

6. The Proposal Preparation Instructions should also require the contractor to provide an outline of the proposed textbook, to indicate how the textbook will be used to support the course presentation, and how the textbook will be written (some textbooks are written in outline form to directly follow and support the instructional presentation, others

are written in narrative form to serve as a reference book after course completion). This part of the successful contractor's proposal should also be incorporated in the SOW before award.

7. In addition to describing the technical requirements, describe any applicable management requirements, such as the submission of progress reports, the use of computer-assisted project management programs, or other management-oriented requirements. In this instance, there is no real need for reports. This is a fixed-price contract so there is no need for financial reports. The contractor is required to deliver draft copies of the course material 30 days before the start of the first course which is 90–120 days after award. The COR can monitor this contract by telephone or periodic visits. Written progress reports will add very little value (but will add cost) to the administration of this contract.

C.2.1 Subparagraphs C.2.1.1 through C.2.1.1.4 were used in paragraph B.2.2.2, Instructor Qualifications, to establish the standards for instructor performance. Subparagraph C.2.1.2 was deleted as being too vague for a valid fixed-price requirement.

C.3 The first paragraph was deleted because it repeated the wording of a contract clause without adding any substance or clarifying the requirement. The second paragraph was deleted because it didn't make sense. Normally the contractor will print all course material as soon as it is first approved (before the first presentation) to take advantage of bulk printing rates. Re-inspection is not necessary. If re-inspection was necessary, the 5-day notification of problems is hardly enough time to do anything about it.

A Contractor-Furnished Materials paragraph (C.3.1) was added to the SOW to offset the Government-Furnished Property and Services clause (C.3.2). This was done to clearly define the respective responsibilities of the parties.

C.4 This paragraph was used in paragraph C.3.2, Government-Furnished Property and Services. The only change made was to add equipment to the first bullet. If the Government is going to contract separately for the training facilities, they must include training equipment in that requirement, or otherwise indicate how the equipment (overhead projector, TV/VCR, etc.) will be provided. Normally the party providing the training facility also provides any necessary equipment. If the Government is not going to provide any equipment, this should be noted in the SOW in the paragraph that addresses contractor-furnished materials.

C.5 This paragraph was deleted. The first sentence is irrelevant and the second sentence is too vague to use.

C.6 This paragraph was deleted. As noted earlier, if meetings are to be a contractual requirement, they must be described in sufficient detail to be priced. In a procurement of this nature, it is doubtful that formal meetings are a valid requirement.

NOTE: The revised SOW added three paragraphs not addressed in the original SOW:

- **C.1 Place of Performance**

This paragraph identifies where contract performance shall take place—in this instance, in two different places. This makes it clear that the Government is responsible for providing the training facilities. Citing the place of performance is part of the description of the requirement, particularly when work will be done in more than one location.

- **C.2 Period of Performance**

Even if the period of performance is stated in a contract clause, it should also be in the SOW, if for no other purpose than to make the SOW a complete document. In this instance the period of performance was cited by a contract clause. It should have also been in the SOW.

- **C.3.3 Qualifications of Key Personnel**

Whenever a Key Personnel clause is used in the contract, the SOW should specify the qualification requirements for each category of key personnel. It will be difficult, during contract performance, to establish that a proposed substitution is not qualified if no qualification requirements have been identified.

INDEX

A

acceptable quality level (AQL), 59, 87–88
acquisition planning
   beginning, 35
   defining requirements, 37–38
   market research, 39–45
   measuring success, 38–39
   team approach, 36
active voice, 231
active work words, 233–234
allowable error rates, 59
ambiguities, 211–212
applicable documents, 154–157
AQL. *See* acceptable quality level
award, 139–140
award incentives, 102–105
award term incentives, 105–109

B

basis of estimate, 65–67
best value evaluation, 137–139
bid samples, 205
buzz words, 231

C

C/SCSC. *See* cost/schedule control system criteria
CDRL. *See* Contract Data Requirements List
change management
   change order form, 249–251
   change order tracker, 252–256
   identifying changes, 242–245
   importance, 239
   lack of adherence to process, 247
   lack of change management section in statement of work, 246
   lack of detailed statement of work, 246
   lack of understanding of statement of work, 248
   legal precedents, 240–242
   managing project changes, 245–249
   misinterpreting changes, 248–249
   poor communications, 247
   triple constraints triangle, 240
clear and concise statement of work
   after award, 6–7
   before award, 5–6
   communicating effectively, 8
   contract baseline, 7–8
   importance, 5
   performance standards, 7–8

colloquialisms, 231
commercial items, 183–185
completion statement of work, 64–67
computer software, 164
constraints, statement of objectives, 123, 130
contract clauses, conflicts with, 223–228
Contract Data Requirements List (CDRL), 190
contract management requirements, 167–170
contract types
   cost-reimbursement, 49–50
   definite-quantity, 52
   delivery-order, 51, 53–54
   fixed-price, 47–49
   indefinite-delivery, 51–55
   indefinite-quantity, 52–53, 55
   labor-hour, 50–51
   requirements, 52
   selecting, 47
   task-order, 51, 54
   time-and-materials, 50–51
contract work products, 176–177
contractor comments
   draft solicitations, 228–229
   obtaining, 228
   preproposal conference, 229–230
   proposal preparation instructions, 230
contractor proposals, incorporating by reference, 61–63
corporate experience, 21
cost, 22–23
cost analysis, 88–89
cost-plus-award fee incentives (CPAF), 60
cost-plus-fixed-fee (CPFF), 63
cost-reimbursement contracts, 49–50
cost/schedule control system criteria (C/SCSC), 170
CPFF. *See* cost-plus-fixed-fee

D

data collection, 179–180
data gathering, 79–81
Data Item Description (DID), 190
deductibles, 112–115
definite-quantity contracts, 52
deliverables
   definition, 195–196
   describing deliverables, 196
   digital media, 196–197
   manufactured products, 196
   marking requirements, 197–198
   packaging, 197–198
   packing, 197–198
   purpose, 195
   written material, 196
delivery-order contracts, 51, 53–54
Department of Defense (DoD)
   disputes, 106
   handbook, 2
   performance work statements, 89–90
descriptive literature, sealed bidding, 205–206
desk audits, 40
DID. *See* Data Item Description
directive analysis, 81
DoD. *See* Department of Defense

draft solicitations, 228–229
due diligence, 132–137

E

early information exchanges, 42–43
executive summary, 174

F

Federal Acquisition Regulation (FAR), 1
final report, 174
five-step approach, statement of objectives, 129
fixed-price contracts, 47–49
follow-on efforts, 69–71
font styles, proposal preparation instructions, 25–26
formal technical meetings, 187–188
format, statement of work, 145–147. *See also* Sections and Parts
formatting proposal preparation instructions, 31–32
formula incentives, 101–102
funding information, 140–141

G

general and administrative expenses (G&A), 8
government-furnished property, 200–201
governmentwide point of entry (GPE), 42

I

IFB. *See* invitation for bids
in-house terminology, 231
incentives
  award, 102–105
  award term, 105–109
  formula, 101–102
  impact of, 109–112
  plan, 75–76, 99–101
inconsistent requirements, 212–213
incorporation by reference, statement of objectives, 125–127
indefinite-delivery contracts, 51–55
indefinite-quantity contracts, 52–53, 55
inexact words, 231
information requirements, proposal preparation instructions, 28–31
initial competition, statement of objectives, 130–132
initial query letters, 44
invitation for bids (IFB), 9
IT systems and software, 181–183

J

jargon, 231
job analysis, 77–78

K

key personnel, 20–21, 201–203

L

labor-hour contracts, 50–51
legal precedents, 240–242
level of effort (LOE)
   basis of estimate, 65–67
   compared to completion statement of work, 64–65
   when to use, 55
long sentences, 222–223

M

management approach, 19
managing project changes, 245–249
manufactured items, 163
market research
   acquisition planning, 39–45
   definition, 39
   desk audits, 40
   documenting, 39
   early information exchanges, 42–43
   effectiveness, 40
   initial query letters, 44
   performance-based service contracting, 81
   preproposal conferences, 44
   purpose, 40
   statement of objectives, 129–130
   techniques, 41–42
   who conducts, 41
misinterpreting changes, 248–249
missing text, 221–222

N

negotiation, 139
non-personal services, 67–69
number of copies, proposal preparation instructions, 25

O

options, 69–71
organizational analysis, 78–79

P

page limits, proposal preparation instructions, 26–28
paper size, proposal preparation instructions, 25–26
Part I: General Information, overview, 147
Part II: Work Requirements, overview, 158
Part III: Supporting Information, overview, 198
past performance, 21–22
PBSC. *See* performance-based service contracting
performance assessment plan, 91
performance-based service contracting (PBSC). *See also* quality assurance plan
   acceptable quality level, 87–88
   award incentives, 102–105
   award term incentives, 105–109
   cost analysis, 88–89
   data gathering, 79–81
   deductibles, 112–115
   definition, 73–74
   Department of Defense, 89–90
   directive analysis, 81
   formula incentives, 101–102
   impact of incentives, 109–112
   importance, 1, 57
   incentive plan, 75–76, 99–101

job analysis, 77–78
market research, 81
organizational analysis, 78–79
performance analysis, 82–83
performance indicators, 83–85
performance requirements summary, 88
performance standards, 85–87
performance work statement, 1, 57, 74–75
when to use, 76–77
work analysis, 82
performance indicators, 83–85
performance objectives, 123
performance requirement analysis, 77
performance requirements summary, 88
performance schedules, 172
performance standards, 7–8, 85–87
performance work statement (PWS), 1, 57, 74–75
period of performance, 123, 199–200
periodic sampling, 92–93
personal services, 67–69
pertinent previous efforts, 164
phrases and terms to avoid, 232, 235–238
place of performance, statement of objectives, 123, 199
planning. *See also* contract types
importance, 35
thinking projects through, 45–46
work breakdown structure, 46–47
poor communications, 247
poor sentence construction, 220–221

preproposal conferences, 44, 229–230
price, 22–23
primary evaluation factors, 15
product description, 3
proposal preparation instructions
contractor comments, 230
corporate experience, 21
cost or price, 22–23
ensuring appropriate coverage, 14–15
font styles, 25–26
importance, 13–14
information requirements, 28–31
key personnel, 20–21
management approach, 19
number of copies, 25
page limits, 26–28
paper size, 25–26
past performance, 21–22
primary evaluation factors, 15
proposal volumes, 24–25
significant sub-factors, 15–18
staffing plan, 19
standardized proposal format, 23–24
type size, 25–26
proposal volumes, 24–25
purchase description, 3
PWS. *See* performance work statement

Q

qualifications of key personnel, 201–203
quality assurance plan (QAP)
100-percent-inspection, 92
customer input, 93
definition, 75

example, 95–99
overview, 90–91
periodic sampling, 92–93
planning, 59–60
random sampling, 92
surveillance methods, 91–94, 91–95
unscheduled inspections, 93–94
query letters, 44

R

random sampling, 92
reliability, 185
request for information (RFI), 40
request for proposal (RFP), 6
requirements. *See also* technical requirements
  acquisition planning, 37–38
  defining, 37–38
  different names for same, 213–214
  Federal Acquisition Regulation, 1
  incomplete descriptions, 216–217
  inconsistent, 212–213
  information, 28–31
  packaging, 197–198
requirements contracts, 52
research, 63, 177–179
RFI. *See* request for information
RFP. *See* request for proposal
risks, 164–165

S

schedules, 214–216
scope, 122, 153–154, 174–175
sealed bidding, 203–204

Section A: Introduction, Part I, 147–151
Section A: Security, Part III, 198–199
Section A: Technical Requirements, Part II
  accuracy, 185
  background, 174
  capacity, 185
  commercial items, 183–185
  compatibility, 186
  computer software, 164
  consistent descriptions, 165
  contract management requirements, 167–170
  contract work products, 176–177
  data collection, 179–180
  defining requirements, 161–162
  describing work requirements, 158–159
  dividing work into tasks, 159–160
  environment, 186
  executive summary, 174
  final report, 174
  formal technical meetings, 187–188
  future direction, 175
  government responsibilities, 171–172
  incorporating other documents, 188–189
  installation, 187
  interchangeability, 186
  interfaces with third parties, 171–172
  IT systems and software, 181–183

known risks, 164–165
manufactured items, 163
manufactured products, 185
materials, 186
performance schedules, 172
pertinent previous efforts, 164
physical restrictions, 186
power, 185
problems encountered and resolutions, 175
project phasing, 167
proposal preparation instructions, 165–166
purpose, 158
quality requirements in functional statement of work, 190–193
quality requirements in performance-based service contracting, 193
reliability, 185
ruggedness, 186
scope, 174–175
sequential task descriptions, 166
special considerations, 177
studies and research efforts, 177–179
success criteria, 190
task descriptions, 160–161
technical data requirements, 189–190
testing requirements, 193–195
training, 163
transportation and storage, 186–187
work elements, 162–163
work performed and results, 175
work plans, 173–174

Section B: Background, Part I, 151–152
Section B: Deliverables, Part II
  definition, 195–196
  describing deliverables, 196
  digital media, 196–197
  manufactured products, 196
  marking requirements, 197–198
  packaging, 197–198
  packing, 197–198
  purpose, 195
  written material, 196
Section B: Place of Performance, Part III, 199
Section C: Period of Performance, Part III, 199–200
Section C: Scope, Part I, 153–154
Section D: Applicable Documents, Part I, 154–157
Section D: Government-Furnished Property, Part III, 200–201
Section E: Qualifications of Key Personnel, Part III, 201–203
Section L, statement of objectives, 124
Section M, statement of objectives, 124–125
security, 198–199
significant sub-factors, 15–18
simple words, 232
sole-source statement of work, 69
solicitation and contract, 9–13
SOO. *See* statement of objectives
specification, 2
staffing plan, 19
standardized proposal format, 23–24
standards, 2

statement of objectives (SOO)
  award, 139–140
  background, 121–122
  best value evaluation, 137–139
  competing, 128
  conducting initial competition, 130–132
  conducting market research, 129–130
  constraints, 123
  definition, 119–121
  developing, 130
  due diligence, 132–137
  five-step approach, 129
  identifying constraints, 130
  incorporation by reference, 125–127
  negotiation, 139
  performance objectives, 123
  period of performance, 123
  place of performance, 123
  purpose, 121
  releasing funding information, 140–141
  scope, 122
  Section L, 124
  Section M, 124–125
  using, 127–128
success criteria, 190
surveillance methods, 91–94

T

task descriptions, 160–161
task-order contracts, 51, 54
team approach, acquisition planning, 36
technical requirements
  accuracy, 185
  background, 174
  capacity, 185
  commercial items, 183–185
  compatibility, 186
  computer software, 164
  consistent descriptions, 165
  contract management requirements, 167–170
  contract work products, 176–177
  data collection, 179–180
  defining requirements, 161–162
  describing work requirements, 158–159
  dividing work into tasks, 159–160
  environment, 186
  executive summary, 174
  final report, 174
  formal technical meetings, 187–188
  future direction, 175
  government responsibilities, 171–172
  incorporating other documents, 188–189
  installation, 187
  interchangeability, 186
  interfaces with third parties, 171–172
  IT systems and software, 181–183
  known risks, 164–165
  manufactured items, 163
  manufactured products, 185
  materials, 186
  performance schedules, 172
  pertinent previous efforts, 164
  physical restrictions, 186
  power, 185
  problems encountered and resolutions, 175

project phasing, 167
proposal preparation instructions, 165–166
purpose, 158
quality requirements in functional statement of work, 190–193
quality requirements in performance-based service contracting, 193
reliability, 185
ruggedness, 186
scope, 174–175
sequential task descriptions, 166
special considerations, 177
studies and research efforts, 177–179
success criteria, 190
task descriptions, 160–161
technical data requirements, 189–190
testing requirements, 193–195
training, 163
transportation and storage, 186–187
work elements, 162–163
work performed and results, 175
work plans, 173–174
testing requirements, 193–195
third parties, 171–172
time-and-materials contracts (T&M), 50–51
trade terminology, 231
training, 163
triple constraints triangle, 240
two-step sealed bidding, 206–207
type size, proposal preparation instructions, 25–26
types, statement of work
   design descriptions, 60–61
   functional descriptions, 55–60
   performance descriptions, 57–60
typos, 221

U

unpriced options, 69–71
unscheduled inspections, 93–94

V

vague language, 217–219
vocabulary, 222
voluntary consensus standards, 3

W

WBS. *See* work breakdown structure
word usage, 230–232
work analysis, 82
work breakdown structure (WBS), 46–47
work effort, 56
work input, 56
work output, 56
writing guidelines, 209–211

Complement Your Federal Contracting Library with These Additional Resources from
MANAGEMENT CONCEPTS PRESS

Federal Statements of Work: A Practical Guide
Michael G. Martin, PMP

When written well, a statement of work (SOW) attracts high-quality, competitive bids. When written poorly, it leads to disputes and protests—and results in bids that do not meet the needs of the government. *Federal Statements of Work: A Practical Guide* is an indispensable reference tool for anyone in the public sector charged with developing, writing, and executing an SOW to procure goods and services.

©2008, 7" x 10" hardcover with CD-ROM, 635 pages ▪ ISBN: 978-1-56726-225-4 ▪ Product code: B254

Delivering Project Excellence with the Statement of Work, Second Edition
Michael G. Martin, PMP

Delivering Project Excellence with the Statement of Work, Second Edition, builds on the foundation of the first edition with a comprehensive yet succinct description of how to apply the statement of work (SOW) to manage projects effectively. With updates throughout and an entirely new chapter on the use and application of the statement of objectives, this book continues to serve as an essential, practical guide for project managers and team members.

©2010, 6" x 9" hardcover, 380 pages ▪ ISBN 978-1-56726-257-5 ▪ Product code: B575

Past Performance Handbook, Second Edition
Joseph W. Beausoleil

This essential resource has been completely updated and revised to bring readers the most up-to-date information they need to conduct past performance evaluations. *Past Performance Handbook: Applying Commercial Practices to Federal Procurement, Second Edition*, not only includes a detailed explanation of the process of past performance evaluation, but also presents new approaches to standardizing assessment areas and rating scales, streamlining the source selection process, and ensuring that awards are made to the most qualified offerors.

©2010, 7" x 10" hardcover, 248 pages ▪ ISBN: 978-1-56726-280-3 ▪ Product code: B803

Source Selection Step by Step: A Working Guide for Every Member of the Acquisition Team
Charles D. Solloway, Jr., CPCM

The path to successful source selection begins with Source Selection Step by Step: A Working Guide for Every Member of the Acquisition Team. Whether you are new to the acquisition team or an experienced practitioner looking to sharpen your skills, this comprehensive, highly readable handbook will guide you through the entire acquisition process, from designing an effective source selection plan, to preparing the solicitation, evaluating proposals, establishing a competitive range, and documenting the source selection decision.

© 2011, 6" x 9" softcover, 407 pages ▪ ISBN 978-1-56726-300-8 ▪ Product Code B008

Federal Acquisition ActionPacks

Federal Acquisition ActionPacks are designed for busy professionals who need to get a working knowledge of government contracting quickly—without a lot of extraneous detail. This ten-book set covers all phases of the acquisition process, grounds you firmly in each topic area, and outlines practical methods for success, from contracting basics to the latest techniques for improving performance.

Each spiral-bound book contains approximately 160 pages of quick-reading information—simple statements, bulleted lists, questions and answers, charts and graphs, and more. Each topic's most important information is distilled to its essence, arranged graphically for easy comprehension and retention, and presented in a user-friendly format designed for quick look-up.

Order the full set of Federal Acquisition ActionPacks to get a comprehensive knowledge of government contracting today.
Full set: ISBN 978-1-56726-198-1 ■ Product Code B981

Order the full set or order the single titles that are most important to your role in the contracting process. Either way, this is the most effective, affordable way for both buyers and sellers to get a broad-based understanding of government contracting—and proven tools for success.

Earned Value Management
Gregory A. Garrett
ISBN 978-1-56726-188-2 ■ Product Code B882
173 Pages

Best-Value Source Selection
Philip E. Salmeri
ISBN 978-1-56726-193-6 ■ Product Code B936
178 Pages

Performance-Based Contracting
Gregory A. Garrett
ISBN 978-1-56726-189-9 ■ Product Code B899
153 Pages

Government Contract Law Basics
Thomas G. Reid
ISBN 978-1-56726-194-3 ■ Product Code B943
175 Pages

Cost Estimating and Pricing
Gregory A. Garrett
ISBN 978-1-56726-190-5 ■ Product Code B905
161 Pages

Government Contracting Basics
Rene G. Rendon
ISBN 978-1-56726-195-0 ■ Product Code B950
176 Pages

Contract Administration and Closeout
Gregory A. Garrett
ISBN 978-1-56726-191-2 ■ Product Code B912
153 Pages

Performance Work Statements
Philip E. Salmeri
ISBN 978-1-56726-196-7 ■ Product Code B967
151 Pages

Contract Formation
Gregory A. Garrett and William C. Pursch
ISBN 978-1-56726-192-9 ■ Product Code B929
163 Pages

Contract Terminations
Thomas G. Reid
ISBN 978-1-56726-197-4 ■ Product Code B974
166 Pages

Order today for a 30-day risk-free trial!
Visit **www.managementconcepts.com/pubs** or call **703-790-9595**